The Battle of Sl

A Step-by-Step Account of One of the Greatest Battles of the Civil War

By Jack Kunkel

Copyright

PEPPER PUBLISHING AND PEPPER STUDIOS
First Printing, September 2012
ISBN: 978-0-9829705-3-9

Table of Contents

Forward

The Battle of Shiloh was fought deep in the Tennessee woods, far away from the intensely-reported, intensely-documented, intensely-visited Civil War battlefields in the East. It lacked the neatness and precision of many of the eastern battles. All battles are chaotic, but Shiloh was more so than most. And though the combatants were North against South, they were all considered "Westerners" by the folks back East. Today of course they would be considered Mid-Westerners. But at the time, the western combatants had more in common with each other than they did with their eastern cousins, including the fact that they all hailed from a more remote, wilder region, nearer to the edge of what was then the American frontier.

By the time the soldiers in the East got around to fighting their bloody battles of Antietam and Gettysburg, most of them at least had some training under McClellan and Lee. By contrast, with the exception of a few West Point graduates at the top of the command structure, the vast majority of the men on the field at Shiloh were complete amateurs at the business of war – mostly local lawyers and politicians leading tens of thousands of their hometown boys into the gates of hell.

Because of their inexperience, combined with a typically straight-forward, Midwestern way of doing things, it's only a mild exaggeration to say that the tactics of the battle of Shiloh boiled down to 80,000 country boys loading their squirrel guns and a couple hundred cannon, and then lining up facing each other and blasting away. What's amazing is the absolute fury and tenacity with which these citizen-soldiers fought, the amount of damage they were willing to do to each other, and the astounding courage most of them displayed.

For those who survived the inferno without an emotional breakdown and without losing important body parts, Shiloh served as an excellent training-ground for future military leaders in the West. But their on-the-job training session certainly left a mess for us writers to explain. Possibly for that reason, many books on the subject tend to shy away from the actual battle, instead focusing heavily on the politics and battles leading up to the fight, so that it's often not until page 100 before anyone takes a shot at anybody at Shiloh.

But in this book I've confined the political foreplay to the first chapter. After that we get down to the battle itself, confusing or not. I've dispensed with footnotes, since this work is not intended to be a scholarly treatise, though I can back up the book-quotes if needed – most of them came from the books listed in the References section. I consider myself a "splainer," rather than a "true" historian. For one thing I've never been to historian school, and for another I haven't spent decades doing in-depth research, pouring over newspapers, letters and journals. I admire those who do, and in my next life I might join them, but right now my object is to synthesize their collective findings and explain things in an interesting manner that readers can understand - taking full advantage of any maps, photos and/or illustrations I can create or lay hands on.

A pet peeve of mine with battle-books is their lack of maps relating to the text. I *hate* thumbing through 20 pages trying to figure out which map belongs to the text I'm reading! For that reason I've included maps in almost every chapter, both close-up and big-picture maps, most big enough to be visible from outer space.

But the participants at Shiloh weren't just pins on a map. So I've tried to include lots of their personal recollections. And since there weren't many photos taken of the field after the battle, and Shiloh's empty fields of today aren't terribly photogenic, I've settled for including numerous illustrations throughout the book.

For those of you reading this book or listening to the audio, my goal is for you to come away with a better understanding of how the battle unfolded, step by step, and more importantly, what it was really like for the men and boys who fought in the terrible Battle of Shiloh.

Jack Kunkel

About the Maps

Books present some challenges in displaying maps, so I thought I'd take a moment to explain how they're set up in this book.

First of all, here's the symbol index for the maps:

Secondly, almost every chapter contains a "Close-up" map that pertains to the subject being discussed. But to give you an idea of where that close-up section of the battle fits into the rest of the battlefield, I've inserted a smaller, "Location map" somewhere above the Close-up map. The small square in the Location map shows where the Close-up map fits into the entire battlefield.

Finally, because there were usually several battles going on at Shiloh at the same time, I've included an Overall map at the end of most chapters that shows you where all the units on the field were at this particular time.

Samples of all these maps are shown below.

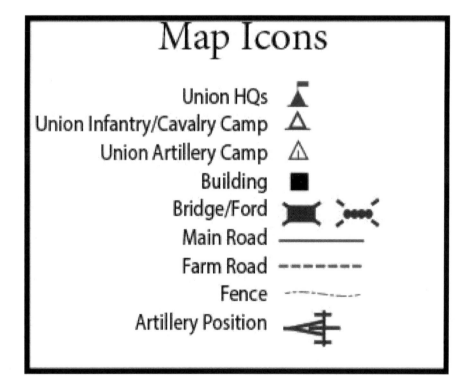

The icons used in the book's maps

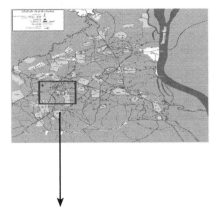

A sample Location map, displaying the battlefield location of the Close-up map shown below.

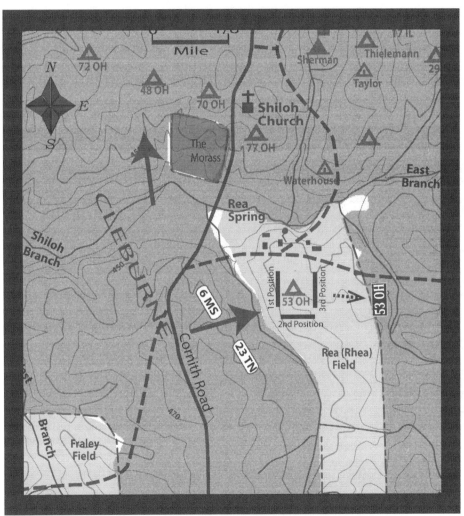

A sample Close-up map, displaying the locations of the units discussed in a specific chapter.

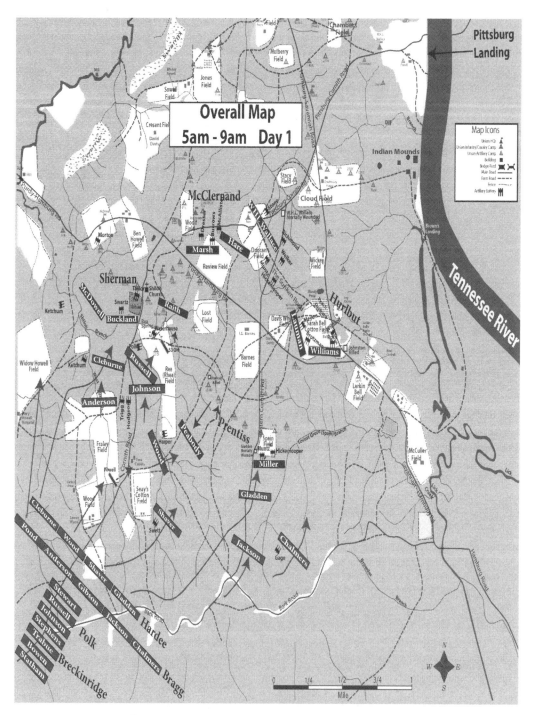

An Overall map usually included at the end of each chapter to display the entire battlefield situation at a certain time.

ONLINE BOOK MAPS

In addition to the maps you find in this book, I also maintain a website which includes one or more maps with markers dedicated to the book topics. You can go to the website, click on the map markers and see the actual battlefield locations in a "live" Google satellite map.

The website address is: www.CivilWarBattles.US

Just go to the website, click the Shiloh tab, and look for an option for "Shiloh Book Map" or wording to that effect (I may be adding more maps later).

OCR MAP ICONS

Last but not least, I have sprinkled OCR (Optical Character Recognition) blocks or tabs (or whatever they're called!) throughout this book so that you can quickly see the discussed locations on a "real time" Google map, if you have a smart cell phone or tablet.

To use the OCR blocks, you need to download an OCR application onto your cell phone. Several are available and they're free. Use your cell phone's standard procedure for locating and downloading apps.

Once you've downloaded the application to your phone, open it and point your cell phone's camera at the OCR tabs in this book. Your cell phone will immediately go to that Google map location, without the need to type in the web location.

Try it on this OCR sample! It leads to my website mentioned above.

CivilWarBattles.us website

Chapter 1   The Road To Shiloh

The Soldiers

Few nations were as unprepared for war, least of all a civil war, as were the combatants in April 1861 when the Slavery-State Rights powder keg exploded at Fort Sumter. At the time the U.S. Army numbered about 16,000 "regulars." The Confederacy possessed no army at all except for the few hundred U.S. Army officers who resigned their commissions and joined the South. Within months, both sides would be training and arming tens of thousands of citizen-soldiers.

Both sides built their armies via a state volunteer system, and both Presidents – Lincoln and Davis – called on their respective states to provide quotas of troops organized into companies – theoretically 100 men per company – and these companies would be combined into regiments – theoretically 10 companies per regiment.

Off to See the Elephant

For the eyeball-to-eyeball business of forming the companies, state governors relied on local politicians and community leaders to recruit volunteers in thousands of towns and villages. For young men who had never set foot outside their county, the prospect of going to war like their revered Revolutionary War forefathers was the thrill of a lifetime - a lot more exciting than milking cows or clerking at the hardware store. Tens of thousands raced to sign up in recruiting drives packed with hometown parades, bands, cheering crowds, absolutions and blessings by local clergy, and stirring speeches by town fathers. The women joined in the excitement by sewing flags and uniforms of every color and design. If their town was big enough to support a photographer, the recruits lined up to have their photo taken. The boys were embarking on a tremendous adventure "to see the elephant," which meant seeing something wondrous – in this case, battle. None of them had ever seen a battle except maybe in a colorful painting of the Revolutionary War or the Battle of Waterloo, where war always looked glorious, and smoky.

Finally the proud companies tramped off to war through their town's streets, hopelessly out of step, past the cheering crowds of mothers and fathers, aunts and uncles and above all, the girls, while being relentlessly serenaded by local bands. The recruits, if they had weapons, were usually armed with shotguns, old muskets, various calibers of squirrel guns, and evil-looking hunting knives. Their officers were local community leaders – usually lawyers/politicians but sometimes school masters and preachers.

These companies would eventually rendezvous at large camps where things were only slightly less festive, with lots of singing, harrahing, and marching. The first order of business was to merge the companies into regiments, the regiments into brigades, the brigades into divisions, and the divisions into corps. The fancy hometown flags were packed up and shipped home; only regiments would carry flags in this war. The officers of the various companies in each regiment gathered and elected a colonel and other field officers from among their number. Few of these officers had any military experience.

It would be a massive understatement to say this recruiting system was imperfect. The North's system was even more imperfect because the legal enlistment-term established by the Uniform Militia Act of 1792 limited the military term of volunteers to 90 days. So when Lincoln called up 75,000 volunteers after Fort Sumter, their terms had expired by the end of summer 1861. Some of these three-month volunteers reenlisted for three years, some didn't.

But this hometown method of building armies had one major advantage: it created tremendous cohesion. Almost every soldier knew his comrades, since they were all from the same community. Each soldier's performance on the battlefield would be relayed to that soldier's family, neighbors and community, and remembered forever. And back then in America, physical cowardice was not considered a virtue.

Through the fall, winter and spring of 1861-1862 the North raised armies and funneled them to jump-off points for a southern offensive. In the western theater, that point was Cairo, Illinois where the Ohio and Mississippi Rivers converge.

Militarization got off to a slightly smoother start in the South due to war-exuberance that gripped Southerners at the time; plus Confederate President Jefferson Davis had the legal ability to summon volunteers for twelve months, not three. Also, due to the Nat Turner slave rebellion of 1831, and John Brown's raid and attempted slave revolt of 1859, many Southern communities had already organized local militias, convenient for fast conversion into military units.

But the lion's share of organized regiments in the Southern states, which included most of those with military training or Mexican War experience, went to Virginia for the defense of Richmond. By the beginning of 1862, the eighth month of the Civil War, many battles had been fought but few were of consequence, except of course to the participants, with the major exception of the First Battle of Bull Run in Virginia and, to a lesser extent, the Battle of Wilson Creek in Missouri.

Both sides, while still hoping knock each other out in a short war, were girding for a long one. And what both sides didn't yet know about conducting wars could have filled volumes.

The Kentucky Shield

Soon after war was declared, Kentucky, a critical border state, proclaimed its "neutrality," and forbade troops from either side from crossing its borders. The Federals had to respect Kentucky's prohibition since Lincoln was determined to avoid any act that might tilt the state into the waiting arms of the South. Kentucky's neutrality was a boon to the Confederacy since it shielded Tennessee's long northern border without the need to station troops there.

But the South threw away its Kentucky shield when, in September 1861, Maj. Gen. Leonidas Polk, the commander of Confederate forces in the Mississippi Valley, took it upon himself to occupy the Mississippi River town of Columbus, Kentucky, thus violating Kentucky neutrality. Polk's move

was logical from a tactical standpoint – Columbus stood on a high bluff which dominated the river for miles. But from a strategic and political standpoint, his move was a disaster because it drove most Kentuckians straight into the arms of the Union (Kentuckians went Union four to one); worse, Tennessee's long, nearly undefended northern border was now fair game for a Union invasion.

The Federals

Through the winter of 1861-1862, the fiercest fighting in the western theater occurred between Union Maj. Gen. Henry W. Halleck in St. Louis and his Ohio rival, Union Maj. Gen. Don Carlos Buell, in their competition to win overall western command. Eventually Halleck won and Buell's army was consolidated into Halleck's Department of Mississippi, which now included all Union forces in the Mississippi and Tennessee River valleys.

The sly, bookish Halleck, was a learned but plodding officer who was far more comfortable mounted on a chair in the office than on a saddle in the battlefield, particularly given his constant battle with hemorrhoids.

But he did have at least one aggressive subordinate – Ulysses S. Grant – a

Maj. Gen. Henry W. Halleck
1815 - 1872

brigadier general commanding forces in Cairo, Illinois. Just over a year earlier, Grant had been feeding his family by peddling firewood on the streets of St. Louis. He was an introvert with a rather dull personality. Quiet and ill at ease in public, he didn't smile much. He was said to be alone, even in a crowd. With the look of a failure, he was someone you might expect to find drinking alone in a tavern. He was in every way perfectly plain and ordinary except, as it would turn out, he had a healthy dose of Midwestern common sense and a logical mind, combined with two extraordi-

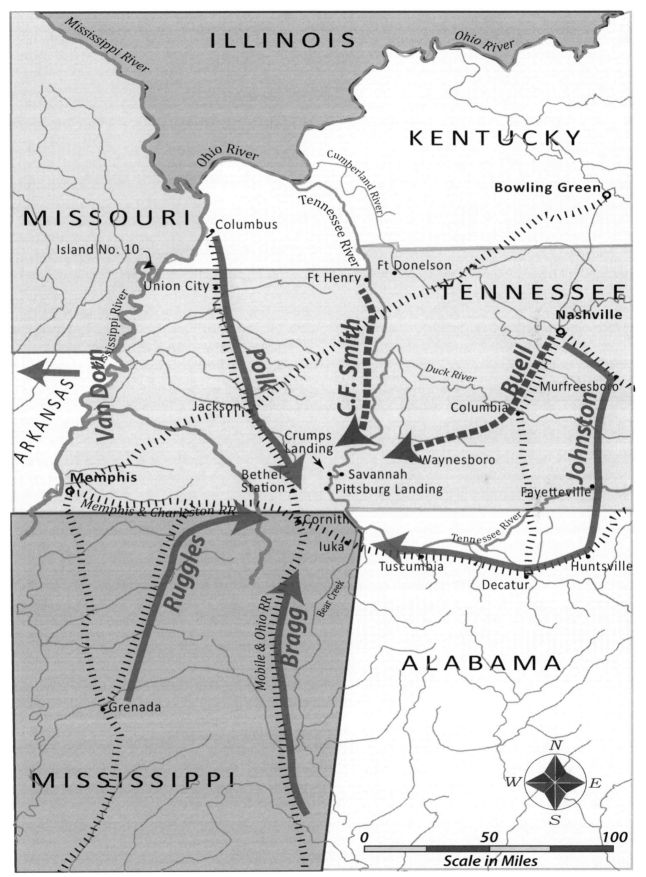

Maj. Gen. Ulysses S. Grant
1822 - 1885

nary talents: a bulldog determination and an uncanny ability to stay calm in situations that would drive most sane men hysterical.

Now, even though he had a reputation as a drunkard, he commanded thousands of men. Soon he would be commanding tens of thousands, and eventually hundreds of thousands.

In November of 1861, before Halleck assumed command, Grant was under the command of Gen. John C. Fremont, who was known as "The Pathfinder" for his conquest of California 15 years earlier. But Fremont was a flop as a Civil War commander; among other problems, he isolated himself in his headquarters in St. Louis and refused to communicate with his generals in the field.

Grant sent Fremont a couple of telegrams, suggesting an attack down the Mississippi River to kick open Confederate defenses in the Mississippi Valley. Fremont didn't respond. Taking that as a "yes,", Grant promptly sailed his troops down the river to Belmont, Missouri, surprising the hell out of Fremont, not to mention the Confederates. In a small scrap of a battle, Grant was winning for the first part of the day, but the Southerners reinforced, and by the end of the day they pushed Grant's men back, forcing him to withdraw. His operation a failure, Grant was roundly criticized in the press. He down-played the whole affair as a mere raid.

But with Halleck now in command, in early 1862 Grant was back at it again, this time with Halleck's full approval and some critical assistance from the U.S. Navy in the form of a squadron of gunboats commanded by Flag Officer Andrew H. Foote. Majestic ships of the line might rule the seas, but drab gunboats - some wooden ("timberclads") and some ironclad - ruled the rivers. These ungainly brutes were really just floating artillery platforms with timber or metal plating, carrying bigger guns than anything the army could drag into the field. The Union could build lots of these boats and the South couldn't, so the South placed its bet on river fortresses, which were to become Grant's chief targets in his western campaigns.

Today, we forget that rivers were the super highways of the 19th century. Boats, powered by steam, chugged up and down these waterways delivering heavy loads faster and cheaper than wagon transport. (Railroads were still something of a novelty, especially in the West). Rivers were also important economically because factories tended to cluster along rivers due to the ease of shipping product and receiving raw materials.

And when war came, big rivers like the Mississippi, the Tennessee, and the Cumberland wriggled like arteries deep into the Confederacy's body. If the Union could seize control of these arteries, it could in a matter of days send soldiers, supplies and armaments flowing down, and land anywhere in Tennessee, Mississippi and Alabama, quickly metastasizing into the Confederate heartland. And once the Federal army landed, it was easy to supply it by river, at least until the troops advanced too deep inland.

The first target on Grant's list was Fort Henry, a poorly situated and incomplete fortification guarding the Tennessee River. The overall Southern commander, Gen. Albert Sidney Johnston had ordered his subordinate, Maj. Gen. Leonidas Polk, to complete the fortifications along the Tennessee River, including Fort Henry, but for whatever reason Polk neglected to do so. The Union gunboats attacked the fort on February 6th and quickly seized it, costing Grant only 40 casualties.

Well! That seemed easy enough! So Grant loaded his men back on the transports and sailed back around a few miles to the east and attacked Fort Donelson on the Cumberland River. But Fort Donelson proved to be a much tougher nut than Fort Henry, as Donelson was well placed and fully manned.

Donelson only had one cannon but it was a big one. Confederate cannoneers fought off the gunboats, negating Grant's naval advantage. Then the

Confederates even sallied out of their fort and attacked Grant's infantry, catching him by surprise – not for the last time – and sending the Federals reeling. But Grant doggedly counterattacked. Finally, Johnston sent orders for the garrison to fight its way out. Nathan Bedford Forrest and about 500 cavalry escaped, but otherwise the local Confederate commanders foolishly ignored the order and instead retreated their 15,000 infantry back *into* the fortress, trapping his men in what was now a prison.

The next morning, February 16th, the garrison was compelled to surrender, costing the South and Johnston 15,000 irreplaceable troops, along with control of the Cumberland River. Those troops might well have changed the outcome of the coming battle at Shiloh.

The loss of the two forts was catastrophic for the South, opening an enormous gash in its western defenses from which it never fully recovered; many historians mark these twin defeats as the beginning of the end of the Confederacy. Now Federal armies, via boat, had free range up the Tennessee River, allowing penetration into Alabama and Mississippi as well as Tennessee; and along the way, the Federals could destroy factories and cut vital bridges used by east-west Confederate railroads. Also, command of the Cumberland River gave the Federals access to Nashville, the capital of Tennessee, which surrendered without a fight on February 25th. Last but not least, Polk's bastion at Columbus – the one he violated Kentucky sovereignty to seize – was now effectively surrounded and had to be abandoned. By the beginning of April, Union naval and army forces were steaming down to Memphis, and that city also appeared doomed.

All of this brought Grant national acclaim and promotion to major general. The media hailed him as "Unconditional Surrender Grant." (He was sent so many boxes of cigars as gifts that he gave up smoking a pipe and switched to more expensive cigars – a habit that would eventually kill him with throat cancer).

The downside to Grant's celebrity was that he incurred the intense jealousy of his boss, Halleck, who was soon sniffing Grant's trail, looking for reasons to eliminate this upstart rival. (Hearing of

Grant's victory at Fort Donelson, Halleck expressed amazement that "a drunkard" could win such a prize).

Halleck ordered Grant's army (which we'll now call the Army of Tennessee, although it didn't officially obtain that name until months after the battle of Shiloh) to proceed up the Tennessee River toward the Mississippi border. (Oddly, the Tennessee River flows south to north, so sailing "up river" means sailing south). There Grant would await Halleck's arrival from St. Louis, as well the arrival of another Union army commanded by Buell, now also under Halleck's command.

Buell's army, the Army of Ohio, marched from central Kentucky into Tennessee where it occupied Nashville after the Confederates abandoned the city. Buell would now march south from Nashville to join Grant and his army on the Tennessee River. And there was yet a third Federal army in eastern Kentucky, commanded by Brig. Gen. John Pope, which was now also under Halleck's orders, and which would also soon be joining Grant and Buell.

Once Halleck arrived, his combined armies - nearly 125,000 strong - would march south toward Cornith, Mississippi - a vital military objective.

Meanwhile, Halleck lost no time in disposing of Grant though manufactured allegations that Grant was drinking again – a supposed relapse to his well-publicized drinking problems in the old army – and also that he was not properly communicating with Halleck. (It would turn out that a telegraph operator stationed somewhere between the two Union headquarters was a Southern sympathizer who, before deserting to the Confederate army, destroyed a number of Grant's cables to Halleck). Halleck relieved Grant and turned over command of the Army of Tennessee to Grant's senior division commander and former West Point Commandant, the much respected Maj. Gen. Charles F. Smith. On March 13th, Smith sailed down to Savannah, Tennessee to take charge of the soon-to-be-arriving Union forces there.

But in the meantime, the Lincoln administration ordered Halleck to either bring formal charges against Grant or return him to command. Grant, after all, had won a battle - something few other Union generals had done. So Halleck grudgingly restored Grant to command of the new Army of Tennessee in late March. Smith was effectively demoted to command Grant's 2nd Division. However, shortly after assuming command of the division, Smith badly scraped his leg while entering a row boat, causing a serious infection that forced him to bed and would eventually kill him. While he was incapacitated, Brig. Gen. W. H. L. Wallace replaced him as commander of the 2nd Division.

So while Grant busied himself with his growing Army of Tennessee, and Buell's Army of Ohio made an unhurried march from Nashville to join Grant, Halleck prepared to sail down from St. Louis to take charge.

Importantly, Halleck gave strict orders to Grant, Smith, Sherman and everyone else that under no circumstances were they to trigger any confrontations with the enemy until Halleck reached the scene.

Cornith - The Backbone of the Confederacy

Today, except for Civil War buffs, few people outside the state have ever heard of Cornith, Mississippi, a sleepy little town on the northeastern edge of the state. But in its day Cornith was almost as important to the Confederacy as Atlanta or Richmond.

While Grant's victory at Fort Donelson threw open the Tennessee River to invasion as far south as Muscle Shoals, Alabama, the primary objective was always Cornith. The town's strategic importance stemmed from the two major railroads that crossed there – the Mobile & Ohio and the Memphis & Charleston. The latter, called the "Confederacy's Backbone," (or "The Vertebrae of the Confederacy") was especially critical to the South since it was the only direct line of communication between the eastern seaboard and the Mississippi River region. Also if the Southerners lost Cornith, the large river port in Memphis would become unusable to them.

Albert Sidney Johnston

The man assigned to stop the Union invasion was Gen. Albert Sidney Johnson, commander of all Southern forces in the west. A charismatic and highly respected West Pointer with a stellar reputation in the pre-war U.S. Army, Johnston was practically a legend in the South. He looked like a hero's supposed to look – handsome and "powerfully made," over six feet tall with wavy gray hair and mustache. One story had him supposedly wading into a fight between a mountain lion and his pack of hunting dogs, and bashing the beast to death with his rifle butt. He had fought a duel and been badly wounded by his opponent after firing his own weapon in the air. He commanded the 2nd U.S. Cavalry, a famous unit that fought numerous Indian battles in Texas and the Great Plains. The regiment was remarkable for the number of prominent Civil War generals it spawned, including Robert E. Lee, who served as Johnston's second in command in the cavalry unit.

In 1860, as a brigadier general, Johnston was appointed U.S. Commander of the Department of the Pacific. He and his family sailed to his new post on Alcatraz Island in San Francisco Bay. But they barely arrived when Texas, Johnston's adopted state, seceded. The Lincoln administration was well aware of Johnston's value. Winfield Scott, the then U.S. Army Commander, considered Johnston "the finest soldier he had ever commanded." When Texas seceded, the administration tried to entice Johnston to stay with the Union by promoting him to Major General. But before the

Gen. Albert Sidney Johnson (k)
1803 - 1862

Pvt. Phillip Stephenson of the 13th Arkansas, hung around Johnston's HQ one day and caught a glimpse of the general. "If ever a man looked the 'great man' Albert Sidney Johnston did. A martial figure, although dressed in civilian clothes. I saw him but once, a black felt 'slouch' hat shaded his features as he walked with head down as though buried in deep thought. He looked like an old Viking king!"

promotion even arrived, Johnston submitted his resignation on April 3, 1861.

The only ships leaving San Francisco sailed for New York City. Fearing he would be arrested if he landed in New York, Johnston decided to travel by horse to Texas. After packing his family on a ship to New York, the 58-year-old Johnston and a dozen officers undertook an incredible two-month, 1,500 mile journey – a trip that would merit a book in itself – across the toughest and hottest desert on the American continent, dodging U.S. Army patrols and Comanches and almost dying of thirst before finally reaching San Antonio, Texas. From there Johnston traveled by train and boat to reach Richmond, where Jeff Davis appointed him commander of the Confederate's Department of the West.

The Confederates Prepare

While the Federals prepared to invade, the Confederates weren't asleep. Johnston, once the darling of the fickle and slightly hysterical Southern media, now became the newspapers' anti-Christ after the debacles at Forts Henry and Donelson. He was under intense pressure to *do* something. But while the press screamed for his head, Jefferson Davis stood by Johnston, stating, "If Sidney Johnston is not a general, I have none." But for his own sake, as well as the sake of the Confederacy, Johnston had to find a way to halt the massive Union tide rolling into the Southern heartland.

The Union advance up the Tennessee River had split the Confederate defenders, with Johnston retaining command of the forces east of the Tennessee River. From Bowling Green, Kentucky, he led his army in a retreat southwest through northern Alabama to the southernmost bend of the Tennessee River.

The Confederate forces west of the Tennessee River were under the command of Gen. Pierre Gustave Toutant Beauregard. "The Great Creole," born in Louisiana, was currently a darling of the Richmond press. He commanded the bombard-

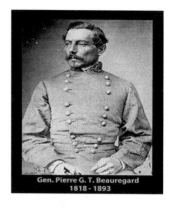

Gen. Pierre G. T. Beauregard
1818 - 1893

ment and surrender of Fort Sumter, and also received undeserved credit for the victory at the First Battle of Bull Run. But he soon made himself a pest in Richmond, spouting off to the newspapers on how the war should be run, irritating the easily-irritated Davis. Johnston had been requesting reinforcements. So, delighted to get Beauregard out of his hair, Davis shipped him off to the beleaguered Johnston as a one-man reinforcement. On Beauregard's arrival, Johnston put him to work supervising Polk's withdrawal of the western segment of the Southern forces, leading the troops southward through west Tennessee into Mississippi.

Partially due to meeting the demands of governors in Florida, Alabama and elsewhere, Davis initially made the mistake of scattering troops around the South's coasts in a vain attempt to defend its entire territory, everywhere. Now, given the debacles in the west, Davis finally relented and agreed, a bit late, to consolidate the western forces into a single, mobile army under Johnston.

And so now more Southern troops were heading to Cornith from Pensacola, Florida; these under the command of Brig. Gen. Braxton Bragg. They had yet to see combat but they were the best trained Southern troops in the western theater since they had little to do in Florida but drill, and Bragg drilled them until they despised him. Bragg's troops rode to battle on boxcars of the Mobile & Ohio Railroad, arriving in Cornith before either Johnston or Beauregard, and securing the critical rail junction, at least for the moment.

Everyone it seemed was heading to Cornith, Mississippi.

Just prior to the outbreak of war, Beauregard accepted the post of Commandant of West Point. He did so knowing that his home state of Louisiana was just days away from seceding from the Union. When it became clear that he would go with his state, the West Point administration fired him, refusing to pay his fare back to Louisiana.

Beauregard filed a suit for damages, which he continued to pursue even after he was a general in the Confederate army.

Google Map Links

Scan with OC Reader to go to Google map locations

Cornith, MS

Fort Donelson

Belmont, MO

Columbus, KY

Cairo, IL

Chapter 2   The Union Encampment

March 17 – April 5

Federals Choose an Encampment

The fall of Forts Donelson and Henry opened a route via the Tennessee River through which Union gunboats and troops could quickly flow into the Confederate heartland. Taking advantage of the situation, the Federals initially planned a simple raid down the Tennessee River to wreck some Rebel railroad iron. But once Halleck was appointed commander of the Department of Missouri in November of 1861, the raid idea mushroomed into a plan for a full scale invasion to seize and hold Cornith and its vital railroad junction. The Confederates were fully aware of the threat, and they began massing forces in Cornith.

On March 13th, Halleck's choice to command the expedition, Brig. Gen. Charles F. Smith, arrived at the river town Savannah, Tennessee, about 30 miles northeast of Cornith. Significantly, the town was on the opposite (east) side of the river from Cornith, which afforded the fledgling Union force some protection from any Confederate surprise attack. While waiting for more troops, Smith ordered two raids: first, he sent Brig. Gen. W. H. L. Wallace and his 2nd Division to Crumps Landing, about four miles south of Savannah, to seize the landing as a beachhead for future inland raids on Confederate railroads. Secondly, Smith ordered Brig. Gen. William T. Sherman to steam south 22 miles up the Tennessee River and wreck some important railroad bridges

Brig. Gen. Charles F. Smith
1807 - 1862

near the small village of Eastport, about 20 miles east of Cornith, after which Sherman and his men would sail back to Savannah.

So on March 14, Sherman and his 5th Division sailed south in 17 transports. Along the way, only about 10 miles south of Savannah, Sherman noticed a small landing on the west side of the river, which the ship's captain explained was the usual landing spot for river travelers heading for Cornith. It was called Pittsburg Landing. It wasn't much to look at; just "three log cabins and a pig sty," according to one traveler. But Sherman sent back word to Smith, suggesting that troops be posted there. Smith complied by sending Brig. Gen. Stephen A. Hurlbut to anchor, but not disembark, his 4th Division at the Landing.

Meanwhile, around 7pm that same evening, Sherman and his men landed at the mouth of Yellow Creek near Eastport, and set off looking for trouble. They found plenty, though not the kind they expected. Sheets of rain churned the roads into muddy quagmires, turning creeks into raging rivers impossible to ford. Sherman and his troops were forced to make a soggy retreat back to the transports without so much as even having seen a railroad track.

Drenched but undaunted, the general and his little armada sailed back north, looking for another spot within an easy march of some Confederate railroad. Remembering that small landing he had passed on his way south, Pittsburg Landing, Sherman decided it just might fit the bill. When he reached the Landing, Hurlbut's division was already anchored there, guarding the place, though his men still remained aboard the transports. So Sherman and his division disembarked there on the 15th, still looking for some Confederate railroad bridges to destroy. But the incessant rain followed Sherman like a curse, causing the usual problems with overflowing creeks blocking his march, and the whole raid was a fiasco. Sherman's cavalry did manage to reach a railroad bridge and burn it, but the Confederates repaired it within a day.

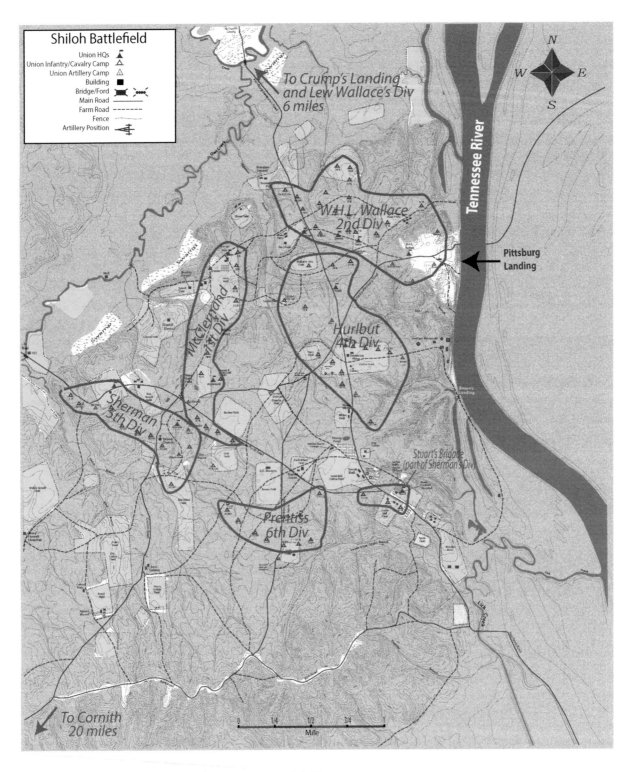

The locations of the division camps at Pittsburg Landing.

But while at Pittsburg Landing, Sherman noticed it that it was an ideal camping location with space to accommodate 100,000 men or more – about the size of Halleck's army once Brig. Gen. John Pope's and Maj. Gen. Don Carlos Buell's forces reached the area. The location's flanks were protected from both the north and southeast by large creeks – the Owl and Snake Creeks to the north, and Lick Creek to the southwest. These moccasin-infested creeks were swampy and nearly impassable, and so, with the river protecting their backs to the northeast, the Federal camp would have natural protection from all sides, except one – the southwest.

Sherman reported all the advantages of the Pittsburg Landing to his superior, Brig. Gen. Smith. Seizing Cornith would require an initial base of operations somewhere on the western side of the Tennessee River, and Pittsburg Landing seemed as good a spot as any. So on March 15, Smith selected it as the concentration point for Union forces. And he now ordered Hurlbut to disembark his 4th Division there, following Sherman's 5th Division.

In the meantime, due to pressure from the Lincoln administration, Halleck was forced to reinstate Grant as commander of the Army of Tennessee, relegating Smith to commander of the 2nd Division. But on March 13th, Smith badly scraped his leg while transferring from one boat to another, causing an infection which incapacitated him and would eventually kill him. In the meantime, Brig. Gen. W. H. L Wallace now assumed command of the 2nd Division.

Grant's First Mistake

Upon Grant's re-assumption of command, he personally inspected the Landing on March 17, approving Smith's choice as the best location for the army's advanced base. This turned out to be his first major mistake. Though the creeks and river provided the Landing with good natural protection, it was still on the west side of the river – as were the Confederates just 22 miles south at Cornith. Had Grant located his army back at Savannah on the *east* side of the river, his men would have been safe from any Confederate surprises. But the new commander was thinking offensively, and deploying his army on the west side of the river at Pittsburg Landing made it easier for him to get at the Confederates. Neither he nor anyone else seemed to give any thought to the possibility that the Confederate Army might strike *him*.

The following day, March 18, more Union troops poured into the Landing. With transports now arriving daily, the Landing's muddy riverfront was soon a hive of activity, crammed with off-loading transports. By the end of March, Grant had about 41,000 men in six divisions in the area – five divisions at Pittsburg Landing, and a sixth one at Crump's Landing five miles downstream (north).

Grant's Second Mistake

Apparently because it was a convenient point to meet Buell, who was expected momentarily, Grant maintained his headquarters at Savannah in a house called the Cherry Mansion, 10 miles north of his troops at the Landing and on the opposite side of the river. This was his second mistake.

A modern photo of the Cherry Mansion in Savannah, TN, about 10 miles north of Pittsburg Landing. This house served as Grant's HQ prior to the battle. Later, two senior Union generals, W. H. L. Wallace and Charles F. Smith, died at the house.

However, he was planning to move his headquarters on the 6th, the day of the attack, not because of any concern about an attack but because one of the division commanders – Brig. Gen. John A. McClernand - had just be promoted to major general, outranking Sherman at the Landing. Grant distrusted McClernand, a political appointee without military training, and so Grant needed to be there in person to prevent McClernand from taking control. Also, a few days prior to the battle, Grant badly sprained his leg when his horse slipped in the mud and fell on him, putting him on crutches throughout the coming battle. This may have contributed to his decision to remain in Savannah a while longer.

McClernand, an ambitious Illinois politician, commanded the 1st Division, now also camped at Pittsburg Landing. His division had done the bulk of the fighting at Fort Donaldson, and so was considered a "veteran" division. Camped next to McClernand's men was another "veteran" division, the 2nd Division. Initially commanded by Charles Smith, but due to Smith's subsequent leg injury, it was now under the command of a man Grant had great faith in – Brig. Gen. William H. L. Wallace. The final veteran division, the 3rd, was commanded by Brig. Gen. Lew Wallace (no relation to W. H. L. Wallace). Lew Wallace, from Indiana, is today best remembered as the author of the novel, *Ben Hur,* which he wrote after the war. It was Lew Wallace's division that was camped five miles north of Pittsburg Landing at Crump's Landing.

The other three divisions at Pittsburg Landing – the 4th (Hurlbut's), 5th (Sherman's) and 6th (Prentiss's) Divisions – couldn't be much greener. The former two were organized just two weeks earlier, just prior to the army's departure up the Tennessee River; and the third one, Brig. Gen. Benjamin Prentiss's 6th Division, was actually formed at the Pittsburg Landing encampment.

This newest of divisions, the 6th, had to pitch its tents on the outskirts of the encampment next to Sherman's greenhorns, because the spots close to the Landing were already taken by the time they arrived.

Sherman's 5th being of the first unit to disembark at the Landing, the then commander, Charles Smith, had ordered Sherman to push farther out from the Landing to allow room for the later arriving divisions. Then, because the spots close to the Landing were already taken by the time it arrived, Prentiss' just-formed 6th division had to pitch its tents on the outskirts of the encampment next to Sherman's greenhorns.

The end result was that the two greenest divisions in Grant's army – 5th and 6th – composed of not much more than armed civilians wearing uniforms, would be smack on the army's front line in the coming battle.

Sherman

Brig. Gen. William T. Sherman was under a cloud. To begin with, he hated journalists ("... *dirty, irresponsible, corrupt, malicious, a shame and a reproach to a civilized people*") perhaps because they kept writing that he was demented. And partly for that reason he attracted them like flies on molasses. But who could blame them? Even in a formal photograph he couldn't keep his red hair from spiking out like a wet chicken. He was wrapped really tight – nervous, profane, sarcastic, bubbling with ideas – some harebrained and some not – and always talking. He had almost talked himself out of the army back in 1861 by making wild statements about the enemy strength. He probably had a nervous breakdown. He apparently considered suicide, and supposedly there was insanity in his family. One general described him as "a splendid piece of machinery with all the screws a little loose."

With the newspapers calling him crazy, it was only due to his excellent political connections – including his brother, John, a U.S. Senator – that his career was salvaged. Despite his brother, Sherman disliked politicians almost as much as journalists.

On top of his insanity-problem, Sherman (along with Halleck) was unlucky in that he had been stuck in California during the Mexican War, which served as sort of a post-graduate course for future Civil War generals.

But with all his faults, there was clearly something special about Sherman.

A West Pointer and professional soldier, he had a low opinion of volunteer troops, and it greatly irritated him having to deal with these amateurs who constantly spooked themselves, spotting phantom Rebels behind every tree.

For all these reasons, plus Halleck's strict order not to engage the enemy before his arrival, Sherman kept his mouth clamped tightly shut, and relentlessly portrayed himself as a model of calm and restraint, serenely unconcerned about reports of nearby enemy forces.

He set up his tent headquarters next to a shady stream that ran near a tiny Methodist meetinghouse called Shiloh Church. Until formal notification of McClernand's promotion to major general (it arrived the day prior to the coming battle), Sherman was senior officer and unofficial camp commander at the Landing in Grant's absence.

One Union private wrote home that "*There is no end to the tents. We can see them scattered in all directions as far as we can see.*" Another private of the 52nd Illinois thought the place reminded him of a religious camp meeting, but much bigger. By the end of March, Sherman was handling the daily activities of five divisions of about 41,000 troops, which included about 34,500 trigger-pullers and 6,500 support troops – medical staff, cooks, teamsters, etc. Sherman gave little thought to a possible enemy attack. He wasn't alone on that score. Even though the Confederates were massing in Cornith, all the Union brass - Grant and Halleck among them - were supremely confident that the recent Confederate defeats in the west had crippled the Southern army, and just one more battle should finish this ridiculous rebellion, at least in the west.

Grant's Third Mistake

Once he had his army at Pittsburg Landing, Grant neglected to construct even the skimpiest defensive fortifications to shield his inexperienced troops. At that stage of the war, most officers frowned on the use of defensive structures. Sherman's opinion at the time was common: "*Such a course would have made our raw men timid.*"

Also Grant, thinking offensively, wanted to use the time to train his raw troops, rather than using them as laborers, felling trees and digging ditches. So the Union encampments sat in the open like a Boy Scout jamboree, as ill prepared to receive a major attack as if the Confederates were a 1,000 miles away, rather than just 20 miles. This would be Grant's third mistake.

The Federal commanders completely convinced themselves that Johnston and his army were gathering in Cornith strictly to defend the town. On April 5th, the day before the attack, Grant sent a telegram to Halleck: "*I have scarcely the faintest idea of an attack (general one) being made on us, but will be prepared should such a thing take place.*"

Grant would rue those words for the rest of his career.

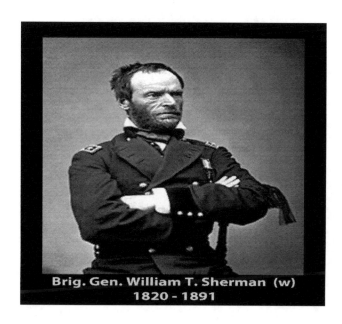

Brig. Gen. William T. Sherman (w)
1820 - 1891

Transports moored at Pittsburg Landing days after the battle. Grant's boat, the Tigress, is second from the right.

Transports at Pittsburg Landing just days after the battle. At far right is the Cincinnati Sanitary Commission's Tyconn, loaded with medical supplies, and next to it is the Tigress, Grant's floating HQ.

Modern photo of the Landing.

Shiloh Church, for which the battle was named, was a rough 25 x 30' log cabin with a clapboard roof built around 1854 by a congregation that was part of the Southern Methodist Episcopal Church. Like many denominations in prewar years, the Methodist Episcopal Church split into Northern and Southern branches, largely over the issue of slavery. The name "Shiloh" came from 1 Samuel and referred to a religious center to which the Hebrews annually made pilgrimage. It roughly translated as "peace."

The original building is long gone, torn apart by Federal soldiers looking for souvenirs. But the church was rebuilt and is the subject of this modern photo.

Google Map Links (scan with OC Reader to go to online maps)

Savannah, TN

Cherry Mansion

Eastport, TN

Pittsburg Landing

Crumps Landing

Shiloh Church

Chapter 3   The March to Shiloh

April 3 - 5

The Confederate Command

When the Confederate armies converged at Cornith in late March, Johnston commanded about 44,700 soldiers. In the Southern armies, troop counts usually included non-combatants – medical, teamsters, etc. – so he probably had about 39,000 trigger-pullers, and five senior officers, described below:

PIERRE G. T. BEAUREGARD

The Southern army had a peculiar command structure. Though Beauregard was technically second-in-command, Johnston effectively appointed him co-commander with the responsibility of organizing the newly concentrated army. Sometimes Johnston was in charge; sometimes Beauregard was in charge. At one point Johnston even offered Beauregard command, which the latter refused. Beauregard was in bad health as he was recovering from recent throat surgery he'd had done in Richmond, and as a result he was now plagued with high fevers and chronic bronchial infections. In fact, the doctors thought he should be in bed. But he pressed on, outfitted in a tailored uniform lavishly adorned with gold braid and a spiffy red cap with a flat brim covered with more gold spaghetti, as worn by French army officers. As a Louisianan fiercely proud of his French heritage, Beauregard was more French than the French.

Though 44,700 troops actually only amounted to four divisions, on March 29th Beauregard divided the army, now designated the Army of Mississippi, into four "corps," hoping to fool the Yankees into thinking the Southern host was twice its actual size (Traditionally a corps, modeled on European military,

Gen. Pierre G. T. Beauregard
1818 - 1893

numbered about 20,000 soldiers, so four Confederate "corps" would appear to be 80,000 troops).

The First Corps was commanded by Leonidas Polk; the Second by Maj. Gen. Braxton Bragg, and the Third by Maj. Gen. William J. Hardee. The fourth corps, designated a "Reserve", was initially under the command of Maj. Gen. George B. Crittenden. But after a minor Confederate defeat in January at Mill Springs, Kentucky, Crittenden was removed from command due to allegations of intoxication – a common problem in all armies at that time. He was replaced on the eve of the coming battle by former U.S. Senator and Vice President, John C. Breckinridge of Kentucky, now a Confederate brigadier general.

Bragg's corps was the largest with approximately 13,000 men; Hardee's was the smallest with about half that number.

Maj. Gen. Braxton Bragg
1817 - 1876

BRAXTON BRAGG

A 42-year-old West Pointer and Mexican War veteran, Bragg was a man who always seemed to travel under a black cloud. He had a well-deserved reputation as a strict disciplinarian – so well deserved that while in the regular army some of his troops tried to kill him on a couple of occasions. He was a sour, irritable man, no doubt due to his numerous health issues, including rheumatism, dyspepsia, nerves, and severe migraine headaches. His temperament probably wasn't improved when his Louisiana plantation was confiscated by the Federals later in 1862. A by-the-book soldier with little imagination, he was almost universally detested, and he fought with his fellow officers nearly as much as he fought with the Yankees. He really had only one supporter, but it was the only one who mattered – President Jefferson Davis.

WILLIAM HARDEE

A 46-year-old, former Commandant of West Point and a Mexican War veteran, Maj. Gen. William Hardee published a book before the war with the catchy title of "*Rifle and Light Infantry Tactics for the Exercise and Maneuvers of Troops When Acting as Light Infantry or Riflemen.*" Better known simply as *Hardee's Tactics*, both sides used his book as their primary drill manual throughout the war. Hardee, a Georgian, was a steady though not

Maj. Gen. William J. Hardee (w)
1815 - 1873

brilliant officer who would serve the Confederacy throughout the war, earning the nickname "Old Reliable."

LEONIDAS POLK

Maj. Gen. Leonidas Polk, 55 years old, owned a Tennessee plantation with 200 to 400 slaves, and was a second cousin of James Polk, the former U.S. President. He attended West Point but resigned his commission immediately after graduation to enter, of all things, a theological seminary, where he would eventually became a bishop in the Episcopal Church. Now known as "The Fighting Bishop," Polk achieved his high military position without prior combat experience because of his friendship with Confederate President Davis. Though person-

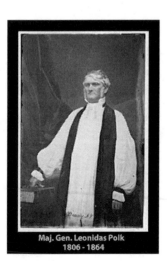

Maj. Gen. Leonidas Polk
1806 - 1864

ally brave and popular with his troops, he was barely competent as a military officer and often dangerously insubordinate, as he had amply demonstrated by attacking that fort in Kentucky, breaking that state's neutrality.

JOHN BRECKINRIDGE

A former U.S. Vice President and member of a prominent Kentucky family, 41-year-old Brig. Gen. John C. Breckinridge had served in the Mexican War. He wasn't a West Pointer but rather a Princeton man and a successful lawyer. In his mid-30s he ran for U.S. President against Lincoln, coming in second in the electoral vote, and third in the popular vote behind Lincoln and Stephen Douglass. Shortly before the battle Breckinridge was selected to command the "Reserve Corps," replacing

Brig. Gen. John C. Breckinridge
1821 - 1875

Maj. Gen. George B. Crittenden who, as discussed earlier, was dismissed on charges of alcoholism. Breckinridge developed into a competent general who would go on to serve the Southern cause throughout the war.

The Objective

Johnston's spies kept him up to date on the progress of Buell's Army of the Ohio as it tramped south to join Grant's Army of Tennessee. Even with his newly consolidated and larger force, Johnston couldn't just sit back and allow the Yankee army to mass at its leisure, swelling into Goliath that would march 20 miles down the road and besiege him at Cornith. Johnston's best hope was to seize the initiative and strike Grant before Buell joined him at Pittsburg Landing. The catch was that he couldn't attack any sooner than absolutely necessary. His army was literally only days old; what he really had was a mob of 44,700 farmers armed with scatter guns. Like Grant, he needed every precious minute to organize his force and provide his raw troops with at least some semblance of training.

So Johnston remained in Cornith, hastily drilling his troops until the very last minute when he was notified that Buell's column was about to reach Grant.

And indeed, late in the evening of April 2nd, Johnston received a message that Buell's troops were nearing Pittsburg Landing. The time to strike had arrived.

Johnston ordered Beauregard to have the army ready to march at daybreak. The idea was simple enough - march the 20 miles to Pittsburg Landing on April 3rd, and strike Grant's sleeping encampment at dawn, Friday, April 4th.

The Battle Formation

Johnston sent a letter to President Davis, outlining a plan of attack, with Polk's Corps on the left, Hardee's in the center, and Bragg's, the largest corps, on the right nearest the river and the Landing. There, Bragg would crush the Union left and drive Grant's army to its destruction in the swampy Owl and Snake Creek bottoms.

It wasn't a bad plan had he stuck to it, but apparently he left the details of drawing up the official orders to Beauregard, who in turn assigned the task to his adjutant, Col. Thomas Jordan, who in turn drew up the orders based on Napoleon's battle plan at Waterloo - which in turn resulted a disaster known as Special Order Number Eight.

Jordan and the French-admiring Beauregard, both Napoleon devotees, completely changed the battle formation. Instead of attacking with three

Col. Thomas Jordan 1818 - 1895

corps left, right and center, the new plan called for an attack in waves, with each corps attacking in successive lines, one behind the other. Jordan and the French-worshipping Beauregard, both ardent Napoleon admirers, completely changed the battle formation. Instead of attacking with three corps left, right and center, the new plan called for an attack in waves, with each corps attacking in succession, one behind the other, like Napoleon apparently did at Waterloo. The problem was that, in the dense terrain of Shiloh,

Col. Jordan had been U.S. Grant's roommate at West Point.

the corps commanders couldn't even *see*, let alone control, their mile-long battle lines. Unlike the gentle, rolling plains of Waterloo, Shiloh was rugged, hilly terrain packed with swamps, steep gullies and creeks in dense underbrush, all randomly interspersed with cotton fields.

Special Order Number Eight guaranteed that once the battle commenced all Confederate organization above the level of brigade, and sometimes even at the regimental level, would dissolve in the rugged terrain as the successive battlelines pancaked into the preceding ranks.

Napoleon's Waterloo plan, which incidentally didn't even work for Napoleon, was a sorry model for the coming fight at Shiloh. If Waterloo resembled a carefully choreographed gentleman's duel, Shiloh would be more like a gun fight in a dark room.

The March

There was yet another flaw in Special Orders Number Eight: the order gave insufficient thought to the limited road network between Cornith and Pittsburg Landing, resulting in overcrowding and massive traffic jams. "Limited" road network is an understatement; there were in fact just two roads - Ridge Road and Monterey Road. The order of march put Polk and Hardee on one road, and Bragg and Breckinridge on the other.

In truth, no one really knew how to move such large bodies of troops at this stage of the war. And so the Confederates' march from Cornith to Shiloh was almost as traumatic as the battle itself. Due to the near-total inexperience of officers and men, combined with the incessant rain, it took three days to cover 20 miles - about 6.7 miles per day. (By the time of Gettysburg just over a year later, large bodies of troops were routinely marching 20 miles a day, and sometimes 25-30 miles a day).

About half of Grant's troops had at least some combat experience at Forts Donelson and Henry, but *none* of Johnston's troops, except for a few of the senior officers, had ever been in battle.

As soon as his army was on the march, Beauragard's and Jordan's Napoleon-marching-plan collapsed. In the first place, there was no way Johnston's raw troops were going to cover 20 miles

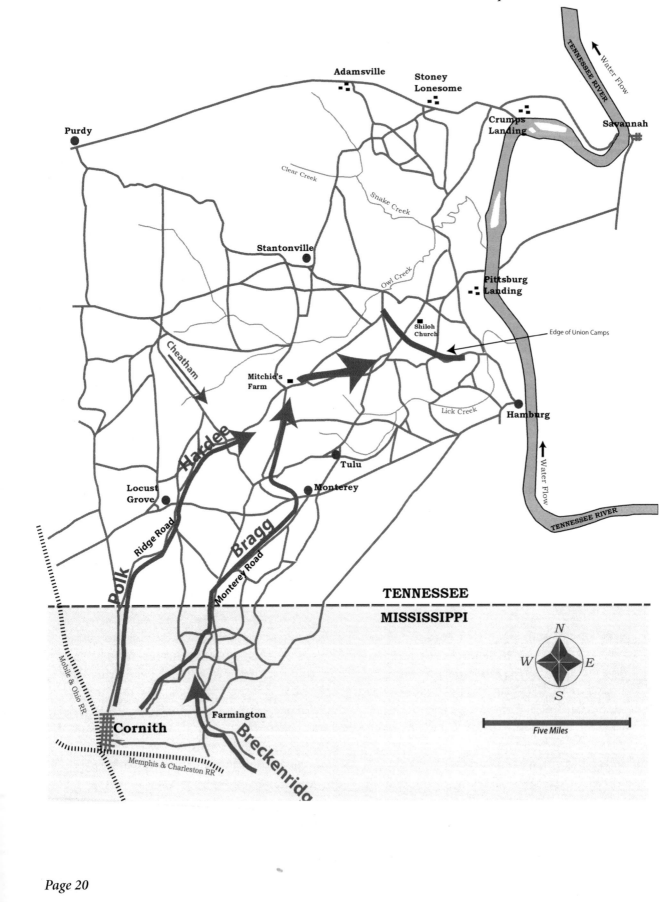

> *Confederate rations on the march usually consisted of a combination of flour and grease, sometimes with molasses. Prior to a march they would fry bacon and use the grease mixed with flour to make biscuits which they wrapped in cloth and stored in their haversacks. They claimed the concoction was "tougher than a mule's ear."*

in one day. These were not the disciplined regular troops he commanded in the prewar years on the Great Plains. Many of these recruits had not even left Cornith until after the time they were supposed to be attacking at Pittsburg Landing. Secondly, Beauregard's marching orders were too complex, with units winding in and out of columns at various road intersections. Even experienced troops would have had a hard time keeping up with such a march schedule.

Last but not least, the Confederates were no sooner on the road than they encountered the same problem that had plagued Sherman – the sky opened, pouring rain, rain, and more rain like a biblical curse. Thirty nine thousand infantry, plus hundreds of horse-drawn wagons, plus horse-drawn artillery (115 cannons), plus 4,300 cavalry, soon churned the roads into a sticky, gooey mess, bogging the march down to a snail's pace. And the rain was bone-chilling, sometimes turning to hail, soaking the troops in their cotton clothing as they stood or sat for hours with their shoes filled with mud, waiting for crossroads to clear, or lying on the soaked ground, wrapped in a soaked blanket.

Adding to their misery, the men were soon famished. They had been issued five days' rations - three in their pack and two on their company wagons. But they weren't used to rationing food, and they gobbled up their five days' rations within a couple of days. By the time they reached Shiloh, the rain-soaked rookies would be fighting on empty bellies.

The delays caused Johnston to postpone his attack from April 4th to April 5th, and then again from April 5th to April 6th.

The delays and problems in the march would leave the Southern troops exhausted and hungry, with many sick with pneumonia before they even fired a shot at Shiloh. Decades later one private from the 16th Louisiana vividly remembered that night before the battle, hungry, wet and shivering in the darkness as he listened at a Yankee band in the distance playing *Home Sweet Home.*

"I would fight them if they were a million."

And there were even greater problems. By now Beauregard was sure that all surprise had been lost, and he had excellent reason to believe it. Among other matters, such as several clashes around Grant's camp, the green Rebel troops kept shooting off their rifles to make sure their powder still worked after all the rain, and they persisted in raising hardy cheers every time a general rode by. Grant's army would have to be not only asleep, but comatose not to have heard the Confederate approach. Late in the evening of April 5, Beauregard, seconded by most of the corps commanders, urged Johnston to call the whole thing off and wade back to Cornith. Johnston, who usually deferred to Beauregard, now had to make an agonizing decision: Should he send his army forward against the advice of most of his generals, into a possible trap and total disaster; or should he turn his army around and make an ignominious retreat back to Cornith?

Finally he stiffened and said, *"I would fight them if they were a million."*

The attack would proceed.

> *On the approach march, the 7,000 men of Hardee's Corps advanced two abreast up the road at dawn on April 5th, heading toward Shiloh.*
> *Presently a lone rider emerged from the brush, blocking their path. His rifle cradled across his saddle, the stranger shouted "Halt! Who are you?" The startled officers replied that it was Hardee's Corps. "Well then," demanded the picket, "advance and give the word." Having no clue of the password, the officers studied the stranger through their field glasses. Seeing he was wearing butternut britches – the uniform of half the Confederate army – they requested he meet them halfway for a pow-wow. He agreed. Finally face-to-face with the diligent sentry, the officers informed him that he was holding up the advance of a quarter of Johnston's army.*
> *Finally, he relented, though he still wasn't too sure about it: "Well, I suppose you can go; but it's agin' orders."*

Chapter 4   First Clash

Fraley Field, April 6

On the afternoon of April 4th, Union Col. Everett Peabody reviewed his brigade in Spain Field, which on the south side of the encampment. His was one of two brigades in Brig. Gen. Benjamin Prentiss's 6th Division. Forced to cancel his review due to heavy rain, Peabody was informed that some of his men had spotted a squad of Rebel cavalry casually observing them from the woods at the south end of the field. Enemy soldiers allowed so close to a Federal encampment? This seemed odd to the Union recruits, and also to Peabody; but the higher command – Sherman – remained unconcerned. In fact, Sherman, who had almost lost his job by getting too animated back in Kentucky, was sick of hearing about the jumpy recruits' sightings of the enemy. He even threatened to arrest anyone who brought him irritating reports like that.

Clearly the new soldiers had a lot to learn about military matters.

The next afternoon, April 5th, back on the same Spain Field, division commander Prentiss reviewed his brigades - Peabody's and Col. Madison Miller's. During the proceedings, Maj. James E. Powell of the 25th Missouri, part of Peabody's brigade, noticed a group of enemy riders again boldly observing the Federals from the southeastern edge of the tree line. Powell reported this to Prentiss, who ordered a 4pm patrol comprised of companies from the 21st and 25th Missouri of Peabody's brigade, led by Col. David Moore.

Moore and his men marched cautiously down the road a mile and a half to Seay Field, on the southwest edge of the encampment. There they encountered several Negro slaves who claimed that earlier in the day they had seen as many as 200 Rebels in the area. But darkness soon fell and the patrol saw nothing, though some of the men claimed they heard thrashing in the woods. Still, they hadn't actually *seen* anything, so when the patrol returned and reported, Prentiss was unimpressed, telling Peabody and his men to forget it.

Powell's Reconnaissance
3 AM – 6:15 AM

But Peabody *couldn't* forget it. He lay awake staring at the tent ceiling, conjuring up images of Rebels lurking nearby in those dark woods. Finally he couldn't stand it! With or without Prentiss' permission, Peabody intended to find out just what in the hell was going on out there in those woods. Around midnight he rousted up Maj. Powell, ordering him to take out a patrol at 3am and make another reconnaissance of Seay Field, hoping to surprise any Rebels lurking at that early hour.

So in the chilly darkness of 3am, Maj. Powell formed up about 250 grumbling soldiers from five companies of the 25th Missouri and 12th Michigan. They marched down the same farm lane Col. Moore had taken the previous evening. (Today that road is named Reconnaissance Road) It led toward Seay Field, and beyond that, another field called Fraley Field. The latter was a 40-acre cotton field once owned by a farmer named James Fraley.

It was spooky out there on that clear, chilly night under a quarter moon. At one point, two nervous Union squads almost blasted each other, which would have required a lot of explaining from Peabody as to why he sent out an unauthorized patrol.

As the sleepy Federals reached Seay Field, they were surprised by Confederate cavalry pickets who, equally surprised, fired off three quick shots before vanishing into the darkness. Powell's men were now wide awake as he formed them into a long skirmish line and advanced warily into Fraley Field. About 200 yards in, the Federals collided with two, seven-man outposts of enemy sentries. These belonged to Maj. Earon Hardcastle's 3rd Mississippi Battalion of Wood's Brigade, Hardee's Corps. Hardcastle's regiment was arrayed about 300 yards behind the pickets, on a slight rise on the edge of an adjoining field owned by a farmer named Wilse Wood.

The Confederate sentries fired off a volley and raced back to Hardcastle's main line, where his 280 men were now fully alert. Powell's men continued

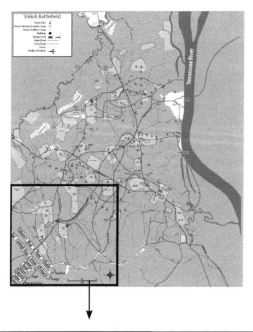

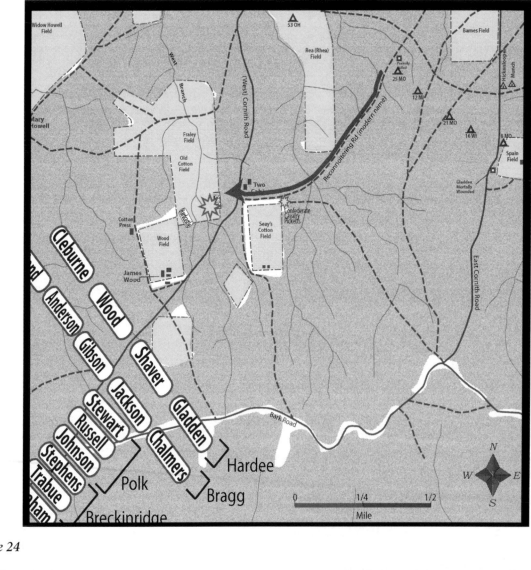

advancing. When they got within 200 yards, the Mississippians opened fired in earnest. The Federals responded. In the darkness both sides blazed away at muzzle flashes for over an hour, from about 5am to 6:15am. Both sides took an unknown number of casualties. In the growing light of dawn, Powell spotted Rebel cavalry about try to curl around his left flank. (Actually it was an escort company, the Jefferson Mounted Rifles, searching for a route through the woods to bring up artillery).

But Powell and his men also were the first Federals to get an idea of what they were really up against when part of Hardee's 9,000 man battleline loomed on the opposite side of Farley Field, the Rebels marching shoulder to shoulder in the standard two-rank battle order and heading straight at Powell and his men. Powell ordered his bugler to sound retreat.

Earlier that morning, back at the intersection of Cornith and Bark Roads at Johnston's headquarters, Beauregard was still trying to convince Johnston to call off the whole attack because he feared they were walking into a trap. Call it off! After that terrible march just to get here? It would break the army's morale.

"Tonight we will water our horses on the Tennessee."

In the middle of their debate, they heard the firing at Fraley Field. It was too late to second-guess themselves now. After listening a few moments, Johnston simply stated, "*Gentleman, the battle has commenced.*" Wearing a big soft hat with a black plum, Johnston mounted his horse, Fire Eater, vowing, "*Tonight we will water our horses on the Tennessee.*"

At around 6:40am, he rode off to the sound of the guns.

And the Battle of Shiloh was on.

Google Map Links (scan with OC Reader to go to online maps)

Spain Field

Seay Field

Fraley Field

Chapter 5   Prentiss Reinforces

7am - 7:30am

Hearing the firing in Fraley Field, 6th Division commander, Brig. Gen. Prentiss, rode into Peabody's camp around 7am, demanding to know what all the shooting was about. Prentiss, a 41-year-old Mexican War veteran, was yet another Illinois lawyer who dabbled in politics, reportedly

Brig. Gen. Benjamin M. Prentiss (c)
1819 - 1901

with ties to President Lincoln. Prentiss had feuded with Grant back in Cairo, Illinois, and a least one newspaper quoted Prentiss as stating that he wouldn't serve "*under a drunkard*." Grant must have read it, but he still had enough confidence in Prentiss to give him command of the 6th Division.

When Peabody confessed that he had sent out a patrol, Prentiss exploded, accusing Peabody of triggering a major engagement and threatening to hold him responsible for his actions. Peabody said nothing, and instead walked over and sat down on his camp chest to begin his breakfast, jamming his spoon into his gruel and muttering that he was always responsible for his actions.

About this time a messenger arrived from Maj. Powell, reporting that he was being driven back by an enemy force of 3,000. Prentiss dispatched five companies from the 21st Missouri commanded by Col. David Moore to reinforce Powell. As these reinforcements headed out, a company of the 16th Wisconsin, just returning to camp from picket duty, decided to join Moore's force.

Around 6:30am Moore and his men encountered Powell's retreating force. A 45-year-old hog farmer from Missouri, Col. Moore was said by one acquaintance to "*get madder and swear longer than any man I ever saw*." And right now Moore was madder than hell, and he ripped into Powell for cowardice. Powell tried to explain that there were a

lot of Rebels out there, but Moore wasn't buying it. He ordered all of Powell's able-bodied men to join his force, and sent Powell back to camp with the wounded. Moore also sent back a courier to Prentiss, requesting the five additional companies of the 21st be brought up, promising that with reinforcements he could "lick 'em."

Back at camp, Peabody could hear the firing intensity growing ever louder. Finally springing to his feet he ordered his drummer boy to sound the "long roll" – the signal for battle. As Peabody sat on his mount on the right side of the line, a furious Prentiss rode up and again accused Peabody of inciting a battle. Peabody responded that it seemed to be the Rebels who were inciting the battle. But in any case, he gave Prentiss a snappy salute and said, "*If I brought on the fight, I am to lead the van*." He then posted the 25th Missouri and 12th Michigan on a low ridge facing the southern direction of the firing. These men were soon joined by the remaining companies of the 16th Wisconsin.

"If I brought on the fight, I am to lead the van."

Meanwhile, Moore's column never made it to Fraley Field. Marching four men abreast about 300 yards down the same road he and Powell had used on their earlier reconnaissances, Moore and his men had almost passed Seay Field around 7am when they took heavy fire from the fence row on the south end of the field. Moore ordered a charge

Col. Everett Peabody (k)
1830 - 1862

from the western side of the field which, given the Confederate numbers, probably would have met disaster. But the charge didn't happen because, just as Moore waved his sword to advance, he shrieked as a bullet shattered his shin bone. Along with thousands

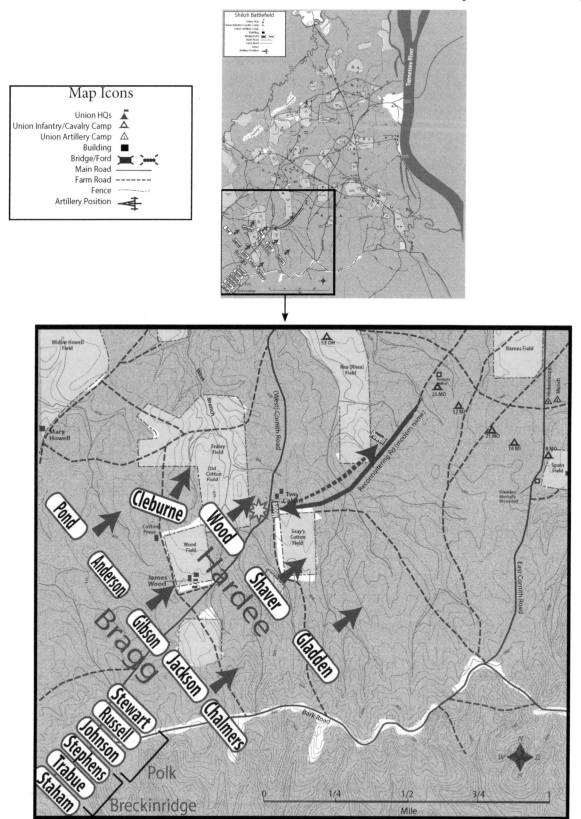

Col. Powell's detail replaces Maj. Moore's, but is soon forced to retreat.

of others, he would lose his leg to amputation that night on a transport.

An officer rushed back to Powell shouting, "*For God's sake, Major, take command quick, the Colonel is wounded.*" But the firing had died down momentarily and Powell, one of the few Federals with no illusions about the size of the enemy force, ordered his men to back to camp.

At about this time, nine miles away, back in Savannah, General Grant was just sitting down to breakfast when he heard a rumbling noise coming from Pittsburg Landing.

It was now around 7:30am.

Google Map Links (scan with OC Reader to go to online maps)

Seay Field

Fraley Field

Chapter 6   Attack into Prentiss' Camp

8am - 9am

Brig. Gen. Prentiss and his two brigade commanders, Col. Peabody and Col. Madison Miller, were uncertain as to whether Peabody's men had just fought a large skirmish that was now ended, or whether there was more to come. Peabody and his four regiments would be the first to be enlightened. Their tent camps, on the southern edge of the Union camp, stretched along Purdy-Hamburg Road, directly in the path of the approaching Confederates.

Peabody, a successful engineer and a Harvard man from a prominent Massachusetts family, had been seriously wounded back in 1861 in a scrap at Lexington, Missouri. Many of the men in his brigade had also been in that fight.

By 7:30am the remainder of his men not involved in the early morning skirmish stood at parade-rest in front of their camp. Suddenly the troops noticed something strange – dozens of terrified rabbits scampering into the troops' formation. Presently they noticed something even stranger – a battleline of several thousand Confederates marching toward them – blood-red banners flapping and bayonets glistening. These were Brig. Gen. S.A.M. Wood's and Col. Robert. G. Shaver's brigades – part of Hardee's mile and a quarter attack wave. One Union private from the 25th Missouri described the Confederate approach as "*A sublime but awful scene, as they advanced slowly, steadily and silently till within about 125 yards.*" Another stated: "*We were dumbfounded at seeing an enormous force of Confederate troops marching directly toward us.*" For an unknown number of moments, the Federals simply gaped, not quite believing their eyes.

"[It was] a sublime but awful scene, as they advanced slowly, steadily and silently till within about 125 yards."

But the Rebels meant business. Once in range, they halted and unleashed a volley, sending Peabody's men bursting back through the camp like a covey of quail. The Union encampments, packed with thousands of tents – teepee-like Sibley Tents for the troops, and wall tents for the officers – had a disorganizing effect on both sides. They broke up the cohesion of the Union ranks as they fled back through the camps in retreat, with many soldiers not stopping until they reached Pittsburg Landing.

But the tents also broke up the lines of the attacking Confederates, mainly because of looting, as the famished Rebel soldiers stopped to pillage the camps, finding a treasure trove of booty. Lt. Liberty I. Nixon of the 26th Alabama noted that the "*Yankees… left everything they had… corn, oats, pants, vests, drawers, shirts, shoes, and a great many other things in great abundance and of the finest quality.*"

Some of the Federal regiments, such as the 25th Missouri, included many former members of the regular army. They held their fire until the enemy came within 125 yards, and then unleashed an effective volley that sent the surprised Rebels racing for the rear. It was all Confederate officers, including Gen. Johnston himself, could do to herd the green troops back into a line of battle. Now the Confederates advanced again, this time to within 75 yards, triggering a heavy firefight which raged until the numerically superior Confederates, specifically S.A.M. Wood's brigade, managed to curl around Peabody's unsupported flanks and force him back.

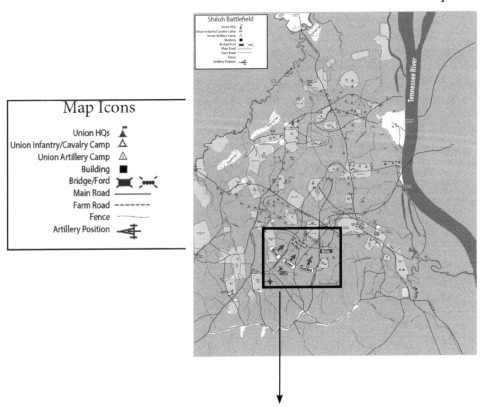

Map Icons

Union HQs	
Union Infantry/Cavalry Camp	
Union Artillery Camp	
Building	
Bridge/Ford	
Main Road	
Farm Road	
Fence	
Artillery Position	

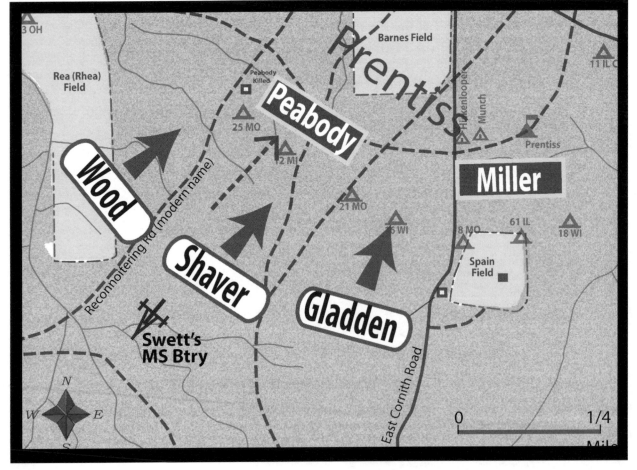

Peabody Falls

Peabody, desperately trying to rally his men, rode to and fro, shouting, "*Remember Lexington!*" In the process he was wounded four times, but remained mounted. Finally, at around 8:45am, seeing his brigade disintegrating, he shouted above the din of battle, "*The 25th Missouri is disgraced!*" Suddenly, his head snapped back and he hurled his sword into the air as a fifth bullet found its mark, striking him in the upper lip and passing through the back of his head, killing him. As he dropped from his horse, it galloped wildly towards the Confederate lines, stirrups flapping in the air.

Maj. Powell, who had earlier been accused of cowardice by Col. Moore, was also killed in this melee while trying to rally the brigade.

Peabody's brigade was wrecked, and most of its survivors now fled toward Pittsburg Landing. Though the Confederate attack was successful so far, it was dangerously behind schedule. Johnston expected his battle line to slam into the Federal encampment at 6am. But here it was 7:30am before they even reached Peabody's camps. They had wasted too much time skirmishing in Seay Field, and that precious hour and a half would be dearly missed later in the day. And even more time was lost as the Confederate troops stopped to pillage the Federal tents.

At about this time, the steamer Tigress, with Grant on board, was just pulling into the Landing.

It was 9am.

Sibley tents were designed by former U.S. Capt. Henry Hopkins Sibley (by 1862, a Confederate brigadier general) and patterned after the teepees of the Plains Indians. A regulation Sibley tent was a large cone of canvas, 18 feet in diameter, 12 feet tall, and supported by center poll, with a circular opening at the top for ventilation and a cone-shaped stove for heat. It could fit 12 men in comfort or, more commonly, 20 men in considerably less.

Each company usually had five Sibley tents, and at the head of the row was a wall tent for the officers. Some ten to fifteen feet separated the companies to allow room for washing and cooking. The quartermaster and hospital tents were located nearby. There were some 5,000 tents packed on almost every open field around Pittsburg Landing. In the middle of the coming battle, they were an impediment to both attacker and defender.

Also intertwined with these Union camps were sutler wagons, which were basically mobile civilian commissaries selling things the soldiers wanted but the army didn't supply - tasty snacks, playing cards, writing paper, envelopes, postage stamps, photos of naked women, and maybe even a shot of whiskey.

Confederates charge into Prentiss's camps early Sunday morning. Apparently this artist wasn't aware that the troops were using Sibley, teepee-style tents, not wall tents. Illustration from Battles & Leaders, Vol 1, p. 472

One of the Confederate soldiers in this attack was an Irish immigrant, Pvt. Henry Morton Stanley. A future journalist–adventurer who, nine years later, would locate and resupply the famed English missionary David Livingstone in central Africa and utter the famous phrase, "Dr. Livingstone, I presume?" On this morning Stanley was a rifleman in the 6th Arkansas in Shaver's Brigade.

"We… loaded, and fired, with such nervous haste as though it depended on each of us how soon the fiendish roar would be hushed. My nerves tingled, my pulses beat double-quick, my heart throbbed loudly, almost painfully… I was angry with my rear rank [the soldier directly behind him], because he made my eyes smart with the powder of his musket; and I felt like cuffing him for deafening my ears!… We continued advancing, step-by-step, loading and firing as we went. To every forward step, they took a backward move, loading and firing as they slowly withdrew… After a steady exchange of musketry, which lasted some time, we heard the order: "Fix bayonets! On the double-quick!"

Pvt. Henry M. Stanley
1841 - 1904

"There was a simultaneous bound forward… The Federals appeared inclined to await us; but, at this juncture, our men raised a yell, thousands responded to it, and burst out into the wildest yelling it has ever been my lot to hear. It served the double purpose of relieving pent-up feelings and transmitting encouragement along the attacking line…

"They fly!" was echoed from lip to lip. It accelerated our pace, and filled us with a noble rage… It deluded us with rapture, and transfigured each Southerner into an exulting victor. At such a moment, nothing could have halted us. Those savage yells, and the sight of thousands of racing figures coming towards them, discomfited the blue-coats, and when we arrived upon the place where they had stood, they had vanished. Then we caught sight of their beautiful array of tents."

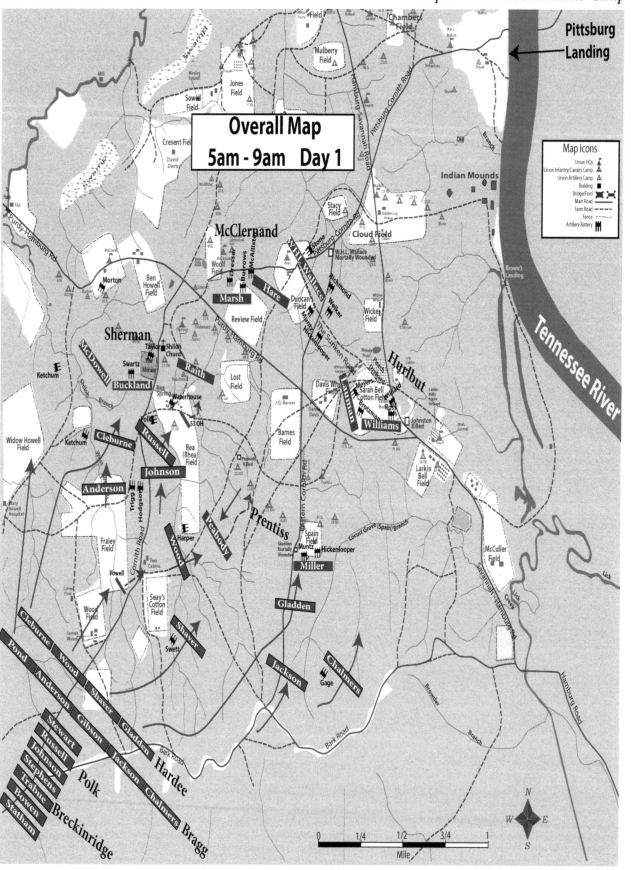

Overall Map
5am - 9am   Day 1

Pittsburg Landing

Indian Mounds

Map Icons
Union HQs
Union Infantry/Cavalry Camp
Union Artillery Camp
Building
Bridge/Ford
Main Road
Farm Road
Fence
Artillery Battery

McClernand

Cloud Field

Stacy Field

Stone

W.H.L. Wallace
W.H. Wallace
W.H.L. Wallace Mortally Wounded

Richmond
Welker

Marsh
Hare
Duncan Field
Review Field

Sherman

McDowell
Taylor
Swartz
Morass
Buckland
Raith
Lost Field
Waterhouse
Rea Spring Branch

Hurlbut

The Sunken Road
Hickenlooper

Davis Wheat Field
Meyers
Sarah Bell
Cotton Field
McArthur
Stuart
Crotzman
Ross
Williams
Johnston Killed

Ketchum
Shiloh Church

Polk
Russell
53 OH

Johnson
Anderson
Ketchum
Trigg
Hodgson
Harper
Wood
Peabody
Powell

Rea (Rhea) Field

Barnes Field
J.G. Barnes
David Davis
Peabody Killed

Prentiss

Spain Field
Muntz
Hickenlooper
Gladden Mortally Wounded
Miller

Locust Grove (Spain) Branch

Larkin Bell Field

McCuller Field

Gladden

Cleburne
Wood
Shaver
Swett

Seay's Cotton Field

Jackson
Gage
Chalmers

Cleburne
Pond
Anderson
Wood
Shaver
Gladden
Jackson
Chalmers
Hardee
Bragg

Stewart
Russell
Johnson
Stephens
Trabue
Bowen
Statham
Polk
Breckinridge

Bark Road

Widow Howell Field
Mary Howell Hospital
Fraley Field
Wood Field

Swartz

Tennessee River

Browns Landing

Lick Creek
Savannah-Hamburg Rd
Hamburg Road

0   1/4   1/2   3/4   1
Mile

N
W   E
S

Chapter 7   The Fighting Spreads East

Miller's Brigade Deploys
7:30am - 8am

Once Peabody's brigade was fully engaged at 7:30am, Prentiss galloped over to his other brigade, Col. Madison Miller's, yelling: "Colonel, get out your brigade! They're fighting on the right!" The 51-year-old Miller, a Mexican War veteran, hastily ordered the 18th Missouri into a line of battle at the north end of Spain field, facing timber. But Prentiss didn't like the position and wisely ordered Miller to redeploy back across the south end of the field where the regiment could command a ravine and have the cleared field to their front.

Col. Madison Miller
1811 - 1866

This new location served as a base for a solid Union battle line. Several companies of the 16th Wisconsin joined Miller's men and extended the line westward across Eastern Corinth Road, while the 18th Wisconsin and 61st Illinois rushed up to extend his line to the east. Two of Prentiss' batteries, Munch's and Hicken-looper's, galloped up and unlimbered on the west and east sides of the road, respectively. And the newly arrived 15th Michigan, as yet unassigned to any brigade, raced up to extend Miller's position farther east. But the 15th had a problem – no ammunition.

Like the "sweep of a midsummer thunder-head rolling across the stubble field," the battle engulfed Miller's brigade.

By 8am Miller's battle line, 3,000 men strong, was as complete as it was ever going to be. The green troops fingered their gun triggers nervously as they waited their turn, listening to the crash of battle grow closer from the direction of Peabody's brigade to the west. Then, *"like the sweep of a midsummer thunderhead rolling across the stubble field,"* the battle rolled east and engulfed them. Soon thousands of men dressed in butternut emerged from the woods in line of battle, their rifles at right shoulder shift, topped off with foot-and-a-half bayonets.

Gladden's Brigade Strikes
8:30am - 9am

Storming Miller's position was Brig. Gen. Jones M. Withers' division, which consisted of three brigades under Brig. Gens. Aldey Gladden, James Chalmers, and John Jackson. These men were part of Bragg's Corps and therefore part of the second wave of the Confederate assault force.

The lieutenant was "fairly wild with excitement, jumping up and down like a hen on a hot griddle."

Waiting to receive the Confederate assault, 18-year-old Cpl. Leander Stillwell of the 61st Illinois, thought they must have disturbed a nest of bees, because of an *"incessant humming above our heads,"* Then he realized those were not bees, but bullets. He also remembered that once the order to fire was given, *"from one end of the regiment to the next leaped a red sheet of flame."* Someone behind him yelled, *"Shoot! Shoot! Why don't you shoot?"* Stillwell looked around to see one of the second lieutenants *"fairly wild with excitement, jumping up an down like a hen on a hot griddle."* Stillwell replied that he couldn't see anything to shoot at because of the smoke. The lieutenant ordered him to shoot anyhow, which he did, though he thought it was ridiculous to fire without a target.

A Confederate cavalryman watching from a rise later wrote, *"We could see the lines of our army for long distances, right and left as they advanced with marvelous precision, with regimental colors flying, and all the bands playing 'Dixie.'"*

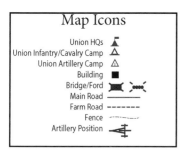

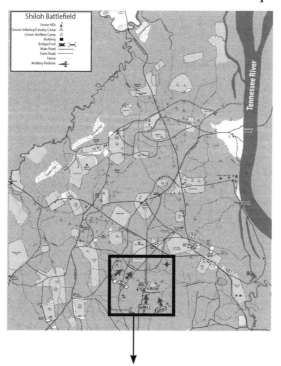

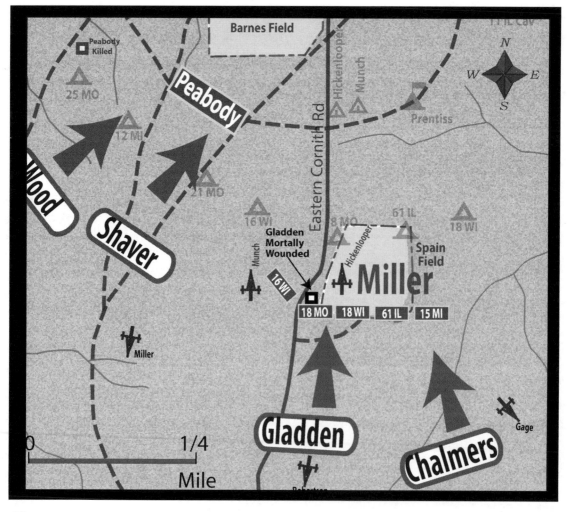

Col. Adley H. Gladden (mw)
1810 - 1862

Gladden's brigade had actually been advanced by Johnston to the east flank of the first wave line (Hardee's Corps), so as to extend the Confederate right flank and secure it along Lick Creek and the Tennessee River. But by 7:30am, Johnston realized that Hardee's attack was veering too far west, and so ordered Chalmers' brigade to fill the gap, once again extending the Confederate right flank so that it remained connected with Lick Creek.

The end result was that Gladden's brigade confronted Miller's Union line thirty minutes before Chalmers arrived to support him. Gladden ordered his Alabama regiments into the fray anyway, but before his attack was even launched, his troops encountered a devastating fire from Miller's infantry and artillery. Capt. Felix Robertson's four-gun Florida battery raced up to support Gladden. Not long after, Capt. Charles P. Gage's Alabama battery from Chalmers' brigade also galloped up, dropping trails within 200 yards of Miller's line.

Both Confederate batteries took heavy infantry fire, but they helped pave the way for Gadden's infantry assault, which began around 8:45am.

The portly, 51-year-old Gladden, a Mexican War veteran and New Orleans merchant, was conspicuously mounted on horseback as he led his men forward into the ferocious fire of Union infantry and artillery. At least one of the batteries switched to canister, and almost immediately Gladden was struck by a shell fragment, nearly tearing his left arm from its shoulder socket. "*Scott,*" he yelled to his aide, "*I'm struck, but let's go on.*" But after moving a few more steps, he admitted, "*It's a serious hurt, help me down, Scott.*" An ambulance carried the mortally wounded colonel to the rear, where a correspondent noted that he was "*pale, faint, but still smiling.*"

With the loss of their leader, the Alabamians fell back. Command passed to the brigade's senior colonel, Daniel Adams of the 1st Louisiana, a former lawyer. Adams grabbed a regimental flag and called for the men to make a second attack. The Alabama men surged forward, supported by Robertson's cannoneers, who pushed their guns almost into point blank range of Miller's line.

Union Cpl. Stillwell saw "*men in gray and brown clothes running through the camp on our right.*" He also remembered, "*I saw something else too, that sent a chill all through me. It was a kind of flag I had never seen before; a gaudy sort of thing with red bars. The smoke around it was low and dense and kept me from seeing the man who was carrying it but I plainly saw the banner. It was going fast, with a jerky motion, which told me that the bearer was at the double quick.*"

> "*It was a kind of flag I had never saw before; a gaudy sort of thing with red bars.*"

Veteran troops might have withstood Adam's assault, but Miller's men were not veterans. Gradually his brigade began leaking men as they drifted to the rear.

The Collapse of Miller's Line
8:30am - 9am

Prentiss' left brigade, Miller's, was facing the storm of Adams's attack; Prentiss' right brigade, Peabody's, was collapsing. To protect Miller's right flank, Prentiss ordered Miller's men to "*change front to the right.*" This was the wrong order to give raw troops in the middle of a battle; worse, at just that moment Adams renewed his assault, putting the Federal recruits under heavy fire and creating even more confusion in their ranks.

> "*[The] Rebel Yell ... caused an involuntary thrill of terror to pass like an electric shock through even the bravest heart.*"

To cap things off, Chalmers' men finally appeared; its men shrieking "*with a Rebel Yell that caused an involuntary thrill of terror to pass like an electric shock through even the bravest heart,*" according to Capt. Andrew Hickenlooper, commanding an Ohio battery. The Confederates poured out

"At intervals we can see the faces of the foe, blackened with powder, and glaring with demonic fury, lost to all human impulses and full of the fiendish desire to kill."

of the wooded ravine on Adam's right and slammed into the 18th Wisconsin. The Wisconsin troops broke and fled, creating a fatal gap in the middle of Miller's line. Immediately Confederate troops flooded into this gap, shattering Miller's entire line.

Pvt. George McBride of the 15th Michigan described it: "*There was the crash of musketry, the roar of artillery, the yells, the smoke, the jar, the terrible energy. At intervals we can see the faces of the foe, blackened with powder, and glaring with demonic fury, lost to all human impulses, and full of the fiendish desire to kill.*"

Prentiss and Miller desperately tried to rally the troops to a new position at the north end of Spain Field, but it was hopeless. By 9am the brigade had been driven through its camp, a terrified mob fleeing toward the Landing.

Federal artillery also suffered heavily. Hickenlooper's Ohio battery was hit by terrible fire that shot down 59 of its 80 horses. Two of the guns fell directly into Confederate hands.

Somehow, Hicken-

Capt. Andrew Hickenlooper
1837 - 1904

looper's men extricated the other four guns by hand, but the loss of the horses would seriously hinder the battery's mobility for the remainder of the day, which is why attacking infantry always targeted the enemy's artillery horses.

As was the story throughout the day, the victorious Confederate attack stalled when the attackers

stopped to plunder the Union camps, saving the fleeing Federals from even greater destruction. In one tent vacated by the 18th Wisconsin, a beaming young lieutenant emerged with an armful of trophies. But his smile froze as he looked up to see Gen. Johnston himself, mounted on his steed, Fire-Eater, and surrounded by his glittering staff. Johnston, intent on stopping the pillaging, must have looked like Jesus and his Apostles to the astonished lieutenant. "*None of that, sir,*" the general bellowed, "*we are not here to plunder!*" The young officer was horrified; to be chewed out by the commanding general for stealing pots and pans in the middle of a battle was never helpful to a lieutenant's career.

Realizing he had been too harsh, Johnston softened the scold by smiling and doing something silly; he leaned over to pick up a tin cup off a table, announcing to all, "*Let this be my share of the spoils today.*"

Johnston packed that cup around for the rest of his life.

Chalmers & Jackson Redeploy
9am - 10am

After destroying the Miller's brigade, and pausing to plunder the Federal camp, the jubilant men of Adams and Chalmers continued surging north to the Purdy-Hamburg Road, where they were reinforced by Jackson's brigade of Wither's division. There they would briefly encounter Hurlbut's Union division at Sarah Bell's Old Cotton Field, before Johnston pulled Jackson and Chalmers's brigades off and sent them farther east to deal with the threat of another Union division, which would turn out to be non-existent. But in this ad hoc way, more by accident than design, Johnston was shifting more attacking power to his right flank, resurrecting his original plan to launch a powerful sweep on the Confederate right toward Pittsburg Landing.

Prentiss' division was wrecked. Of the 5,400 men in his division, only about 1,000 continued fighting as Prentiss fell back to what would soon be called the Sunken Road.

Union Pvt. McBride described the collapse of Miller's defense: "The enemy flank us and are moving to our rear; someone calls out 'Everybody for himself!' The line breaks, I go with others, back and down the hill, across a small ravine, and into the camp of the 11th Illinois Calvary with the howling, rushing mass of the enemy pressing in close pursuit... The striking of shot on the ground threw up little clouds of dust, and the falling of men all around me impressed me with the desire to get out of there... I felt sure that a cannonball was close behind me, giving me chase as I started for the river... I never ran so fast before."

Canister is basically a tin can containing anywhere from 26 to 30 one-inch iron balls packed with sawdust. About two-and-half pounds of gunpowder is first rammed down the cannon barrel, followed by the canister can. When ignited, the canister balls spew out like a shotgun blast with 26 to 30 iron golf-balls flying into densely packed infantry lines. It was said that just one of these balls could cut a man` in half at 500 yards.

Civil War canister, dug up and placed in a basket.

A Mississippi cavalryman was under artillery fire while watching the fighting from a distant hill. "Many solid shot we saw strike the ground," he said, "bounding like rubber balls, passing over our heads, making a hideous music in their course."

But one of the cannon balls struck the tail of his horse, Bremer. The horse was holding his tail high in the air due to the excitement and the cannonball "cut away about half of it, bone and all."

From then on Bremer was known as "Bobtail Bremer."

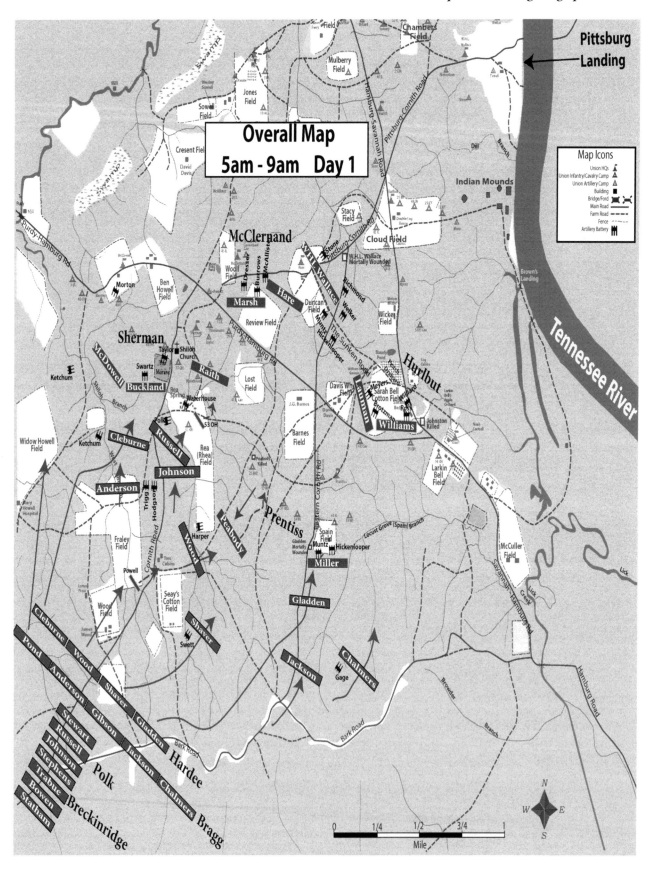

**Overall Map
5am - 9am   Day 1**

Pittsburg
Landing

Tennessee River

Map Icons

Union HQs
Union Infantry/Cavalry Camp
Union Artillery Camp
Building
Bridge/Ford
Main Road
Farm Road
Fence
Artillery Battery

Indian Mounds

McClernand

Sherman

McDowell

Buckland

Raith

Marsh

Hare

W.H.L. Wallace

W.H.L. Wallace
Mortally Wounded

Richmond

Welker

Wicker
Field

Hurlbut

Stuart

Williams

Ross

Johnston Killed

Larkin
Bell
Field

McCuller
Field

Ketchum

Widow Howell
Field

Cleburne

Russell

Johnson

Anderson

Polk

Hodgson

Trigg

Wood

Harper

Peabody

Prentiss

Miller

Gladden

Gladden
Mortally
Wounded

Muntz

Hickenlooper

Shaver

Swett

Jackson

Chalmers

Gage

Cleburne

Pond

Wood

Anderson

Shaver

Gibson

Stewart

Russell

Johnson

Stephens

Trabue

Bowen

Statham

Polk

Jackson

Gladden

Chalmers

Hardee

Breckinridge

Bragg

Purdy-Hamburg Rd

Bark Road

Hamburg Road

0   1/4   1/2   3/4   1
Mile

N
W   E
S

Google Map Links (scan with OC Reader to go to online maps)

Spain Field

Sarah Bell's Old Cotton Field

Chapter 8   Sherman Attacked

6am - 8am

Attack on the 53rd Ohio

Around 4pm on Saturday afternoon, April 5th, the day before the battle, Col. Jesse R. Appler, a 31-year-old former Ohio probate judge and auditor, now commanding the 53rd Ohio, received a report that Rebel cavalry had been spotted snooping around the south end of Rea Field. Appler continued drilling his troops, but he sent a platoon to investigate. Suddenly shots rang out from the platoon's vicinity. An officer came racing back, yelling that they had been fired on "*by a line of men in butternut clothes.*" "*There're Rebs out there ,*" he exclaimed, "*thicker'n fleas on a dog's back!*" Appler instantly ordered the long drum-roll sounded to form his men into ranks, and dispatched a messenger to Sherman.

"There're Rebs out there thicker'n fleas on a dog's back."

The colonel was standing at the head of his regiment when the courier promptly returned and announced in a sarcastic, twangy voice, loud enough to be heard by all, "*Colonel Appler, General Sherman says: 'Take your damn regiment back to Ohio. There ain't no enemy closer'n Cornith!*" The regiment roared with laughter. A humiliated Appler dismissed his regiment.

"Take your damn regiment back to Ohio. There ain't no enemy closer'n Cornith!"

Sherman had scornfully dismissed several warnings of the enemy proximity in the past two days, and he'd soon have to eat his words, being particularly mortified to see them widely printed in newspapers by those dirty, irresponsible, corrupt, malicious reporters.

Like Col. Peabody in Prentiss' division, Appler remained uneasy about an enemy wandering so close to his camp, regardless of Sherman's sneering, so he established a small outpost near the south end of Rea Field. Early the next morning,

Sunday, April 6th, these pickets came racing back to the camp, breathlessly reporting Rebel troops on the Cornith Road just west of the field. Then Appler heard firing to the southwest in Fraley Field. The colonel was still contemplating this when a wounded soldier of Prentiss' division limped into camp announcing fighting on Prentiss' front.

Sherman or no Sherman, Appler ordered the drum roll again, and the 53rd fell into line directly in front of its camp, facing west toward Fraley Field. No sooner was this done than someone spotted Confederate troops advancing across the south end of Rea Field, toward the regiment's right flank. Appler therefore pivoted his line to face south, ordering his men forward just beyond the camp. But now Confederate skirmishers appeared in the woods around Shiloh Branch, directly to the *east.* There were enemy approaching on three sides of Appler's regiment. The whole place was *infested* with Rebels!

"*This is no place for us*" muttered the increasingly rattled Appler, who pivoted his regiment back through its camp and withdrew into the edge of the woods, now facing his men east. Helping buck up Appler and his frightened men, a 2-gun section of Capt. Allen Waterhouse's battery, rolled into position at the edge of the woods on Appler's right.

In the midst of all this pivoting, Appler dispatched a courier to Sherman, reporting the enemy sightings. Incredibly, especially given the level of firing he must have been hearing, which had been going on for nearly an hour, Sherman scoffed at the 53rd's courier, "*You must be mighty scared over there.*"

But now, finally, around 7am when the shooting on Fraley and Seay fields had been going on for almost an hour, Sherman and his staff rode over to Rae Field, trotting into the field about 200 yards south of Appler's tent camp. Using his field glass, Sherman studied the south end of the field, trying to identify the soldiers advancing east across it. Just then, one of his aides called out to look to the right.

What Sherman saw to his right were troops of Brig. Generals S.A.M. Wood's and Patrick Cle-

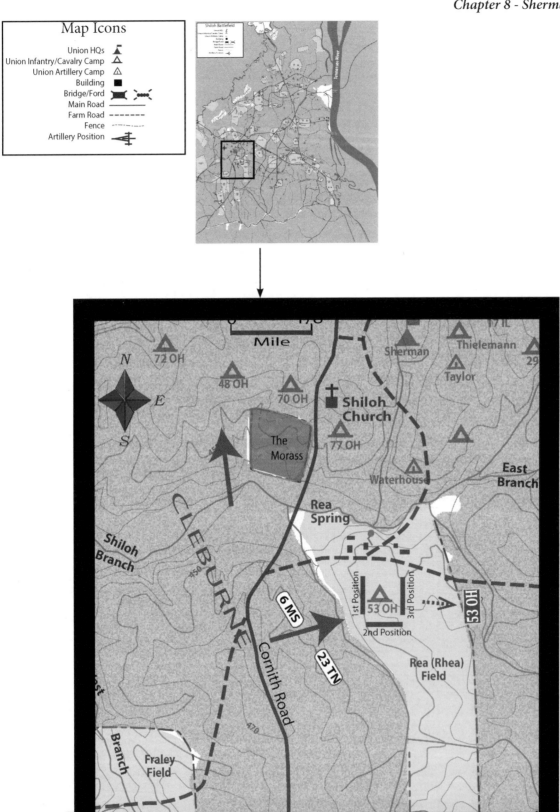

Map Icons

Union HQs
Union Infantry/Cavalry Camp
Union Artillery Camp
Building
Bridge/Ford
Main Road
Farm Road
Fence
Artillery Position

The 53rd Ohio shifts position three times in the face of Confederates attacking, seemingly from every direction.

burne's Confederate brigades, currently in the process of shooting him. Sherman instinctively threw up his arm in a defensive motion as the Rebels fired. A bullet, or more likely buckshot, struck Sherman's upraised hand; another bullet, likely meant for Sherman, cracked open the head of his orderly, Sgt. Thomas Holiday, killing him. "My God, we're attacked!," Sherman exclaimed as he beat a hasty retreat back to Appler's camp. There he ordered the colonel to hold his position, promising to support him. With that, Sherman galloped off to direct the rest of his division. *Finally,* the scales had dropped from his eyes!

IN HINDSIGHT

Sherman's reckless disregard of enemy movements until his ride into Rae Field was probably the worst performance of his career. Had he been killed in that initial salvo, history would remember him as a fool. What saved his career and possibly Grant's army, besides the Confederates' poor aim, was Sherman's outstanding performance throughout the rest of the battle.

The 53rd Ohio Fights & Retreats
7am – 8am

Modern Changes in Rea Field
Running through the north end of Rea Field (sometimes spelled Rhea Field) is a ridge that composed part of the first position of Sherman's 5th Division at the start of the battle. The Rea cabin stood just north of the road. Farther in that northern direction, in the ravine, are Rea Springs and the east fork of Shiloh Branch. Out of sight today on the ridge beyond that ravine (but quite visible in the thinner forest growth of the 1860s) is Shiloh Church, near where Sherman made his headquarters. The 53rd Ohio, on what would soon be the left flank of Sherman's division, made its camp along the northern section of Rea Field, just south of the farm lane that cut through the field.

Looking down the length of Rea Field, in 1862 the open field extended much farther south than it does today. The far tree-line was then about 900 yards from the farm lane instead of the 200 or so yards today. To the southwest about 1,500 yards away is Fraley Field, out of sight beyond the trees today as it was then.

Soon after Sherman's departure, the 53rd Ohio suffered the full fury of the Confederate attack.

At least some companies of the 53rd were protected by hastily erected breastworks formed by throwing additional rails on the five-foot high snake-rail fence bordering the field. They also used bales of hay and perhaps a few logs to bolster their line.

Zeroing in on them in from the high ground across Shiloh Branch, 800 yards to the southwest, was Maj. Frances Shoup, commander of an Arkansas artillery battalion. With a deafening explosion Shoup's 12 guns opened fire on the Buckeyes as well as other Union positions around Shiloh Church. After firing only two rounds in reply, the 2-gun section of Waterhouse's battery, acting on orders from Sherman's Chief of Artillery, Maj. Ezra Taylor, limbered up and raced off to join the rest of the battery farther north, on the high ground on the other side of Rea Springs and the east fork of Shiloh Branch.

Even as they watched their artillery protection racing for the rear while enemy shells rained in, the Ohioans saw large formations of Rebel infantry advancing toward them from the thickets along the main fork of Shiloh Branch – soldiers of the 6th Mississippi and 23rd Tennessee of Cleburne's brigade. But the obstructing brush and the tents of the camp disorganized the Confederate lines, causing the Southerners to attack in a piecemeal fashion. The 53rd held its fire until the enemy closed to 50 yards, then blasted them with a devastating volley. The 6th Mississippi also had its left flank raked by Union artillery around Shiloh Church. By now, artillery iron – cannon balls, explosions and canister – poured into the ranks of both infantry lines, but the men just had to ignore it and focus on shooting at each other.

But the Confederates were the more exposed as they crossed the open field. Their attacking wave broke and fled back over the crest, only to reform and come again, but more cautiously, settling for a gunfight instead of an attack. A more sustained firefight now raged at murderous range, with even more devastating results to the Confederate attackers, who finally fled in disorder, leaving the ground littered with 300 dead and wounded out of their initial muster of 425. The 6th Mississippi was the

"Cap'n, give me a gun. This blamed fight ain't got no rear!"

first of many Southern units that day to discover that whipping Yankees was far easier in theory than practice.

Union casualties were comparatively light. The men, the ones still there, had stood their ground. They had some barricade protection. The Confederates weren't attacking at the moment. All and all, the 53rd Ohio seemed to be more than holding its own. But suddenly, for no apparent reason, Col. Appler's nerve cracked. Shouting "*Fall back and save yourselves,*" he led the way in a race to the rear, the regiment following in a disorderly retreat. Capt. Wells S. Jones, the senior captain, took command and tried to rally what was left of the 53rd, with limited success. But the ones he did rally were the bravest of the regiment – those still willing to fight.

By now, Confederate bullets were snapping in from all points of the compass. One soldier was shot in the shin. Capt. Wells ordered him to the rear. The man hobbled off. Presently he hobbled back, disgusted. "*Cap'n, give me a gun,*" he said. "*This blamed fight ain't got no rear!*"

IN HINDSIGHT

After the collapse of the 53rd Ohio, the Union line fell like stacked dominoes, starting at Rea Field and running from east to west along Sherman's line, eventually forcing Sherman to abandon his initial position along the ridge of his camp. But the 53rd would have been broken sooner or later anyway. Unnoticed by the Confederates because of the dense terrain, a yawning 600 yard gap in the Federal line stretched from Appler's left flank to the right of Prentiss' division. Eventually the Confederates would have discovered that hole, allowing them to easily turn the Ohioans' left flank.

Disarray in Southern ranks due to the looting of Union camps and the rough terrain, combined with an outstanding performance of Waterhouse's and Capt. Samuel Barrett's Illinois batteries posted on high ground near Shiloh Church, had allowed Sherman to hold his first position at the church for two hours.

After Col. Appler called for a retreat of the 53rd Ohio, one of the regimental officers, Lt. Ephraim Dawes, ran "to where the colonel [Appler] was lying on the ground behind a tree, stooping over." Dawes said, "Colonel, let us go and help the fifty-seventh. They are falling back." According to Dawes, Appler "looked up; his face was like ashes; the fear of death was upon it; he pointed over his shoulder in an indefinite direction and squeaked out in a trembling voice: 'No, form the men back here." The suggestion was ridiculous. The lieutenant cursed the colonel and refused the order. At which point Appler "jumped to his feet and literally ran away."

As the 53rd Ohio broke into a disordered retreat, Dawes and seven other men, one of whom had been captured and escaped, wandered about the smoke-filled chaos searching for the Union lines. At one point in their odyssey they came upon an artilleryman astride a horse, crying; the brass cannon he was dragging was jammed between two trees. Dawes and his little band helped free the cannon, making the cannoneer feel better, and then moved on.

Eventually they spotted a mounted man wearing a long duster (a long coat, sort of like a rain coat), about 200 yards distant. Thinking it was a major from their unit, Dawes waved his hat to catch his attention and approached him. Saluting, Dawes asked, "Major, where is our brigade?" The man glumly answered, "I don't know where anybody is." As he turned toward him, Dawes was shocked to see the man's uniform under that duster was Confederate gray.

"At just that moment, " Dawes said, "a stand of grape [canister shot] came whirring through the air and struck just under his horse, the horse ran away and I never heard the rest of the story."

Later, Dawes learned that he had reported to Confederate Brig. Gen. Thomas Hindman.

Union Artillery Battery. Note the Sibley tents in the background.

Looking south into Rea Field. At the time of the battle, this field extended over twice as far as that tree line. Most of this upper area would have been packed with the tents of the 53rd Ohio. Farther south where the trees are today is where Sherman rode out and was struck in the hand by a Confederate bullet. About where you see that monument in the distance is one of the five Confederate mass graves marked by the Park Service.

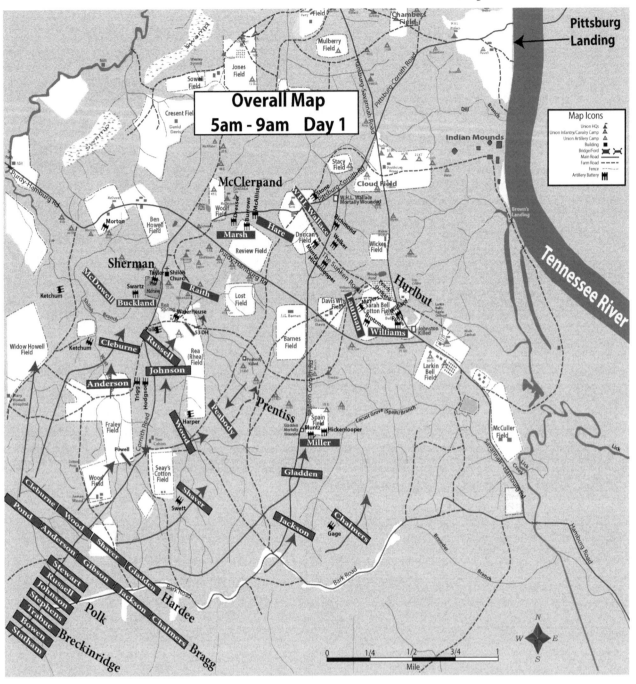

Overall Map
5am - 9am   Day 1

Google Map Links (scan with OC Reader to go to online maps)

Fraley Field

Rea Field

Chapter 9 Fight at Shiloh Branch

Brig. Gen. Pat Cleburne's Confederate brigade was the left flank of Hardee's first attack wave. The 33-year-old officer, an Irishman who had served in the British army, was a prominent Arkansas attorney before the war. Incredibly bashful around women, he was a fierce fighter and a rising star in the Confederate army.

His men would strike the Yankees at Shiloh Branch – a creek just south of Shiloh Church. Initially the wild, broken woods and ravines helped by concealing Cleburne's approach. But when he and his men reached the creek, they encountered the "Morass" – a "marsh" or swamp that was impassable. Cleburne proved it when he plunged into the swamp at the head of his troops. His horse soon became mired up to its belly in something like quicksand; it reared, and flung Cleburne on his back into the stagnant muck.

His dignity dented – this was not how battles looked in the paintings – and his boots filled with slime, the determined Cleburne slithered out of the mud "with great difficulty" and slid back on his mount. But the best he could do with the Morass was divide his brigade, with the two halves passing around the swamp on opposite sides. On the right side, the 6th Mississippi and 23rd Tennessee attacked east of Cornith Road, advancing through Rea Field against the 53rd Ohio (discussed in the previous chapter), while the 2nd, 5th, and 24th Tennessee, along with the 15th Arkansas, worked their way around the quagmire west of Cornith Road. Meanwhile, the mud-caked Cleburne galloped back and forth between the two sides of the swamp, desperately trying to lead both

Brig. Gen. Patrick Cleburne (w)
1828 - 1864

sections of his brigade. But the two sections never again rejoined tactically that day.

The Confederates' path on the west side of the swamp was blocked by three Ohio regiments of Col. Ralph Buckland's brigade, well placed at the top of a ridge. The four Confederate regiments, one at a time, charged up the thicket-covered slope multiple times, only to be beaten back in bloody repulses.

Col. Ralph P. Buckland
1812 - 1892

Finally, Cleburne's exhausted regiments were replaced by troops arriving in the second attack wave – Brig. Gen. Bushrod Johnson's brigade of Bragg's division. But Johnson's men couldn't make headway either. So after Johnson's men were chewed up, they were replaced by Brig. Gen. Patton Anderson's brigade of Polk's third assault wave. None of them was able to crack Buckland's line.

The stubborn Federals holding the line – the 72nd, 48th and 70th Ohio – were green, but they held an excellent defensive position, and they were ably supported by two artillery batteries (Capt. Samuel Barrett's and Maj. Adolph Schwartz's). Often under the personal supervision of Sherman himself, they managed to hold their position for two solid hours, beating back assault after assault. When they finally retreated, it wasn't due to pressure from their front, but due to the collapse of the brigade across the Cornith Road to their left - Col. Jesse Hildebrand's brigade.

As discussed in a previous chapter, Hildebrand's men began their fight at Rea Field where they were badly mauled; then they made a fighting retreat north directly past Shiloh Church, more or less forming in line to the east of Buckland's men, with their right flank connected to the left flank of Buckland's line.

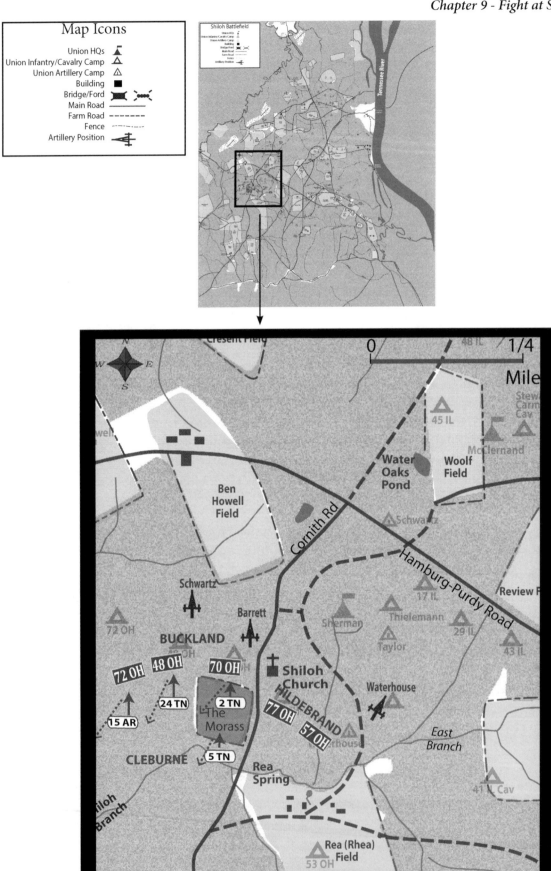

"If they were willing to do that to themselves, what would they have done to us?"

The Union gunners of Barrett's and Waterhouse's batteries on the north side of Shiloh Church alternately blasted the surging Rebel infantry charging up on the ridge to their front, as well as dueling with Confederate Shoup's Battery (and other Confederate batteries arriving later) on the rise on the opposite side of Shiloh Branch.

For some time after Appler's 53rd Ohio fled the fight, the Federal gunners here put the Confederates in Rea Field under a devastating fire. (In 1862, unlike today, the timber was sparser, and Sherman and his cannoneers could easily see the Rebel infantry advancing across Rea Field). One Union soldier, watching the Confederate lines storm forward into almost certain death, wondered, "If they were willing to do that to themselves, what would they have done to *us*?"

But the Federals could only delay, not stop, the Rebel tidal wave. Eventually Southern troops attacked north up Rea Field and across the east fork of the Shiloh Creek, forcing the collapse, one after the other, of the remaining two regiments of Hildebrand's brigade – the 57th and 77th Ohio. This in turn unraveled Sherman's left flank.

His line crumbling, Sherman ordered what remained of his division – the artillery, Buckland's brigade, the fragments of Hildebrand's brigade, and the still-fresh brigade of Col. John D. McDowell – to fall back about 600 yards to an area known as "The Crossroads" where the Cornith Road and the Purdy-Hamburg Road intersected.

"We're holding them pretty well just now, but it's hot as hell."

Sherman sent Grant a message: "*Tell Grant if he has any men to spare I can use them. If not, I'll do the best I can. We're holding them pretty well just now, but it's hot as hell.*"

According to the caption in Battles & Leaders, Vol 1, p471, this is an illustration of "Waterhouse's battery's first position." It looks rather serene, and so must have been drawn prior to the battle. If so, that may be the 53rd Ohio camp in the far left distance, and the 57th Ohio on the near right.

On Sherman's order, Barrett's battery pulled out. Waterhouse's battery was in the process of following when Sherman's Chief of Artillery, Ezra Taylor, galloped up and demanded that every inch of ground be defended as long as possible. He ordered the battery to unlimber and deploy just 100 yards from its previous location. Waterhouse followed orders, but the maneuver was suicidal in the face of the Confederate onslaught. Finally, after Waterhouse and a 1st lieutenant were sufficiently wounded and the battery had lost three guns, Taylor allowed Waterhouse and his remaining guns to withdraw.

A Federal officer, Lt. Dawes (the same one who cursed Col. Appler for cowardice as discussed in the previous chapter), watched as the Southerners of the 13th Tennessee *"swarmed around them [Waterhouse's guns] like beasts. They jumped up on the guns and on the hay bales in the battery camp, and yelled like crazy men."*

"They jumped up on the guns and on the hay bales in the battery camp, and yelled like crazy men."

Barrett's and Waterhouse's batteries, like Buckland's infantry brigade, preformed heroically and deserve great credit for prolonging Sherman's stand here. It's all the more amazing considering the complete lack of experience of Waterhouse's men. The Chicagoans received their horses only 10 days prior to the battle and drilled with them only three times. And Sherman's tenacious stand at Shiloh Branch, a full hour after the collapse of Prentiss' division, and his fighting retreat back to the Cross-roads, bought the Union army precious time to collect itself from the initial shock of the attack.

One Federal described Sherman at this time, on his mount with his injured hand wrapped in a handkerchief and stuck inside his tunic, sitting "ramrod straight," facing the Confederate fire.

In Hindsight

Cleburne's problem at the Morass again illustrates the bigger problem with the Confederate's attack deployment, where each of three corps stretched across the entire battlefield. This deployment meant that Cleburne's brigade also had to stretch out some 1,500 yards wide, in a line too long for Cleburne to control.

Had the three corps instead been attacking side by side, per Johnston's original plan, Cleburne's men could have advanced along a much narrower front in battalion column (each regiment in line of battle, one behind the other), or possibly with a couple of regiments deployed side by side and each of the other four in a compact column behind, ready to be brought up and deployed as needed.

A second problem was that Beauregard should have been funneling the bulk of his reinforcements to the Confederate right, in compliance with Johnston's plan of crushing the Union line next to the river. Instead Beauregard sent reinforcements toward the sound of the heaviest firing, and Buckland's well-defended line provided lots of heavy firing. Rather than throwing more troops against the stoutly defended Federal line at Shiloh Branch, Beauregard would have been wiser to send troops to the quieter sections, since the latter might indicate the areas of weak resistance, or maybe even no resistance.

Under fire from Confederate Cleburne's men, a private in the 77th Ohio, John McInerney of Hildebrand's Division, was struck by a ball just over his right eye. With his face a bloody horror, McInerney casually walked back to the file closer, Lt. Jack Henricle and asked, "Lutenant, do you think that went in dape?" The shocked lieutenant waved McInerney to the rear.

It turned out to be only a glancing wound, and McInerney managed to survive the war.

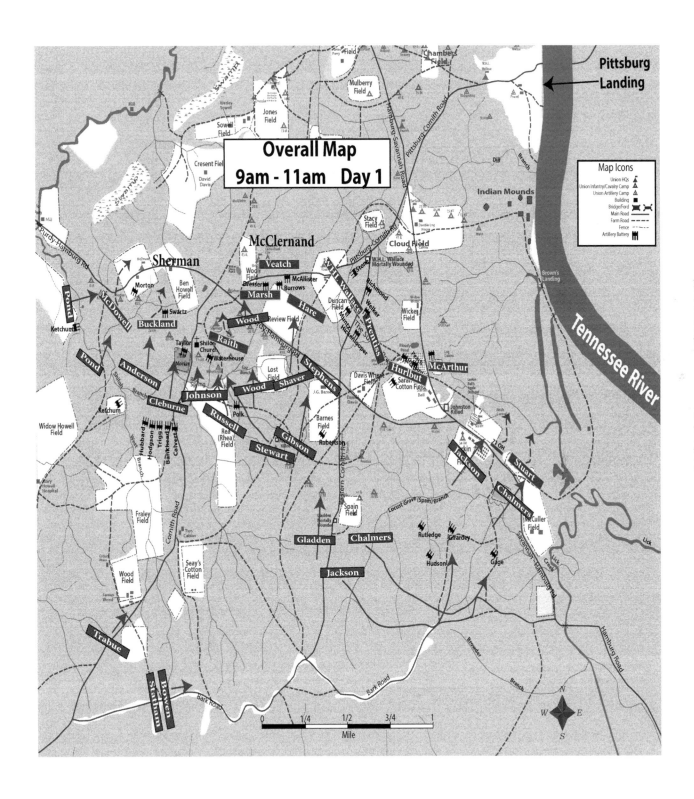

Overall Map
9am - 11am   Day 1

Google Map Links (scan with OC Reader to go to online maps)

The Morass

Rea Field

The Crossroads

Chapter 10   McClernand Joins the Fight

10:30 AM – 11:30 AM

One of the major problems for the Union army during the morning's fighting was that Sherman's 5th Division never tied into its closest neighbor to the east, Prentiss' 6th Division. Instead there was a dangerous 600 yard gap between the two divisions. Fortunately for the Union cause, the Confederates failed to capitalize on this vulnerable point because it remained hidden in the dense timber.

In any case, neither Sherman nor Prentiss were in any position to address the gap-issue as they were fully occupied just holding the lines to their front. Sherman, for example, already nicked in the hand at the start of the battle, had received another painful wound when a bullet bounced off one of his metal buckles; still another bullet cut his horse's rein as he held it with his good hand; and before the day was out he would be on his fourth horse – the previous three having been shot from under him.

Not all his men were as brave as Sherman's horses. Capt. Frederick Behr raced up with his 6th Indiana Battery. Sherman had no sooner pointed out where the battery should deploy than a Rebel bullet struck down the captain. To Sherman's enormous disgust, the entire battery fled, abandoning five of its six guns.

McClernand's 1st Division, camped north of Woolf Field, was the obvious candidate to plug the gap in the Federal line between Sherman and the remnants of Prentiss' division, though the task was difficult because McClernand's camps ran in a vertical, north-south direction. So while Sherman's men made a fighting retreat back to new positions along the Purdy-Hamburg Road, McClernand's division advanced from its camps and deployed along Purdy-Hamburg Road in a line that extended from Sherman's left at Cornith Road to Prentiss' right at Duncan Field.

McClernand, a good friend of Lincoln and a Democrat, is invariably described as an "ambitious" Illinois lawyer/politician, as if political ambition was a rarity in the Union army. In fact, due to the acute shortage of professional military men, nearly the entire volunteer officer corps of Union army, not to mention the Confederate army, consisted of ambitious lawyer/politicians at the middle and lower officer grades. (There weren't too many dentists leading brigades and regiments in that war.) McClernand stood out because of his rapid promotion to major general, and Grant's other division commanders, mostly West Pointers and/or Mexican War veterans, saw McClernand as an unctuous politician who weaseled his way into command because of his Lincoln-connection. On top of that, apparently he was insufferable schemer.

Maj. Gen. John A. McClernand
1812 - 1900

That said, he seems to have conducted himself reasonably well at Fort Donelson – well enough to earn another star – and in the chaos and fury of this first day at Shiloh, his division would fight side by side next to Sherman's throughout the battle, all the way back to Pittsburg Landing. And McClernand, not Sherman, was technically the senior commander.

In any case, now at least the Federals had a continuous line across the western half of the battlefield, held by five brigades and parts of a sixth (the remnants of Hildebrand's shattered command).

McClernand arranged his brigades with Col. Julius Raith's (pronounced 'right') at the Crossroads – the intersection of Cornith Road and the Purdy-Hamburg Roads next to Sherman; in the center was Col. C. Carroll Marsh's brigade and on the left flank, Col. Abraham Hare's brigade, north of a pasture the Federals called Review Field.

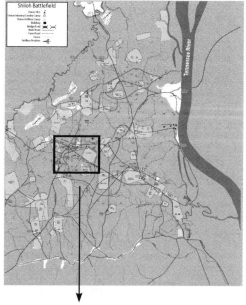

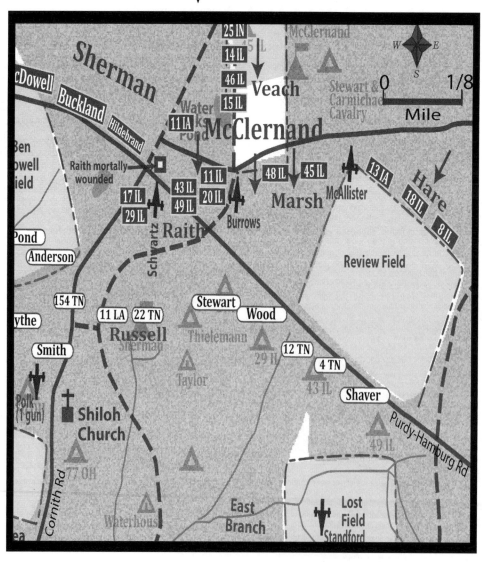

Unlike Sherman's and Prentiss' men, the soldiers of McClernand's division were reasonably battle hardened, having fought at Fort Donelson, though of course Fort Donelson was nothing like this. But unlike Sherman's defensive line perched atop a steep ravine, McClernand's line rested on flat ground with no terrain advantage.

Around 11am, the Confederates troops, now a mishmash of regiments from four different brigades – Russell's, Stewart's, Wood's and Shaver's – continued advancing from around Shiloh Church, striking McClernand's line at the Crossroads.

As the 1st Tennessee of Maney's brigade marched to the front, General Johnston halted the regiment to give the men a pep talk. Informing them that he had personally selected them for this post of honor, he explained the importance of defeating Grant's army before Buell's reinforcements arrived. He directed the Tennesseans to hold their positions no matter what the price. Winding up his speech, he cautioned the soldiers to check their ammo pouches to be sure they had their required 40 rounds. In that solemn moment, most of the soldiers just patted their ammo pouch. But Pvt. David Adams, deeply impressed with the gravity of the situation, carefully counted all his bullets. Alarmed, he piped up, "General, I ain't got but 38!"

Johnston smiled and sent him back to the quartermaster to get two more bullets.

"The Crossroads" This modern photo on Cornith Road looks NE toward the intersection with the Purdy-Hamburg Road . Shiloh Church is about 200 yards behind the camera. Sherman's tent location is off the photo to the right about 150 yards. On the right just across the road where you see those black triangles (they're cannon balls) marks the location where Col. Raith was killed. Out of view in this photo, on the right across the road, is Water Oaks Pond and Woolf Field.

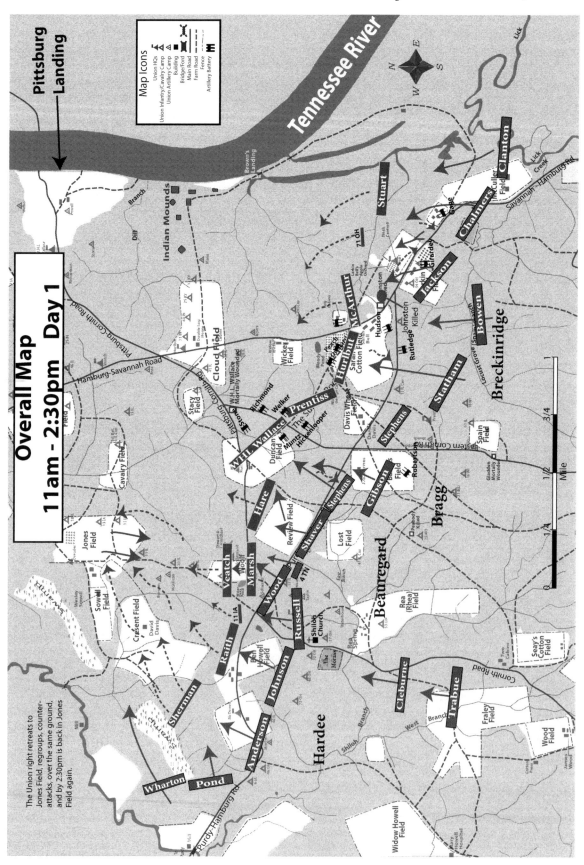

Overall Map
11am - 2:30pm Day 1

The Union right retreats to Jones Field, regroups, counter-attacks, over the same ground, and by 2:30pm is back in Jones Field again.

Google Map Links (scan with OC Reader to go to online maps)

Woolf Field

Duncan Field

The Crossroads

Review Field

Shiloh Church

Chapter 11   Collapse of the Union Right

Along the Purdy-Hamburg Road, Sherman's two exhausted brigades, Buckland's and the remnants of Hildebrand's, stubbornly held their own against fierce Rebel assaults. But farther down the line to the east along Pittsburg-Cornith Road, McClernand's recently arrived division was soon in big trouble. For one thing, McClernand's battle line had a poor field of fire compared to Sherman's position. A private in Marsh's Illinois brigade explained: *"We could not see them [the Rebels] as they crouched down behind the rising ground, while we were entirely exposed within easy range of their guns… We had to load on our backs and fire on our knees to keep from all being killed, so our fire was not so rapid."*

Having wrecked Prentiss' division, Johnston assumed he was on the right flank of the Union line, and so around 9:30am or 10am, he ordered five brigades (Woods, Shaver, Stewart, Gibson and Stephens) to advance east of Shiloh Church and strike Raith's brigade of Sherman's division and all the brigades of McClernand's division.

A motley collection of Confederate units, including Wood's and Shaver's brigades, and two Tennessee regiments – the 4th of Stewart's brigade and 12th of Russell's brigade - surged across the Purdy-Hamburg Road and into Review Field (the Federals gave the field its name after using it for that purpose). The Rebels struck Marsh's brigade and, to its right, Hare's brigade – both of McClernand's division.

Here, where the open ground in front allowed an excellent field of fire for the artillery supporting McClernand - Capt. Edward McAllister's Illinois battery of four 24-pounder howitzers. At

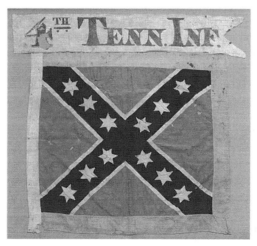

Battle flag of the 4th Tennessee. Delivered to the unit in April 1862 and carried until its surrender in Greensboro, NC on April 26, 1865. The flag is 35.5" X 37". Initially blood red, it's now a faded orange.

some point, McAllister's battery was challenged by Thomas J. Sanford's Mississippi Battery, but McAllister's guns soon won the duel, silencing Sanford's guns.

But the Confederates wanted McAllister's guns, and the 4th and 12th Tennessee got the assignment to seize them. Leading the two regiments was

Brig. Gen. Thomas C. Hindman Jr. (w)
1828 - 1868

hot-tempered Brig. Gen. Thomas C. Hindman of Hardee's Corps. Conspicuous in his white, oilcloth poncho, Hindman galloped about in the hail of bullets, deploying his two regiments for the attack while *"whooping like a Comanche, and with his horse on the dead run."* Finally a shot from one of McAllister's guns smashed directly into the chest of Hindman's horse, bringing the beast to an abrupt halt and hurling the general 10 feet through the air in a spectacular forward somersault. When he slammed to ground he had just enough juice left to stagger to his feet, wave his sword and shout *"Tennesseans, take that battery!"* before collapsing.

His two regiments, now led by Col. Robert Shaver, kept up their attack. Marsh would later confess that Shaver's men advanced *"with a steadiness and precision which I had hardly anticipated."* McAllister's canister induced the 12th Tennessee to swerve to its left into the cover of timber, where Confederate S.A.M. Wood's brigade was also attacking toward Marsh's

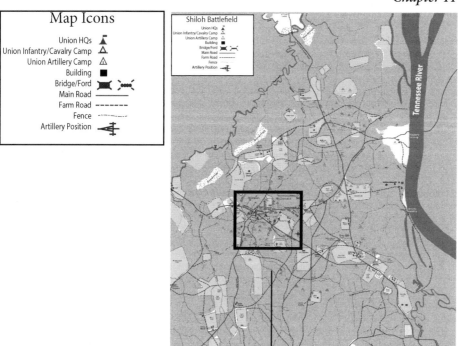

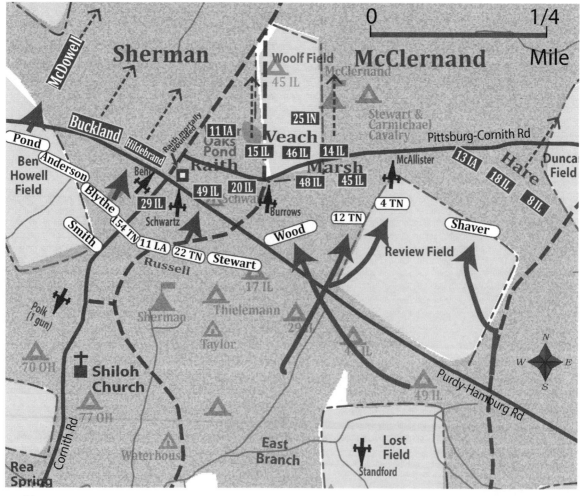

brigade. More by luck than design, this brought an overwhelming force against the two defending regiments in that area – the 45th and 48th Illinois – giving the attackers a three to one numerical advantage. The two Union regiments began taking heavy casualties, especially among their officers. The 48th Illinois finally broke, leaving the 45th with no choice but to follow. This left its supporting battery, Lt. Jerome Burrow's 14th Ohio, unprotected, and the battery was soon overrun with the loss of all six guns.

With Marsh's brigade collapsing, Hare's brigade and McAllister's battery had to retire. McAllister managed to get three of his four guns out. Too many horses had been killed to pull out the fourth gun.

McClernand's line was cracked.

Into McClernand's Camps
11am - 11:30am

McClernand and his brigadiers - Marsh, Raith and Hare - desperately tried to rally the men, but it was hopeless – the troops were too panicked and the Confederates too close. Col. Raith, who had just assumed command of his brigade, was mortally wounded in the chaos at the Crossroads. Hare's brigade headed northwest towards Pittsburg Landing, but Marsh and Raith's troops fled directly north through Marsh's camp, not slowing down for another 750 yards until they reached Jones Field – the tent campsite of Hare's brigade.

Earlier in the fighting Sherman had sent an urgent message to 4th Division commander Hurlbut bivouacked near the river, requesting reinforcements. Hurlbut responded by dispatching one of his three brigades, commanded by Col. James C. Veatch. The colonel and his men reached McClernand's vicinity about the time the Federal line collapsed there.

Veatch's men fought just long enough to cover McClernand's retreat before falling back in disorder themselves.

With McClernand's line broken, Sherman's weary division had no choice but to withdraw. He and his men also headed north toward Jones Field, using a country lane (today called "Sherman Road").

As usual, the fleeing Federals got a reprieve when the triumphant Confederates paused after entering Marsh's camps around Woolf Field, partially because by now the Southerners were badly disorganized, and partially because they couldn't resist plundering the camp. The inexperienced Confederate officers would not or could not get the men moving again, prolonging the pause even more.

Russell's Confederate brigade did probe ahead, but got a bloody nose near the south end of Jones Field when it ran into the recently-arrived 15th and 16th Iowa regiments which Grant had dispatched to reinforce McClernand.

While the Confederates wasted precious time ransacking Marsh's camps, Sherman and McClernand back at Jones Field made good use of the lull to regroup their mauled units. Welcome artillery support arrived in the form of Maj. Taylor, who scrounged up nine cannon – Barrett's battery and orphaned guns from other batteries – and deployed them on a rise on the south edge of Jones Field. Taylor's guns were soon in a fierce duel with Capt. Robert Cobb's Kentucky Battery at the north end of Woolf Field.

Though the Federals at Jones Field were given a respite to catch their breath, it was clear that this right flank of Grant's army was being pushed back, ever closer to its destruction in the swamps to the north, or to Pittsburg Landing and the river to the east.

Lt. Col Camm's 14th Illinois was one of Hurlbut's regiments sent west to assist Sherman and McClernand. On the way, Camm and his regiment passed a wagon carrying wounded. One soldier's leg was blown off below the knee. "He stuck the stump, with the shattered bone almost sticking out into my face," Camm said, "and in a strong voice he cried above the din, 'Give'em hell for that, Colonel!' "

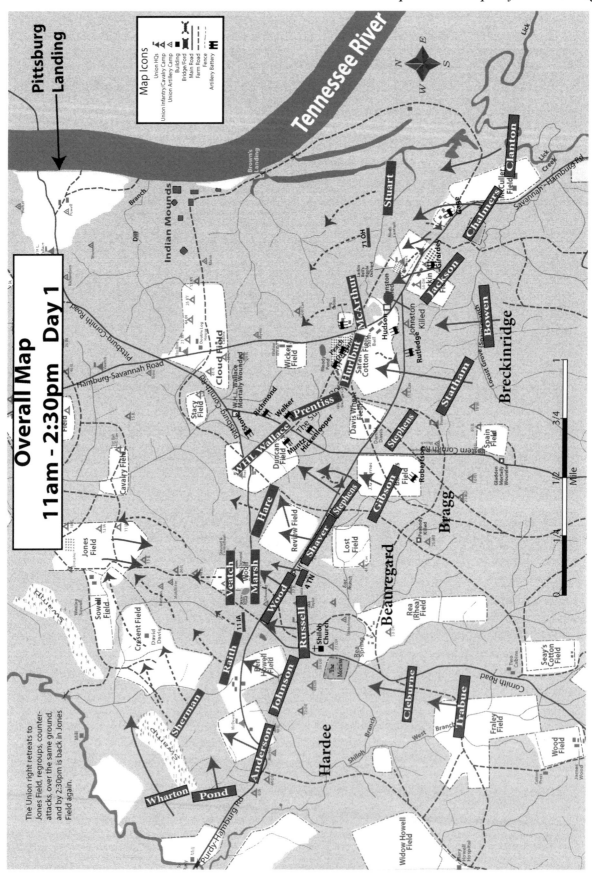

Map Icons

- Union HQs
- Union Infantry/Cavalry Camp
- Union Artillery Camp
- Building
- Bridge/Ford
- Main Road
- Farm Road
- Fence
- Artillery Battery

Overall Map
11am - 2:30pm Day 1

Pittsburg Landing

Tennessee River

The Union right retreats to Jones Field, regroups, counter-attacks, over the same ground, and by 2:30pm is back in Jones Field again.

Indian Mounds

Stuart

Chalmers

Clanton

McCuller Field

Jackson

Bowen

Breckinridge

McArthur

Hurlbut

Statham

Cloud Field

Wicker Field

Stacy Field

Prentiss

W.H.L. Wallace Mortally Wounded

Richmond

Walker

Will Wallace

Duncan Field

Hickenlooper

Stephens

Spain Field

Bragg

Cavalry Field

Hare

Review Field

Stephens

Gibson

Robertson

Lost Field

Jones Field

Veatch

Wood

Marsh

Shaver

4 TN

11 IA

Beauregard

Rea (Rhea) Field

Sowell Field

Crescent Field

Raith

Russell

Shiloh Church

The Morass

Seay's Cotton Field

Sherman

Johnson

Hardee

Cleburne

Trabue

Wharton

Pond

Anderson

Purdy-Hamburg Rd

Corinth Road

Wood Field

Fraley Field

Widow Howell Field

0   1/4   1/2   3/4   Mile

Google Map Links (scan with OC Reader to go to online maps)

Shiloh Church

Review Field

The Crossroads

Jones Field

Woolf Field

Pittsburg Landing

Chapter 12   Union Counterattack

11:30am - 1pm

Thanks to a Confederate pause to raid the Union camps, by 11:30am Sherman and McClernand, now pushed back to Jones Field, had time to reorganize their shattered divisions. Casualties and deserters decimated their force, and many regiments were out of ammunition; but the two generals managed to round up about two thirds of their commands and coax the men back into battle formation. On the bright side, through trial by fire, the Union ranks were now weeded down to its toughest soldiers – the ones who didn't run. Sherman's third brigade, commanded by Col. John McDowell (brother of Irvin McDowell who lost the 1st Battle of Bull Run), was still fresh, having occupied the right of the Union line which saw no action, allowing McDowell's brigade to simply fall back with the rest of the division, unscathed.

McClernand also received some much-needed help in the form of an artillery battery and two fresh Iowa regiments – the 15th and 16th Iowa – gifts from Grant.

Meanwhile the Southern attack paused, not just for the usual reason – to pillage Union camps – but also to allow ammunition wagons to catch up, and to reorganize the jumbled Confederate battleline.

Amazingly, given what they had already been through and with just a bit of time to reorganize, Sherman and McClernand now felt confident enough to launch a counterattack. In what would be the only significant Federal attack of the day,

---

Following Sherman's order, McDowell withdrew his brigade toward Crescent Field. Lt. Col. Morkoe Cummings, commanding McDowell's old regiment, the 6th Iowa, suddenly about-faced the left wing of his regiment and marched it back to a fence, leaving the remainder of the regiment standing in line in the woods. An irritated McDowell rode back and demanded to know what it meant. "It means, sir," replied an officer, "that the Colonel is drunk."

McDowell relieved Cummings and placed Capt. John Williams in command.

---

around noon the Federals came roaring back south toward Woolf Field. The Confederates had by now grown accustomed to chasing Yankees, and the plucky counterattack caught them completely off guard. In fact, the charge knocked the Southerners back a half mile to Woolf Field in such disorder that McClernand's troops overran Cobb's Kentucky Battery and captured all six guns.

Brig. Gen. Alexander P. Stewart
1821 - 1908

But the Confederates soon recovered and launched a counterattack of their own with a motley collection of brigades scraped together from the three main Confederate assault waves – Russell, Stewart and Johnson's brigades from Polk's Corps; Pond and Anderson's brigades of Bragg's Corps; and Col. Robert Trabue's brigade from Breckenridge's Reserve Corps. Galloping up to support the infantry, Capt. W. Irving Hodgson's Washington Artillery Battery (a Confederate battery from New Orleans) deployed only about 200 yards from the Union line, blasting canister into Mc-

Brig. Gen. Bushrod R. Johnson
1817 - 1880

Clernand's men. But accurate Union rifle fire soon forced the Southern battery back out of range.

The Southern numbers were overwhelming but, having survived the initial shock and surprise of the Confederate early morning attack, the Federals were growing increasingly stubborn, and the battle slowly degenerated into a toe-to-toe slugging

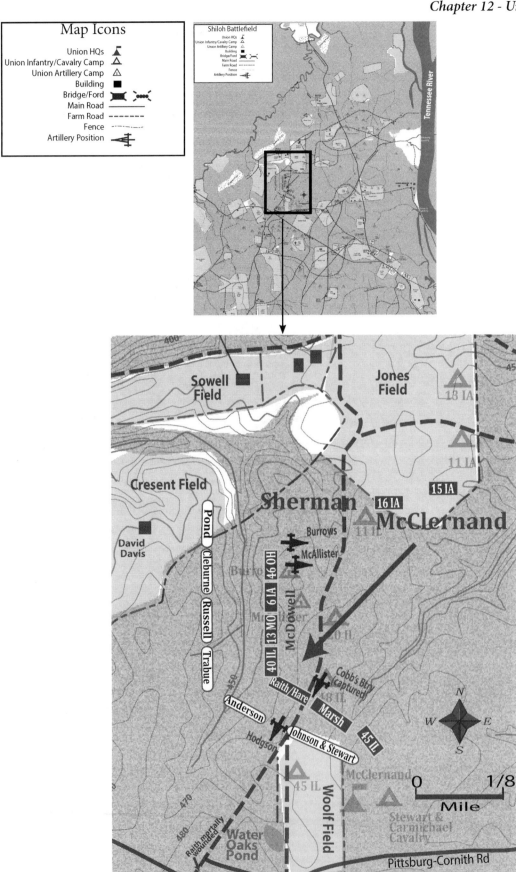

Map Icons

Union HQs
Union Infantry/Cavalry Camp
Union Artillery Camp
Building
Bridge/Ford
Main Road
Farm Road
Fence
Artillery Position

Shiloh Battlefield

Tennessee River

Sowell Field

Jones Field

18 IA

Cresent Field

11 IA

15 IA

Sherman

16 IA

McClernand

David Davis

Burrows

11 IL

McAllister

Burrows

46 OH

6 IA

McDowell

13 MO

40 IL

Cobb's Btry (Captured)

Raith/Hare

Anderson

18 IL

Marsh

Johnson & Stewart

45 IL

Hodgson

N

W   E

S

McClernand

45 IL

Stewart & Carmichael Cavalry

Raith mortally wounded

Water Oaks Pond

Woolf Field

0   1/8

Mile

Pittsburg-Cornith Rd

match. Both sides slammed away at each other for over an hour – sometimes fighting hand to hand – which is to say fighting with gun butts and bayonets and both sides taking heavy casualties. (Grant would later write that there were more bodies collected after the battle on this side of the field than any other). Finally, the Confederate brigades of Trabue and Pond stretched farther west than did McDowell's brigade on the far right of the Union line, allowing the Southerners to outflank McDowell's line. McDowell's brigade, virtually untouched until the counter-attack, was now a shambles.

The Confederates now battled their way back north. One Ohio soldier watched as the Rebels swarmed forward into a muddy pond (Water Oaks Pond), and then into an open field, Woolf Field. *"Without a waver the long line of glittering steel moved steadily forward, while overall the silken folds of the Confederate flag floated gracefully on the morning air."*

The Federals grudgingly gave ground until they were pushed back to their starting point at Jones Field around 1pm. Along the way, the Confederates recovered the guns of Cobb's battery. After Sherman and McClernand's men withdrew, the Confederates took time to rest, gulp down some pond water and refill their ammo pouches. Then most of the Southern brigades on this part of the line shifted southeast, toward the big fight now shaping up in the center of the Union line at the Sunken Road.

Around 2pm, Sherman and McClernand decided to fall back from Jones Field to the rugged Tilghman Branch ravine, which offered a much better defensive position. Later in the day, around 4pm, Confederate Col. Preston Pond found out just how good a defensive position Tilghman Branch was when his Louisiana units attempted to seize it, only to be thrown back by a storm of fire from Sherman's and McClernand's men.

Though the Federal counterattack failed, it did drain off Confederate brigades which might otherwise have been used to attack the Federal left, per Johnston's original plan. The stubborn Union resistance here also bought Grant time to build a defensive line back at Pittsburg Landing. Last but not least, the fight also shattered several Confederate units – leaving Cleburne's brigade completely wrecked, and S.A.M. Wood's brigade with a 62% casualty rate.

As Union artillery pounded Cobb's Kentucky Battery and its supporting infantry, Confederate Kentuckian, Johnny Green, saw three of the four men in the file next to his killed by a single shell. Another shell killed two of Cobb's gunners and tore both hands off a third. Looking at the bloody stumps, the stunned artillerymen gasped, "My Lord, that stops my fighting!"

Confederate battery being overrun.   *Battles & Leaders, Vol 1, pg 527*

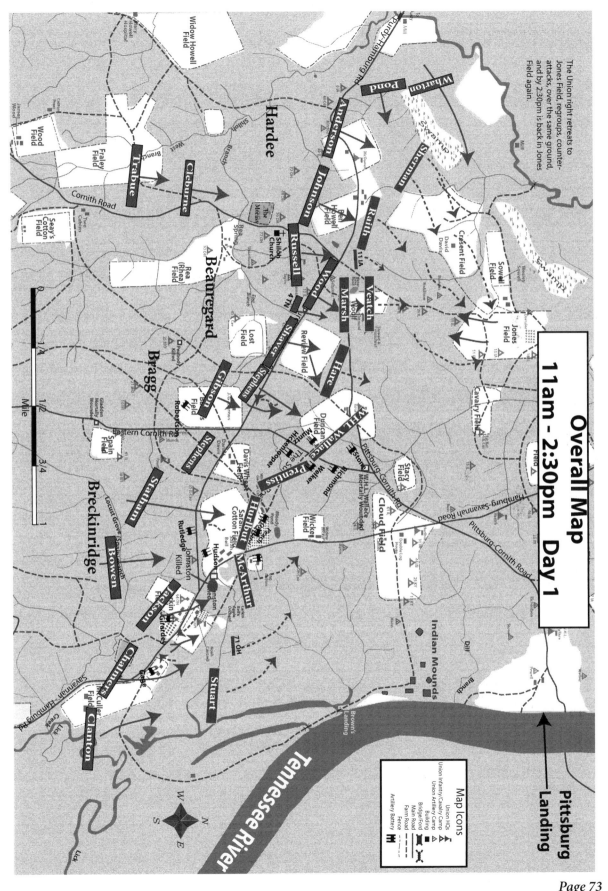

Overall Map
11am - 2:30pm Day 1

The Union right retreats to Jones Field, regroups, counterattacks, over the same ground, and by 2:30pm is back in Jones Field again.

Pittsburg Landing

Tennessee River

Map Icons

Union HQs
Union Infantry/Cavalry Camp
Union Artillery Camp
Building
Bridge/Ford
Main Road
Farm Road
Fence
Artillery Battery

Google Map Links (scan with OC Reader to go to online maps)

Jones Field	Water Oaks Pond	Pittsburg Landing

Chapter 13   Sarah Bell's Cotton Field

7:30am - 10am

Camped in and around Cloud Field near Pittsburg Landing was the Grant's 4th Division, commanded by 47-year-old Brig. Gen. Stephen A. Hurlbut – a South Carolina-born, political appointee, notorious for his drinking binges and shady real estate deals. Col. Isaac Pugh, commanding the 41st Illinois regiment, confided to his wife on March 22: "*Genl Hurlbut is a drunkard & is drunk all the time when he can get anything to drink on.*" Someone circulated a petition throughout the division to request his resignation but nothing came of it.

But on this day at least, drunk or sober, Stephen Hurlbut would earn his pay.

At 7:30am, about two hours after the first shots, Hurlbut received almost simultaneous urgent requests for help – the first from Sherman on the Union right and a second one from Prentiss on the Union left. Both of these officers' inexperienced divisions took the brunt of the initial Confederate assault, and they were in serious trouble. Hurlbut immediately dispatched his 2nd Brigade – 2,700 troops under Col. James C. Veatch – to reinforce Sherman. The camps of Hurlbut's two remaining brigades were widely scattered around the Landing, so it took him another half hour to notify and assemble these men, plus three artillery batteries and two cavalry battalions – about 4,100 men in all – in preparation for a march to Prentiss' support.

Just after 8am Hurlbut and his men marched off toward the sound of the guns, south down Savannah-Hamburg Road through a steady stream of dazed men from Prentiss' division, all heading in the opposite direction. Some of these men were wounded, but most had simply fled the battle; many had thrown away their rifles. They warned Hurlbut's men, by way of self-justification, "*You' catch hell – we're all cut to pieces – the Rebs are coming!*" Disgusted, one of Hurlbut's captains loudly sneered that if any of his men ran, he'd shoot them. His men actually cheered, relieved to hear a note of determination in their march toward the inferno.

In another case, a hysterical colonel rode up, shouting "*We're whipped! We're all cut to pieces.*" One of Hurlbut's lieutenants grabbed the horse's bridal and drew his revolver, threatening to shoot the colonel if he didn't shut his mouth.

By 8:30am, Hurlbut and his reinforcements reached Sarah Bell's Cotton Field and peach orchard, soon to be known as *The* Peach Orchard. The southeast edge of Mrs. Bell's cotton field fronted the important intersection of Purdy-Hamburg and the Savannah-Hamburg roads.

Brig. Gen. Stephen A. Hurlbut
1815 - 1882

> *"Genl Hurlbut is a drunkard & is drunk all the time when he can get anything to drink on."*

Hurlbut Deploys
8:30am-9:30am

At the Peach Orchard, Hurlbut filed his two brigades (the 1st under Col. N. G. Williams, and the 3rd under Brig. Gen. J. G. Lauman) onto the country lane leading to a cabin owned by one W. Manse George at the northern edge of the cotton field. This lane was the beginning of what we today call the Sunken Road, now famous as a key part of the Union defensive line. But at this point Hurlbut didn't stop at the lane, but instead advanced his men south across Ms. Bell's cotton field. Reaching the post and rail fence at the south edge, Hurlbut faced Williams's men south and Laumen's west, with both units facing timber directly to their front.

He would soon regret this move, as his initial position on the Sunken Road with its clear field of

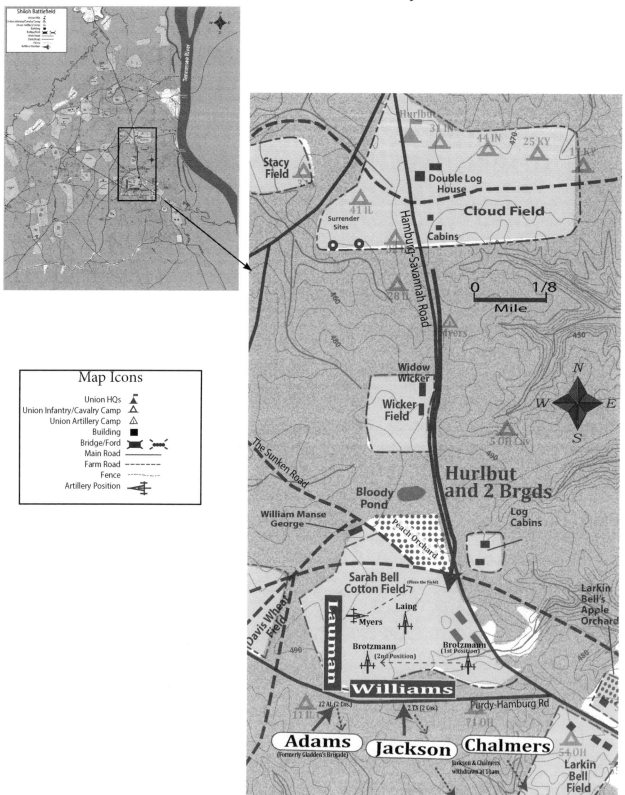

Hurlbut and his two brigades join the fight at Sarah Bell's cotton field.

fire across the cotton field offered an ideal location compared to where he now deployed with his troops facing timber. Also, his new position created a salient – a right angle between his two brigades. Salients were militarily weak because they allowed the enemy to cross-fire into the backs of each brigade. He would have been better off maintaining his line along the Sunken Road and deploying a few skirmishers on this south side of the field to give warning of the enemy approach.

In any case, as his artillery rolled up, Hurlbut located Lt. Culbert Laing's Michigan battery behind William's line, and Lt. Edward Brotzmann's Missouri battery near the intersection of the Purdy-Hamburg and Savannah-Hamburg Roads. But the general soon changed his mind and moved Brotzmann's guns over to the apex of his line between the two brigades. He strung out his cavalry behind the division to serve as a straggler line, which was about the only use for cavalry in Shiloh's forested terrain.

But Hurlbut's third artillery battery, the 13th Ohio, commanded by Capt. John B. Myers, still hadn't arrived. This was odd because of all the units in Hurlbut's division, this battery's camp was the closest to the cotton field, and conveniently adjacent to the Savannah-Hamburg Road.

Finally, after the general had sent repeated messengers, the battery finally showed up around 9:30am, over 30 minutes late. Hurlbut ordered the battery to face the timberline behind Laumen's brigade. Myers objected, arguing the battery should be placed farther back on more open ground, but the general insisted.

W. H. L. Wallace Deploys

Meanwhile, around 8:30, while Hurlbut deployed around Sarah Bell's field, 2nd Division commander W. H. L. Wallace arrived with his three brigades and placed two of them – Cols. James Tuttle's and Thomas Sweeny's – to the west of Hurlbut along the same country lane, the Sunken Road. Wallace kept the third brigade, McArthur's, in reserve for the moment.

The First "Attack"
9:30 AM to 10 AM

Hurlbut's Federals got their first look at the enemy emerging through the woods south of the Purdy-Hamburg Road. *"His regiments with their red banners were flashing in the morning sun"* according to one 3rd Iowa lieutenant.

"... his regiments with their red banners flashing in the morning sun."

William's and Laumen's brigades began receiving peppering fire from the surrounding woods. The Federals answered, but with little effect. Soon they began taking some scattered artillery fire from an unseen battery (probably Capt. Felix Robertson's Alabama battery). The incoming rounds did little harm, with two major exceptions:

First, a shell fragment sliced through Col. Williams' horse, slamming both rider and horse to the ground and paralyzing Williams for weeks, eventually forcing his resignation from the army. The loss of Williams, a classmate of Grant's at West Point before he quit because of poor math grades, was not mourned by men

Col. Isaac C. Pugh
1805 - 1874

and officers of his brigade, who thoroughly hated him because of his harsh discipline. Col. Isaac Pugh of the 41st Illinois now took command of William's brigade.

Another casualty of an incoming shell was Myers' battery. Just as Myers was deploying his guns, an incoming round scored a direct hit on one of his battery caissons. Packed with powder and ammo, the caisson erupted in a tremendous blast, killing one gunner and wounding eight. This in turn sent Myers and his remaining gun crews flying to the rear, along with at least one team of horses, which dragged a gun and caisson along with it. That left five guns on the field with no artillerymen to serve them, so gunners from the other two batteries rushed over to spike the guns and cut the horses from their harnesses. ("Spiking" a cannon renders it inoperable, usually by hammering a metal spike down the vent in the breach.) After the battle Hurlbut angrily urged that the 13th Ohio battery be disbanded and Capt. Myers cashiered from the army, which he was, sort of. But the governor of Ohio stoutly defended Myers, and pulled strings to have the captain reinstated. The argument dragged on for years.

Strangely, from the Federals' point of view, the expected Confederate assault didn't occur, at least not yet. As it turned out, the Confederates – men of Wither's Division, exhausted and disorganized by their costly victory at Spain Field – were at the moment more concerned about Hurlbut attacking *them*!

Around 9:30am, Johnston received an alarming message from a Capt. Samuel Lockett, one of Hardee's engineers, who reported spotting a full Yankee division near the river – in fact it was only an under-strength brigade, and a frightened one at that. (A division normally includes three brigades). But now, thinking that there was a full enemy division on his right, Johnston pulled Jackson's and Chalmer's brigades off of the line here at the cotton field, as well as Capt. Charles Gage's and Capt. Isadore Girardey's batteries, and deployed them farther east, leaving only Adam's (formerly Gladden's) lone Confederate brigade to confront Hurlbut's two fresh brigades.

In one of the great might-have-beens of the battle, if the three Confederate brigades had attacked Hurlbut's two brigades in their vulnerable, salient formation, the Southerners would very possibly have smashed the Federals here at the cotton field, with little to stop them from pushing straight up the Savannah-Hamburg Road to Pittsburg Landing.

But the Confederate pause gave Hurlbut time to reconsider his position. A brief flurry of confusion caused Pugh to withdraw one of his left-flank regiments back to the Peach Orchard at the north end of the cotton field. Thinking about it, Hurlbut decided to move his entire force back to the orchard, which provided a much better defensive position with a clear field of fire across the cotton field, and no vulnerable salients or right angles in the Federal line.

So now his men quickly took up position behind an old fence along the edge of a timber, on the country lane eventually known as the Sunken Road.

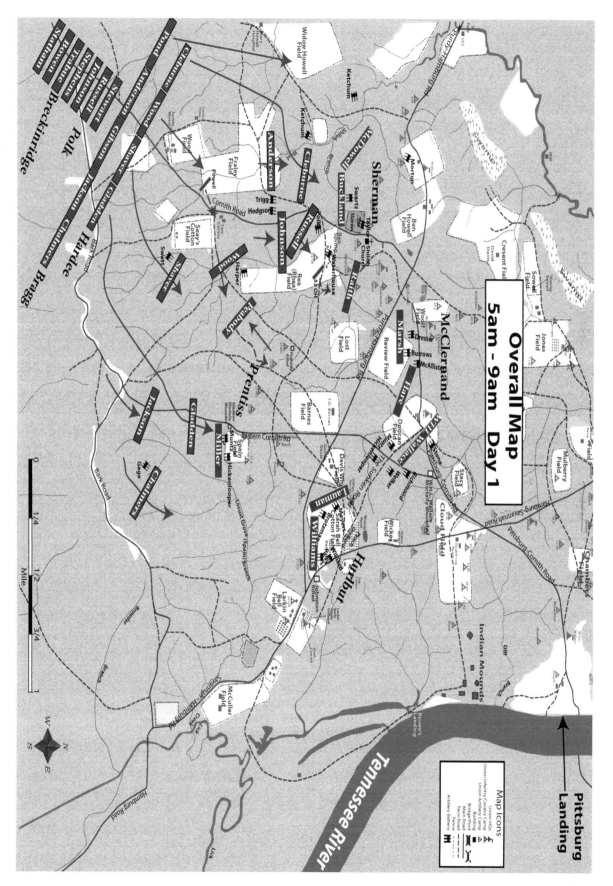

**Overall Map
5am - 9am Day 1**

Pittsburg Landing

Tennessee River

Looking north from the Confederate position across Sarah Bell's Old Cotton Field. That's the William Manse George's cabin on the opposite side of the field. The Sunken Road runs just behind the cabin.

Google Map Links (scan with OC Reader to go to online maps)

Cloud Field

Sarah Bell's Cotton Field

W. George Manse Cabin

Spain Field

The Peach Orchard

Chapter 14   The Peach Orchard

10am - 2:30pm

The Union Line Stiffens
10am to 11am

The Sunken Road was a farm lane used for decades, maybe for generations, by farmers and stage coach drivers as a shortcut connecting the Eastern Cornith Road and the Savannah-Hamburg Road. This ordinary lane – really just a wagon path – would become known rather grandly as "The Sunken Road," though in fact it wasn't very sunken. Its main attraction to the Federals was that it provided a tangible line to rally upon.

Hurlbut's redeployment began the Union migration to the Sunken Road, which became the center of the battlefield and the focus of the entire battle by noon of that first day. His two brigades anchored the east end of the line. They were soon joined by the shattered fragments of Prentiss' division, now reduced to about 600 men, which formed on the road to Hurlbut's right. Prentiss would eventually be reinforced by the 23rd Missouri, bringing his strength on this part of the line to 1,200 men.

Extending Prentiss' line farther west were 5,800 men of Brig. Gen. W. H. L. Wallace's 2nd Division, which had been camped nearest to the Landing. Wallace's division extended the Sunken Road position all the way west to the Cornith Road.

Around 10:30am, Wallace loaned two of his regiments, the 9th and 11th Illinois, led by Brig. Gen. John A. McArthur, to extend Hurlbut's left flank east of the Savannah-Hamburg Road. Accompanying McArthur was Lt. Peter Wood's (aka Willard's) Chicago battery. Along the way, McArthur accidentally picked up a bonus regiment – the 50th Illinois – which somehow strayed from its parent brigade and ended up tagging along behind McArthur, who would put it to good use. All three regiments took up position behind a deeply wooded, 40 foot ravine to the east of Hurlbut's line. Wood's battery set up shop east of the Peach Orchard and slightly in front of McArthur's infantry.

Farther to McArthur's left, near the river, was a very lonely brigade commanded by Col. David Stuart, sent there by Sherman prior to the battle to guard the ford at Lick Creek.

Including Hurlbut's two batteries, the Federals' Sunken Road position was eventually supported by eight batteries totaling 33 guns. And so by 11am the Federals had themselves a formidable line, three-quarter miles long, strung along that road.

"Only A Few More Charges"
12:30pm to 2:30pm

By now fighting also erupted farther down the Sunken Road in Duncan Field to the west, which we will discuss in a later chapter. But back here to the east, around 12:30pm the Confederate brigade of Col. Winfield Statham reached the southern edge of Sarah Bell's cotton field and filed into position to the right of Col. William H. Stevens' brigade (now under Col.

Col. George Maney
1826 - 1901

George Maney). Maney's men had suffered severe losses on the western side of the Sunken Road near the Eastern Cornith Road. They now shifted into position facing the southwestern corner of the Sarah Bell's field.

Part of Breckenridge's Reserve Corps, Statham's Confederates took cover under a ridge at the southern end of the cotton field, in the tent camp formerly occupied by the 71st Ohio. (That camp is today hidden by a belt of trees that wasn't there during the battle.). From that protected position they initially sparred with Pugh's Federals at a range of about 450 yards. Out of Statham's six

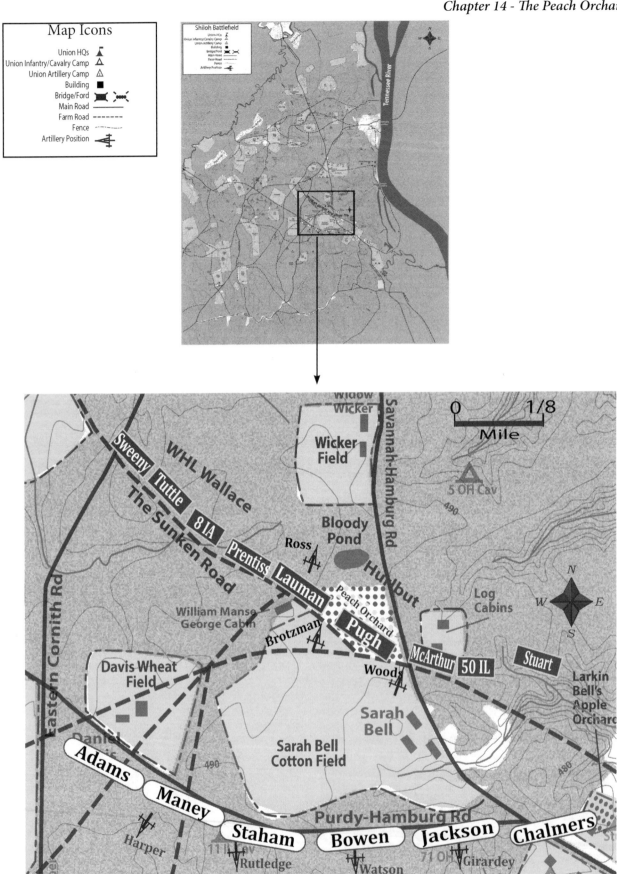

regiments, only the right-most of them, the 20th Tennessee, got into a serious scrap with the enemy – elements of McArthur's brigade – and might have gotten into serious trouble had not a regiment from another brigade (probably Jackson's) arrived to shore up its exposed flank.

Perhaps 30 minutes later Gen. Johnston himself led another brigade - commanded by Brig. Gen. John S. Bowen - onto the field and extended the Confederate line to the east. "*Only a few more charges,*" John-

> ### "Only a few more charges and the day is won!"

ston assured them, "*and the day is won.*" Soon two regiments from Jackson's brigade arrived as well, so that by 1:30 PM the Confederates arrayed 4,000 troops in line of battle, ready to push up the Savannah-Hamburg Road and drive the Yankees into the river.

But Breckinridge, former Vice President of the United States, was having problems getting his exhausted men to form up and advance across

Brig. Gen. John S. Bowen (w)
1830 - 1863

that murderous field. He approached Johnston in a huff, "*General Johnston, I cannot get my men to make the charge.*" Johnston replied calmly, "*Then I will help you.*"

Riding along Bowen's line, the commander clinked the soldiers' bayonets with the tin cup he had taken in the 18th Wisconsin's camp as his share of the "spoils". "*Men of Missouri and Arkansas,*" he boomed, "*the enemy is stubborn. I want you to show General Beauregard and General Bragg what you can do with your bayonets and toothpicks [Bowie Knives].*" Then, galloping over to Statham's brigade, he made a similar speech: "*Men, they are stubborn; we must use the bayonet.*" He reached the center of the line and cried, "*I will lead you!*" With a wild cheer, the Confederate battle-line surged forward.

Assaults on the Peach Orchard Line
2pm to 2:30pm

At around 2pm, Pugh's Federal brigade in the Peach Orchard watched as rank upon rank of Confederate troops of Statham's brigade emerged from the tree line on the south end of the cotton field with their blood-red, Stars & Bars flapping. (In 1862 the tree line was farther back than it is today, beyond the Purdy-Hamburg Road).

Wood's Federal battery opened fire with canister. Pugh's infantry held their fire until the Confederates got within 200 yards, then unleashed a terrific volley. The Rebels wavered but kept coming. Presently they forced Brotzman's Union gunners to abandon their field pieces and flee to the rear. As the Confederates angled toward the abandoned guns and the nearby 41st Illinois, Hurlbut desperately reshuffled his line, placing the 42nd Illinois in support of its fellow Illinois regiment, and extended the 3rd Iowa's line to cover the gap thus created. Together, the three regiments managed to repel Statham's Confederates.

A few minutes later the Southerners rallied and came on again, this time to the west of the cotton field, partially concealed within some timber

Col. Zachariah C. Deas (w)
1819 - 1882

that was soon to be known as the Hornet's Nest. Facing them on this sector of the Federal line was Lauman's brigade. The attackers included Stephens' brigade (now under Col. George Maney) and the remnants of Gladden's Brigade (now led by Col. Zachariah C. Deas, its third commander of the day). The assault didn't get far, however, before the Confederates were stopped by a blistering crossfire. They laid down and began a steady but inconclusive gunfight with Lauman's men. The firing was so fierce that eventually the woods caught fire in front of Laumen's line, broiling an unknown number of wounded. In the smoke their screams could be heard even through the roaring gunfire.

Hurlbut's Division repelling Confederate assaults at the Peach Orchard and Sarah Bell's Cotton Field

Officers and NCOs of Capt Arthur Rutledge's Tennessee Battery, which supported the Confederate attack on the Peach Orchard.

Google Map Links (scan with OC Reader to go to online maps)

The Peach Orchard	Sarah Bell's Cotton Field	Duncan Field

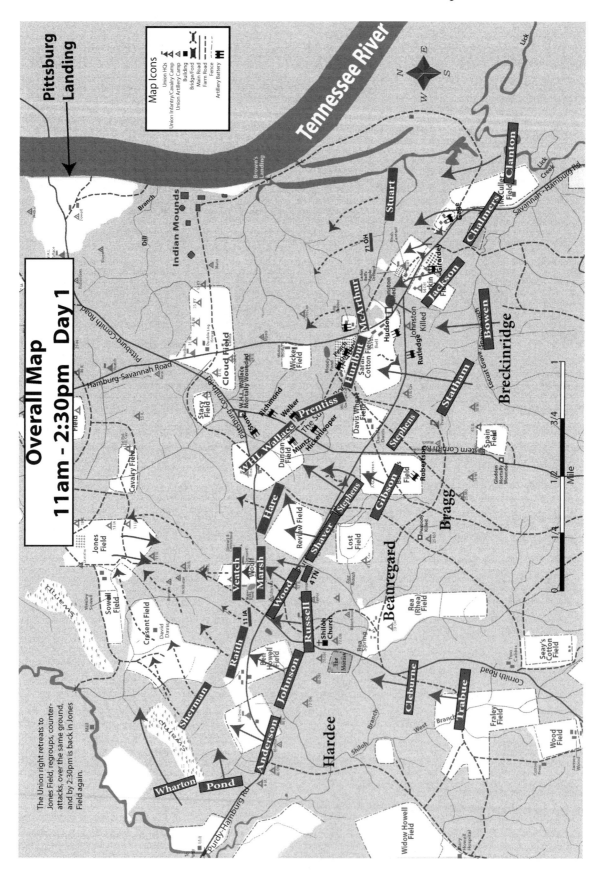

Overall Map
11am - 2:30pm Day 1

Pittsburg Landing

Tennessee River

Map Icons
Union HQs
Union Infantry/Cavalry Camp
Union Artillery Camp
Building
Bridge/Ford
Main Road
Farm Road
Fence
Artillery Battery

The Union right retreats to Jones Field, regroups, counter-attacks, over the same ground, and by 2:30pm is back in Jones Field again.

Pittsburg-Corinth Road

Hamburg-Savannah Road

Cloud Field

Indian Mounds

Stacy Field

Cavalry Field

Jones Field

Sowell Field

Cresent Field

Wharton

Pond

Sherman

Anderson

Johnson

Raith

Russell

Wood

Marsh

Veatch

Hare

Shaver

Stephens

Gibson

Russell

11 IA

4 TN

Shiloh Church

Rea Spring

Review Field

Lost Field

Duncan Field

The Sunken
Hickenlooper

Prentiss

WHL Wallace

Richmond

Welker

W.H.L. Wallace
Mortally Wounded

Hurlbut

McArnt

Sarah Bell
Cotton Field

Hudson

Johnston
Killed

Rutledge

Stephens

Robertson

Spain Field

Statham

Gladden
Mortally
Wounded

Bragg

Beauregard

Hardee

Cleburne

Trabue

Fraley Field

Wood Field

Widow Howell Field

Seay's Cotton Field

Rea (Rhea) Field

Corinth Road

Stuart

Chalmers

Clanton

Cullen
Field

Jackson

Bowen

Breckinridge

Savannah-Hamburg Rd

Purdy-Hamburg Rd

0   1/4   1/2   3/4   Mile

Chapter 15   Attack on the Union Left

10:30am to 11:30am

Stewart's Defense

Several days prior to the battle, before most of the other divisions had arrived at the Landing, Sherman split off one of his four brigades – Col. David Stuart's – and ordered it to set up camp near the river, nearly two miles east of Sherman's main position at Shiloh Church. Stuart's job was to guard the ford where the Savannah-Hamburg Road crossed Lick Creek. As a result, when the Confederate attack began, Stuart and his men were separated not only from Sherman, but from the rest of the army as well; by default they were the left flank of the Union line, smack in the bull's eye of Confederate Johnston's original plan to concentrate his attack on the Union left.

Col. David Stuart (w)
1816 - 1868

David Stuart was "a man with a past." He had once been a Michigan congressman and wealthy Chicago attorney. But he entangled himself in a noisy divorce where, to the horror of proper Chicago society, it came out that the cad had strayed from the arms of his dutiful wife, entering a love affair so torrid that it apparently frightened even the horses. When war came he attempted to raise a regiment but the newspapers raised such an outcry that the governor denied him the honor. However, the U.S. government desperately needed troops and was far less picky about how it got them, so now Stuart quickly got permission to form a brigade. He expected the war

to be the re-launch of his public career. Despite the scandal, or perhaps because of it, Stuart was wildly popular with his men.

Hearing the firing early that Sunday morning, and receiving a message that Prentiss was under attack, Stuart deployed his three regiments facing southwest. In doing so, he stretched out his line over 600 yards, apparently still trying to keep his far left regiment – the 54th Ohio – anchored on the Lick Creek ford, per Sherman's orders. The deployment was a fiasco. Stuart's line was simply too long for three regiments to defend. He should have pulled his small force back to a more consolidated position.

Facing him were two Confederate brigades dispatched by Johnston to take on what they had been told was an entire Yankee division (A division usually consists of at least three brigades), but which turned out to be only Stuart's brigade.

The Confederate brigade to the east, commanded by Brig. Gen. John Jackson, formerly a Georgia lawyer, angled toward Larkin Bell Field and the 71st Ohio, Stuart's right-most regiment. The other Southern brigade, commanded by Brig. Gen. James Chalmers – another lawyer, this time from Mississippi – headed straight north up McCuller Field toward the 54th Ohio.

Two Confederate batteries, Girardey's and Gage's, quickly deployed on the heights south of Locust Grove Branch and set to work blasting Stuart's formation, and in the process, chasing off four companies of skirmishers from the 55th Illinois

Brig. Gen. John K. Jackson
1828 - 1866

stationed along the creek. The gunners now turned their attention to the 71st Ohio, lobbing shells into the Federals. Under the support of that artillery, Jackson's brigade charged the 71st across Larkin

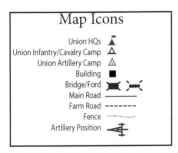

Map Icons

Union HQs	⚑
Union Infantry/Cavalry Camp	△
Union Artillery Camp	△
Building	■
Bridge/Ford	⬗ ⠿
Main Road	———
Farm Road	-------
Fence	—·—·—
Artillery Position	⚏

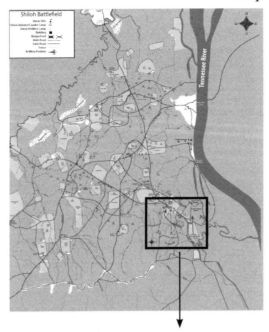

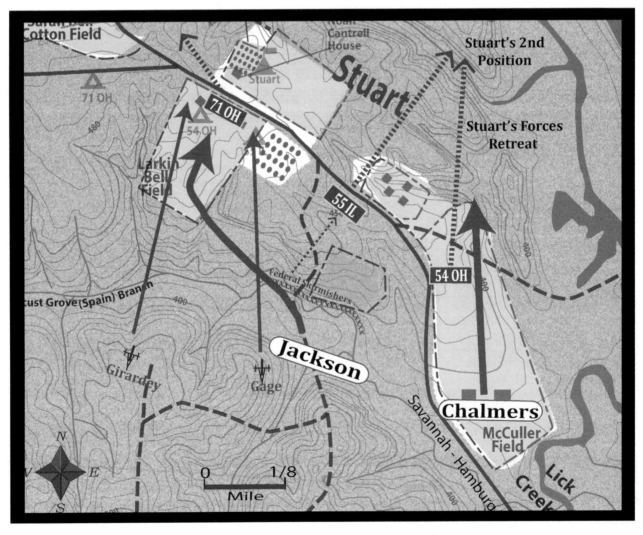

Bell Field. After firing two or three volleys at the Confederates, the regiment's commander, Col. Rodney Mason, panicked and allowed, if not led, a headlong race to the rear; the regiment didn't stop and reform until about 500 yards farther back, though apparently without Mason.

After the battle, Mason went to Grant with tears in his eyes, claiming extenuating circumstances and pleading for a second chance. Grant agreed. But four months later, while commanding an outpost in Clarksville, TN, Mason surrendered half of the 72nd Ohio and some other troops to a band of Rebel partisans. Humiliated and disgraced, he was cashiered from the army.

Meanwhile, on the southeast end of Stuart's line, Chalmer's brigade worked its way through the brush toward the 54th Ohio, which was defending a fence at the north end of an orchard on a slight slope, offering them some protection. But when Chalmer's troops got within 40 yards, the Federals retreated. At some point Stuart was hit in the shoulder but remained in command as much as possible in the chaotic situation.

With its sister regiments on its right and left retreating, the 55th Illinois in the middle began feeling lonely. The regiment commander, Lt. Col. Oscar Malmborg, ordered the men to do a "half wheel left" – a moderately complicated maneuver – attempting to face his attackers with his full battleline. But with artillery shells exploding and the enemy charging, Malmborg's raw troops were unable to perform the maneuver; the regiment's companies were soon colliding into each other, creating panic,

Col. Oscar Malmborg
1820 - 1880

and the men broke for the rear. A furious Stuart, his budding army career dissolving before his eyes, cursed the Illinoisans as cowards. But his curses were premature, at least regarding most of the men, as about 500 of them, along with 300 from the 54th Ohio, rallied about a quarter mile to the north along the lip of a deep ravine. Once secure in a protected position, the recruits stood their ground and continued fighting for several hours.

Around 11:30am, Jackson's men stormed through Stuart's camps, advancing north with their left astride the Savannah-Hamburg road. McArthur's Federals, assisted by oblique fire from Hurlbut's division, fended off the attack, though with heavy losses.

Still, the bulk of Jackson's and Chalmer's brigades where now able to swing west and join the fight at the Sunken Road.

In Hindsight

The Federals weren't the only ones with problems with raw troops performing complex maneuvers under fire. Chalmer's 52nd Tennessee crossed the Spain (Locust Grove) Branch Bridge in the early stages of the attack on the 54th Ohio. Upon reaching the other side, the Tennesseans were ordered to lie down and allow the rear rank to fire over them. Then they were told to fall back across the stream to clear a field of fire for Gage's artillery. Apparently mistaking the order as a retreat, the green regiment broke and fled. Chalmers frantically tried to rally the unit but only succeeded in corralling a couple of the companies. Disgusted, he attached the two companies to a different regiment and refused to allow the 52nd back into the fight, which apparently suited the 52nd Tennessee just fine.

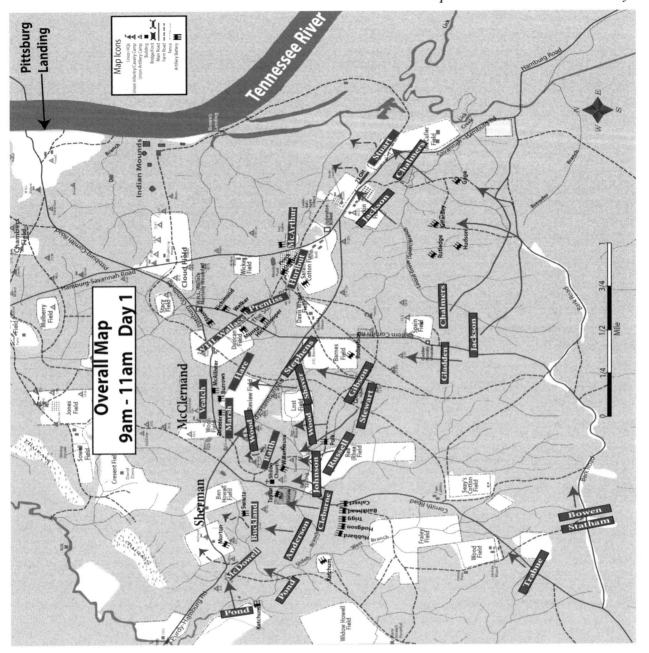

Google Map Links (scan with OC Reader to go to online maps)

Larkin Bell Field

McCuller Field

Lick Creek ford at
Savannah-Hamburg Road

Chapter 16   The Hornet's Nest

Duncan Field, 10am – 4:30pm

The fight along the center of the Sunken Road – the eastern portion of it called the "Hornet's Nest" by the Confederates because of the whirring sound of bullets flying about in the brush – is probably the best known aspect of the Shiloh battle, and one of the few scenes of the Shiloh battle glorified with a painting.

As mentioned in an earlier chapter, the Sunken Road wasn't very sunken; being a three-quarter mile long, it was just an old stagecoach shortcut that intersected with the Pittsburg-Cornith Road to the west in front of Duncan Field, and with the Savannah-Hamburg Road in the east in front of the Sarah Bell's Cotton Field. Also as mentioned in an earlier chapter, Gen. Hurlbut initiated the Federals' Sunken Road position at the eastern end of the road, where he was soon joined by the battered remnants of Prentiss' division, and then by W.H.L. Wallace's division.

The Federals formed up here not because the road was sunken or offered any protection, but rather because it was a handy line to rally on.

Wallace's two brigades – commanded by Brig. Gen. Thomas Sweeny and Col. James Tuttle – formed along the lane in front of Duncan Field.

Col. James M. Tuttle
1823 - 1892

Tuttle's Iowa regiments, particularly the 2nd and 7th directly in front of Duncan Field, would see some of the hottest fighting along the lane.

At the time of the battle Duncan Field was an old cotton field overgrown with weeds, in some places as high as a man's head. Spiking south into the field from the Sunken Road was a large, thickly forested gully and creek bed. The gully almost split off the eastern third of the field into a separate field of its own.

As early as 10am Confederate troops began massing in this vicinity, with Confederate artillery sparring with Federal cannon across the field. Beginning around 10:30am the Confederates began launching assaults against the Sunken Road. Once Sherman and McClernand fell back to Jones Field around 1pm, even

Brig. Gen. Thomas W. Sweeny
1820 - 1892

more Confederates turned their attention to the Sunken Road line. In all, the Confederates would assault the Sunken Road at least eight times (some historians say nine or ten times), mostly across Duncan Field and the woods to the east – the Hornet's Nest. That number does not include the assaults made across Sarah Bell's Cotton Field.

1st Attack 10:30am – Stephen's Brigade

Confederate division commander, Maj. Gen. Benjamin Cheatham – a popular and hard-drinking Tennessee planter-aristocrat who had participated in the Gold Rush of 1849 – led Stephen's brigade, about 1,350 men in three regiments in an attack across Duncan field. But unknown to the Confederates, the Federals had infiltrated the thicket-

Maj. Gen. Benjamin F. Cheatham (w)
1820 - 1886

filled ravine which cut through southeastern side of the field, allowing them to fire into the right flank of the attackers.

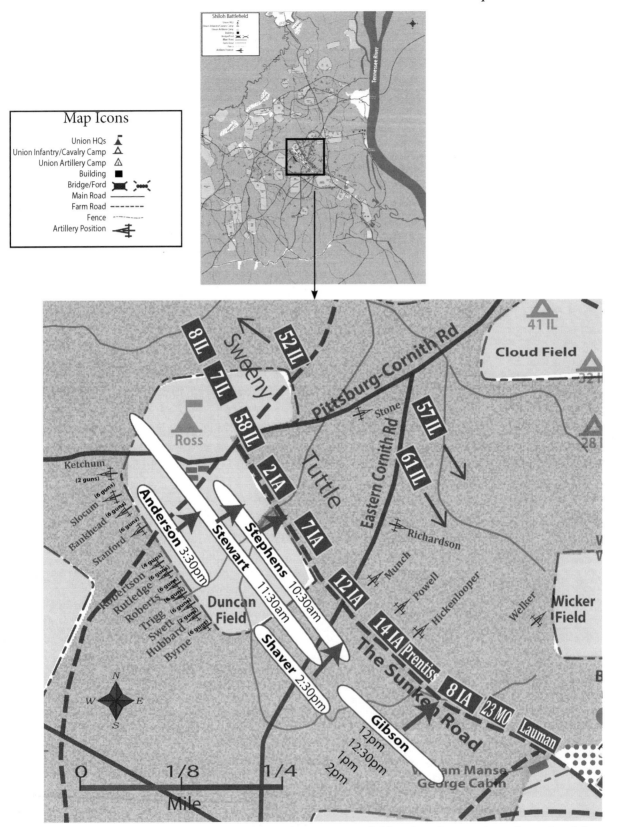

Map Icons

Union HQs	
Union Infantry/Cavalry Camp	
Union Artillery Camp	
Building	
Bridge/Ford	
Main Road	
Farm Road	
Fence	
Artillery Position	

Confederates attacked at least eight times across Duncan field and in the woods to the right of the field, the latter called the "Hornet's Nest."

"*All was silent in front until our ranks were near*," wrote 6th Tennessee Pvt. R. W. Hurdle. Then the men came under a "*murderous crossfire*," both from artillery and from infantry to the front and from the ravine to the Confederate right. The 6th Tennessee charged against the 14th Iowa, commanded by Col. William Shaw, a Mexican War veteran. To his youthful troops, Shaw seemed a strange old geezer who walked with a gimp and cussed like a sailor. But he was plenty tough.

Shaw ordered his men to lay down and hold their fire; when the Confederates got within 30 paces, the blue line rose up and loosed a devastating volley, "*leaving the dead laying in line of battle, as if on dress parade.*" Shaw even ordered a counterattack, but quickly thought better of it and ordered his men back to the road.

In 30 minutes, the 6th Tennessee lost 250 men, including 14 officers and the entire 12-man color guard. The regimental flag was shredded beyond recognition. The other two regiments fared little better. Cheatham was shot in the ear. Stephens, his horse shot from under him, collapsed from exhaustion. His son William, who served as his aide, was severely wounded.

2nd Attack 11:30am – Stewart's Reinforced Brigade

This second attack was clearly the most formidable assault on the Sunken Road line that day. On Bragg's order, Brig. Gen. Stewart led approximately 3,600 Confederates - the bulk of 10 regiments - in an attack that stretched from Prentiss' command to the far end of Duncan Field, west of the Pittsburg-Cornith Road. But the Federals, numbering about 4,300 men and 19 guns in this sector, held their ground, hurling deafening barrages at the attackers. The attack, which lasted about a half hour, failed. Few of the Southern attackers managed to get much more than half way into smoke-covered Duncan field before being driven back by the storm of fire.

3rd Attack 12pm – Gibson's Brigade

Around noon, Bragg assumed command of this sector and immediately ordered Col. Randall Gibson to lead his 2,400 man brigade in an attack

against the section of the line held by Prentiss and Lauman. The Rebels clawed their way through heavy thicket. "*It was almost impossible to walk through it,*" according to a 4th Louisiana soldier. The undergrowth was so dense that soldiers were firing into their own ranks. It was this densely wooded sector, to the southeast of Duncan field, that the Confederates called "The Hornet's Nest."

**Col. Randall L. Gibson
1832 - 1892**

Gibson's men were walking into an ambush.

"*Men fell around us like leaves.*"

When they got with 80-100 yards of the Union line, the Federals opened up with "*a perfect tornado of rifle fire ... in our very faces,*" according to a Louisiana soldier. "*Men fell around us like leaves,*" according to another. A single artillery blast took out six Zouaves of the 13th Louisiana, splattering brain matter over their captain, Capt. Edgar M. Dubroea. The woods in front of Lauman's position caught fire once again, roasting to death many of the wounded who were too crippled to crawl away.

The attack stalled.

4th Attack 12:30pm – Gibson's Brigade

Gibson rode back to Bragg and requested artillery support, but Bragg simply ordered him to renew the attack.

Gibson's men attacked again, but this time they kept a greater distance from the enemy, satisfied to trade gunfire with the Yankees. It was still hell, given that there was plenty of Federal artillery in this area. The Yankees "*mowed us down at every volley,*" according to Pvt. Robertson of the 4th Louisiana. The 4th fired off two or three volleys and then withdrew, but the 19th Louisiana kept fighting for another 30 minutes before withdrawing.

For decades, historians assumed that the fiercest fighting of the day occurred along the Sunken Road, and specifically the Hornet's Nest. However, recent historians have questioned the ferocity of fighting here compared to the rest of the battlefield. For one thing, of the five Confederate mass graves currently identified on the battlefield, four of them are on the west side of the battlefield and the fifth is farther north of the Sunken Road. If the fighting in the Sunken Road was so bloody, why no mass grave sites near it? Also, Grant in his memoirs said the most bodies were collected on the west side of the field, in and around the Water Oaks Pond area.

The new theory is that the over-emphasis of the Hornet's Nest occurred in the late 1800s when it's most prominent survivor, Prentiss, formed an organization dedicated to the Sunken Road survivors. This group naturally emphasized their part of the battle, and thus the Hornet's Nest legend grew.

All of that sounds logical, and it's hard to argue with U. S. Grant. Still, no one really knows how many Confederate mass graves were dug after the battle. The five currently identified grave locations are not only distant from the Hornet's Nest, but also distant from Duncan Field and Sarah Bell's Cotton Field – scenes of bloody fighting on both days of the battle. There surely must have been a significant body count from those locations. So where are their grave sites? No one knows.

So, the Confederate mass grave sites we know of today may not be the best gauge for judging the ferocity of fighting in the Hornet's Nest.

5th Attack 1pm Gibson's Brigade

As the exhausted troops came running back after the failed assault, Bragg rode up to Col. Henry Allen, commander of the 4th Louisiana regiment, and ordered his and the 13th Louisiana to ambush the enemy, whom Bragg incorrectly believed to be advancing. "*Serve them as they have served you,*" Bragg advised. Allen also requested artillery support. Bragg admonished him, "*Colonel Allen, I want no faltering now.*" With that, Allen returned to his men, gave them a pep talk, and once again charged into the inferno, this time advancing against the Sunken Road from across Davis

Wheatfield. The engagement soon degenerated into a long distance, hour-long gun fight. Allen was hit with a bullet that passed through both cheeks, which must have done wonders for his dental work. The commander of the 1st Louisiana, Col. James Fagan, leaped from his horse as it was shot dead.

> *"Colonel. Allen, I want no faltering now."*

Again the Confederates were driven back, this time breaking into unorganized groups. Many of the men had enough, vowing they would not attack that line again.

6th Attack 2pm – Gibson's Brigade

Seeing the troops streaming back across the Davis Wheat Field, Bragg called for Capt. Samuel Lockett - the same man who had earlier passed the incorrect report to Johnston that there was a Union division on the far eastern flank. Bragg ordered Lockett to seize the banner of one of the regiments and lead it forward, stating "*The flag must not go back again.*"

> *"Here boys is as good a place as any to die!"*

Lockett grabbed the banner of the 4th Louisiana just as the color bearer was shot down. A few moments later Col. Allen, blood steaming from the holes in his cheeks, rode up to Lockett and indignantly inquired, "*What are you doing with my colors, Sir?*"

Grasping the flag from Lockett, Allen defiantly rode out in the field and faced the enemy, calling out to his men, "*Forward! Here boys, is as good a place as any to die!*" The colonel waved his sword and led his men through the underbrush and dense smoke to within 50 feet of the Federals on the Sunken Road. In the midst of the fight, as a Louisiana soldier rose to advance, a cannon ball snapped off his head. With a blood geyser shooting out

Col. Henry W. Allen (w)
1820 - 1866

of his neck, his comrades watched in amazement as he continued to walk two or three steps before dropping.

But soon this attack also broke, with the entire brigade falling back, leaving about 700 dead and wounded on the field.

Col. Allen would survive the battle and go on to be elected governor of Louisiana in 1864.

7th Attack 2:30pm – Shaver's Brigade

Bragg now sent in Shaver's (formerly Hindman's) Arkansas Brigade, which had already fought heavy engagements in front of Peabody's camp and in Review Field. Shaver's 1,500 men struck the center of the Sunken Road line, manned by the 12th and 14th Iowa and Prentiss' survivors. The Southerners got within 60 yards before being hit by a wall of infantry and artillery fire, breaking their attack.

Bragg would later write to his wife that Gibson, who led four charges against the Sunken Road, and who would lead more the next day, "was an arrant coward."

8th Attack 3:30pm – Anderson's Brigade

Finally, Patton Anderson's brigade, reinforced with the Crescent Regiment – about 1,300 men in all – advanced once again across Duncan Field, only to meet the same blistering response from the Federals that had broken all the previous attacks. This attack also failed, with particularly heavy losses to the 20th Louisiana, which had struck the 2nd Iowa.

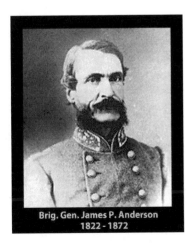

Brig. Gen. James P. Anderson
1822 - 1872

In the attack, Lt. Col. John A. Dean of the 7th Arkansas fell mortally wounded, shot through the neck. As the Confederates withdrew, Capt. Warren C. Jones of the 14th Iowa ran between the lines and spoke briefly to Dean before the Southerner died. Jones crossed the dead man's arms and placed a handkerchief across his face before dashing back to his line.

RUGGLES' BARRAGE

After at least eight failed attacks, there was a lull in the fighting as the Confederates once again regrouped. But they were still determined to crack that damn Yankee line if took all summer, and now they began dragging up every piece of artillery they could lay hands on. Brig. Gen. Daniel Ruggles, one of Bragg's division commanders, a crabby 51-year-old in poor health and generally detested by his troops, usually gets credit for organizing this cannonade, although some Confederate accounts state that it was a group effort by

Brig. Gen. Daniel Ruggles
1810 - 1897

several officers, with Ruggles being just one of the participants, or possibly just a spectator.

In any case, the Southerners eventually lined up 53 guns – give or take one or two – hub to hub along the southern edge of Duncan Field. At the time it was the largest concentration of artillery ever seen on the American continent. Shortly after 4pm, these guns, which could fire about three rounds a minute, unleashed a storm of fire on the Federal line, including explosive shells, canister and round shot that brought down tree limbs on the heads of the defenders.

The massive barrage continued about 20 minutes, until 4:30pm, by which time the Federals retreated.

Some argue that the barrage actually had little to do with the Federal withdrawal from the Sunken Road, since the retreat of McClernand to the west in the early afternoon, and Hurlbut in the east, exposed both flanks on the Sunken Road line and made it inevitable that the Union troops there would have to retreat.

But while the Sunken Road defenders may have been retreating anyway, the cannonade created a hell on earth along the line, and undoubtedly hastened their departure.

In the meantime, the Confederates were also taking incoming shells. W. A. Howard wrote to his wife: "*It was an awful thing to hear no intermission in firing and hear the clatter of small arms and the whizzing Minnie balls and rifle shot and the sing of grape shot, the hum of cannon balls and the roaring of the bomb shell and explosion of same, seeming to be a thousand every minute.*"

The stubborn Union defense of the Sunken Road cost the Confederates precious time and men, and undoubtedly helped make the difference between success and failure of Johnston's grand offensive of the first day.

Assuming three rounds per minute per cannon, in 20 minutes the math works out to about 3,180 incoming shells – some of which would have been exploding shells and others would have been solid shot (cannon balls) – the latter very effective against troops in timber since the cannon balls knocked down trees and limbs, crushing soldiers below and raining down wooden splinters.

This is probably the most famous of the few paintings of the Battle of Shiloh; it's by an artist named Thure de Thulstrup, and it shows the Union line on the Sunken Road in the Hornet's Nest.

While under the Confederate artillery barrage, an officer of the 2nd Iowa later wrote: "It seemed like a mighty hurricane sweeping everything before it… The great storm of cannonballs made the forest in places fall before its sweep, … men and horses were dying, and a blaze of unearthly fire lit up the scene. [Yet] at this moment of horror, when our regiment was lying close to the ground to avoid the storm of balls, the little birds were singing in the green trees over our heads!"

Modern picture of Duncan Field, standing on the Sunken Road, looking southwest toward the Confederate position.

The Phantom of Duncan Field

In one of Gibson's attacks, the 4th Louisiana, led by Col. Allen, was positioned on the far left of the brigade line. In the confusion and smoke, a section of Cheatham's men fired into the rear of the Allen's regiment, killing and wounding at least 27 men. The enraged Louisianans, mostly French Creoles who didn't speak English, raised their guns to fire at Cheatham's men, who were in the process of firing again.

Suddenly in the middle of the two lines came (You probably guessed!) a woman in sunbonnet, wearing a long dress. In a scene both comical and eerie, the amazed soldiers held their fire while the woman, seemingly oblivious to her surroundings, walked across the field with great purpose as if on a vital mission, before finally disappearing into the smoke on the opposite side.

No one ever knew who she was, or what she was doing, or what happened to her. One possible clue, as good as any other, comes from Elsie Duncan in a letter written decades after the battle. Elsie, 9 years old at the time, was one of the many Duncans and others who had houses around Duncan field, all of which were destroyed or appropriated as hospitals. In her letter Elsie describes her mother, who also had a son in the battle, trying to comfort a hysterical woman in "a house filled with wounded and dead men and the floor covered with blood." The woman was "screaming and wringing her hands" because her two sons had joined the battle on opposites sides. Possibly that woman went looking for her sons.

In any event, apparently the mystery woman prevented the two Confederate units from firing upon each other.

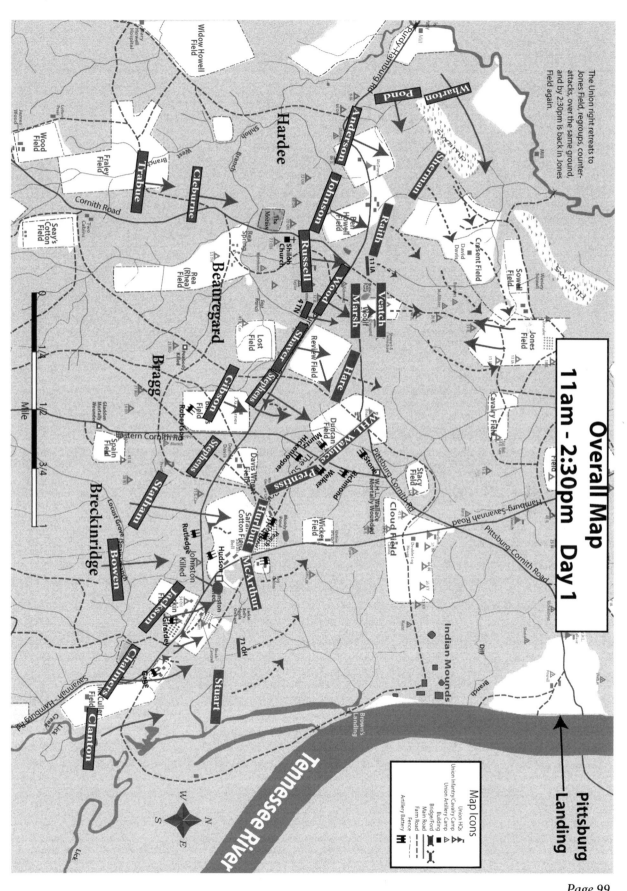

Overall Map
11am - 2:30pm Day 1

The Union right retreats to Jones Field, regroups, counter-attacks, over the same ground, and by 2:30pm is back in Jones Field again.

Pittsburg Landing

Tennessee River

Map Icons
Union HQs
Union Infantry/Cavalry Camp
Union Artillery Camp
Building
Bridge/Ford
Main Road
Farm Road
Fence
Artillery Battery

Google Map Links (scan with OC Reader to go to online maps)

Duncan Field

Sarah Bell's Cotton Field

The Hornet's Nest

Davis Wheat Field

Review Field

Chapter 17　Collapse of the Sunken Road Line

2pm to 4pm

The western side of the Union line at the Sunken Road – the area facing Duncan Field – was repelling attack after attack until finally blasted out of the position around 4:30pm. Meanwhile, the eastern end of the Union line on the Sunken Road, held by Hurlbut's division and Brig. Gen. John McArthur's small brigade, were locked in their own separate battle.

Pugh's brigade of Hurlbut's division, directly in front of the Peach Orchard, was struck by the better part of three Confederate brigades – Maney's (formerly Stephens') , Statham's, and Bowen's, all well supported by artillery. Pugh's men began falling back. Hurlbut desperately reorganized by pulling back his whole line, reshuffling his units to bolster Pugh and forming a new line across the southern end of Wicker Field, facing the Bloody Pond.

Meanwhile, on the left flank of Hulburt's line, McArthur's three Federal regiments, decked out in Scottish tams and marching to bagpipes, had their own problems. Around 10:30am, McArthur and his 1,200 men had been sent there by W. H. L. Wallace to extend the Federal line eastward, becoming the left flank of Hurlbut's line and in fact the left flank of the entire Union line on the Sunken Road.

But now they were being overwhelmed and flanked by fierce attacks hurled at them by Jackson's, Chalmer's and part of Bowen's Confederate brigades. Also the Federals were running low on ammunition. A Union soldier with McArthur's brigade later wrote: "*I saw the gray dirty uniforms of the enemy. I heard their fierce yells. I saw their flags flapping in the grimy atmosphere. That was a sight I have never forgotten. I can see the tiger ferocity in those faces yet; I can see them in my dreams.*"

McArthur did receive some much needed assistance from the 57th Illinois, plus Hurlbut sent Laumen's brigade to plug the gap between Hurlbut's and McArthur's line. Nonetheless, McArthur's force began falling back, either due to pressure or simply to stay abreast of Hurlbut's line.

Chalmer's Confederate brigade soon swarmed around the east side McArthur's line, continuing to force the Federals back and exposing Hurlbut's left flank. By now, around 4pm, it was clear that the Federal left flank had collapsed. Hurlbut decided to withdraw to Pittsburg Landing. His two brigades and McArthur's men retreated in fairly good order – making a running fight back toward the Landing, though not sure exactly what they were going to do once they got there.

Fortunately, Grant had been busy at the Landing, preparing for this moment by building what is now known, and probably was then known, as "*Grant's Last Line.*" Once behind this final line, the Federals had nowhere else to retreat, except to plunge into the Tennessee River or flee into the swamps north of Pittsburg Landing.

In any case, the left flank of the Federal line on the Sunken Road was shattered beyond repair. The remainder of the Federals on that road would now have to retreat as well.

"I can see the tiger ferocity in those faces yet; I can see them in my dreams."

Bloody Pond got its name from the number of wounded and dying men from both sides who crawled there, desperately thirsty; many supposedly died half submerged in the water, turning the pond pink with blood.

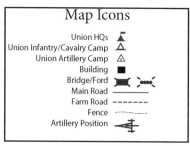

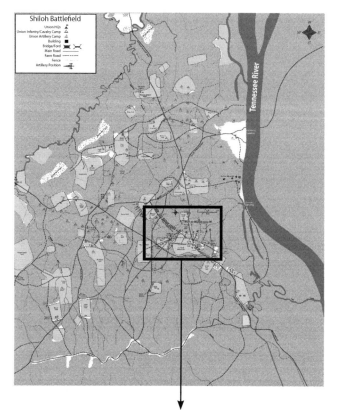

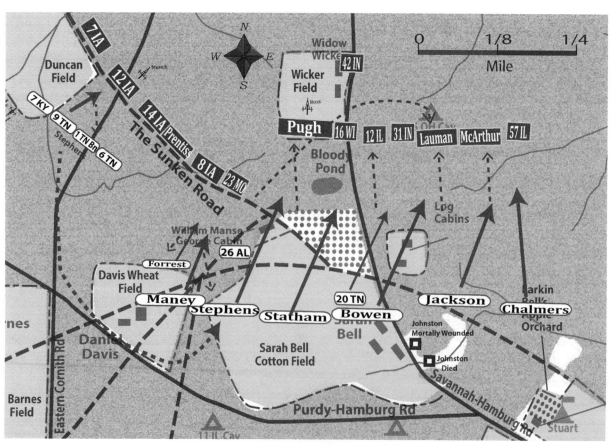

Johnston's Death

2:30pm

Johnston joined Statham's Confederate brigade during its 2:30pm assault. Thinking it was succeeding, the commander galloped to the south end of the cotton field where he encountered a member of his staff, volunteer aide and Tennessee governor, Isham G. Harris, *"a thin man wearing a white coat and riding a mule."*

**Gov. Isham G. Harris
1818 - 1897**

Johnston showed off his polished riding boot with its sole split open from toe to heel by a bullet, remarking cheerfully, *"Governor, they came very near putting me hors de combat in that charge!"* Concerned, Harris asked Johnston if he was wounded. The general assured him he wasn't, and sent Harris off to deliver a message to Statham. The governor later recalled that he had *"never in his life seen Johnston looking more bright, joyous and happy."*

After delivering the message to Statham about 200 yards away, Harris no sooner returned when he saw Johnston swaying in his saddle. Harris and other aides lifted Johnston from his horse.

"General, are you wounded?" asked the governor. *"Yes, and I fear seriously,"* Johnston admitted. He was right. The bullet had cut an artery behind his right knee; he was rapidly bleeding to death.

> ***"Ravine, 2:30pm General Johnston has fallen, mortally wounded, after a victorious attack on the left of the enemy. It now devolves on you to complete the victory."***

(Johnston may not have even been aware he was hit until he became weak from loss of blood. Years before he had been wounded in his right hip in a duel which damaged the sciatic nerve. Ever since then he had always had numbness to heat, pain and cold in that leg.)

Harris led the general's horse into the ravine about 40 yards away, where they laid Johnston down. He was clearly dying but the staff officers could find no wound – the blood was draining into his boot, unseen. His brother-in-law, Col. William Preston, arrived and propped the general's head in his lap, asking repeatedly, *"Johnston, do you know me?* But the general died without another word.

Everyone was crying, Preston most of all. *"Pardon me, gentlemen,"* he sobbed, *"but you all know how I loved him."* Then, back to business, he removed his notebook from his pocket and scrawled a message to Beauregard:

> *"Ravine, 2:30pm General Johnston has fallen, mortally wounded, after a victorious attack on the left of the enemy. It now devolves on you to complete the victory."*

Beauregard calmly received the news around 3pm. Johnston's body was wrapped in a blanket and removed from the field without ceremony to keep his death a secret from the troops. But word gradually spread around the battlefield.

It would later turn out that he had been hit four times – twice by bullets to the body that failed to penetrate, once in the sole of his boot, and the fatal shot to the back of his knee.

Painting of Johnston's Death. National Park Service

In Hindsight

The jury is out, and will forever be, on what kind of leader Johnston might have become had he lived. He certainly had charisma, and after Shiloh no one could doubt his willingness to fight. True, like almost every officer on both sides at this early stage of the war, Johnston made serious mistakes, but probably no more than did Grant and Sherman, who went on to become the top generals in the their army.

The jury will also forever be out on the question of whether the Confederates would have won the battle had Johnston remained in command. In another of those might-have-beens, many Southerners contend then and now that Johnston's death cost them the battle. But that's a stretch.

Johnston died at 2:30pm. If the Confederate drive failed to reach Pittsburg Landing by 3pm, most likely it never would. By then Grant's Last Line was well under construction. Packed with artillery, including siege guns, and supporting naval gunboats; the troops gathering on the Last Line were now concentrated and fighting with their back to the wall, or at least to the river. It took the exhausted Confederates six hours to break the Sunken Road Line, and they only did so by eventually curling around the ends of the Federal line. Grant's Last Line had no flanks – with one end protected by the river and the other end by the swamp. Very likely his line could have held on for three hours – until nightfall and/or until Buell's, and eventually Lew Wallace's, troops arrived.

After his death, Johnston was criticized for having put so much energy in smashing the heavily defended Peach Orchard position, rather than striking farther east, where there were fewer Federals – namely McArthur and Stuart's battered brigades. But the Peach Orchard was critical to Johnston because it commanded the Savannah-Hamburg Road, which was the fastest route to Pittsburg Landing. Though Johnston initially planned to attack on the east side of this road near the river, once he was on location he could plainly see the deep, swampy ravines at right angles to the river – four of them – blocking the Confederates' route to Pittsburg Landing. Had Johnston attempted to go off road and attack through these jungle-like ravines, his troops would have had an extremely tough fight. From the opposite banks of these deep ravines even a small Union force could put up a stout defense.

Johnston's understandable but fatal mistake was his midmorning decision to shift forces (Jackson and Chalmers brigades) to attack Stuart – based on false information that there was a Union division lurking there to threaten his right flank. Ideally he should have continued his attack straight ahead, against Hurlbut's poorly-deployed and understrength division at the south end of Sarah Bell's Cotton Field.

Earlier that morning Johnston had sent his own surgeon, Dr. D. W. Yandell, to treat wounded Federal prisoners of the 18th Wisconsin. When the doctor protested that his duty was to stay with the commanding general, Johnston said, "No, those men were our enemies but are our prisoners now, and deserve our protection." The decision to dispense with his doctor proved fatal.

Modern photo of ravine where Johnston died. The view faces east.

Illustration of the Bloody Pond, looking west. There was much fighting around this pond as the two sides surged back and forth. Both sides drank here even though the water was tinged pink with blood..

Modern view of the Bloody Pond.

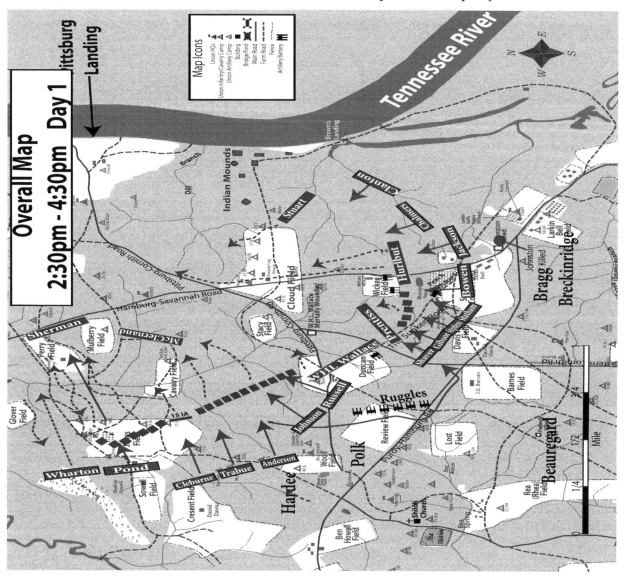

Overall Map 2:30pm - 4:30pm Day 1

Google Map Links (scan with OC Reader to go to online maps)

Duncan Field

Sarah Bell's Cotton Field

The Peach Orchard

Bloody Pond

Wicker Field

Pittsburg Landing

Ravine where Johnston died

Chapter 18   Surrender at Hell's Hollow

4pm – 5:45pm

By 4pm it was clear to W. H. L. Wallace that his division's position at the Sunken Road was collapsing. Sweeney's brigade on the right flank was faltering; Hurlbut's division on the left was retreating. Across Duncan Field, the Confederates were lining up enough cannon to pulverize anything that stood it their way.

Wallace ordered a withdrawal up Pittsburg-Cornith Road, but in the process of standing up in his stirrups to take a look back, a bullet slammed through his head. His brother-in-law, Cyrus Dick-

Brig. Gen. W.H.L. Wallace (mw)
1821 - 1862

ey, with the aid of three soldiers, tried to carry the general to the rear. But Confederate troops were surrounding the vacated Sunken Road position – creating a trap for any lingering Yankees – and the three helpers dropped Wallace and ran. Dickey couldn't carry Wallace by himself; thinking him dead anyway, he left the general on the side of the road near some ammo crates.

At least some of Wallace's troops withdrew in fairly good order, making a fighting retreat. Around 4:15pm, for example, the 2nd and 7th Iowa retreated through the southwest side of Cloud Field – today known as "Hell's Hollow." There they encountered Confederates in Stacy Field blocking their retreat. The two Iowa regiments formed a battleline, drove the Confederates off, and broke through to Pittsburg Landing.

By 4:45pm eleven of Wallace's fifteen regiments and his division artillery had escaped the Sunken Road position. One of the regiments that didn't make it was the 58th Illinois, which had manned the far right flank of the Union line on the Sunken

Road, and at one point had even briefly charged out on Duncan field to seize some farm buildings. But as the regiment's 300 survivors attempted to retreat through Hell's Hollow they found their path hopelessly blocked by Confederates surging in and around them. It was the same story for the 8th Iowa and 23rd Missouri. The 12th Iowa, also trapped, laid down its weapons in the abandoned camp of the 41st Illinois. A triumphant Confederate cavalry trooper dragged the Iowans' regimental flag back and forth in a mud puddle.

By 5:45pm Prentiss and all the units still within Hell's Hollow had surrendered.

In Hindsight

Once Sherman's and McClernand's divisions were driven back from their positions in Woolf Field, and McArthur's brigade was pushed back east of the Peach Orchard, the collapse of the Sunken Road position was inevitable. Confederate forces began to flow around both the left and right flanks of the defenders. For example, Trabue's Kentucky brigade, which had been fighting McClernand's division in Woolf Field, shifted southeastward and eventually took a position clear up on the north end of Cloud Field, blocking the Union retreat up Savannah-Hamburg Road. Other Confederate units made similar deployments.

Nevertheless, the six hours during which Wallace's division, along with Hurlbut's and the remnants of Prentiss', stalled the Confederate advance were probably decisive in saving Grant's army. Prentiss

---

While raiding the Yankee camps, Sgt. Henry Cowling of the 5th Kentucky of Trabue's Confederate brigade discovered a true prize – a big hunk of Ohio cheese. Unwilling to relinquish such a feast, and with no other way to carry it, he stuck it on the end of his bayonet. Not long after, the 5th Kentucky formed up to attack. Its commander, Col. Thomas Hunt, rode down the battle line for a last minute inspection, during which he spotted Cowling's bayonet – it being the only one with cheese on it.

The colonel "almost took Sgt. Cowling's head off and made him throw the cheese away."

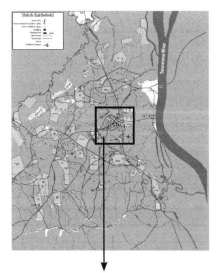

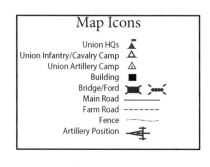

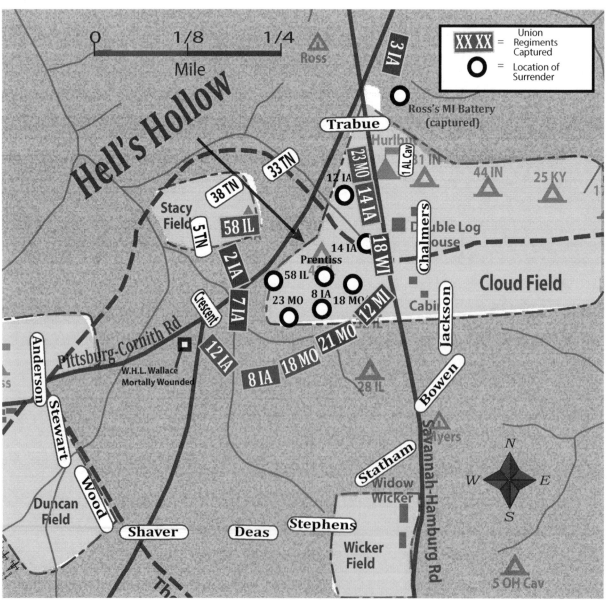

had followed Grant's order to hold at all costs, but Grant never fully appreciated it. His memoirs criticized Prentiss in a backhanded way for having allowed himself and 2,200 men to be captured.

Aftermath

Contrary to the expectations of his brother-in-law, W. H. L. Wallace hadn't died on the field, though he was horribly wounded – a musket ball had hit him above and behind the left ear, passing through his skull and out his left eye. Like hundreds and probably thousands of wounded soldiers, he lay on the battlefield in the pouring rain throughout the night of April 6-7. Around 10am the following day, when Union troops retook the ground, they found Wallace still clinging to life.

Early on the morning of the 6th, Wallace's wife, Ann, had arrived by steamboat at Pittsburg Landing to pay her husband a surprise visit, and also her father, a colonel, and both her brothers who were officers, and two of her husband's brothers, as well as a number of other distant relatives, all in Grant's army.

The outbreak of the battle prevented her from entering the camps, and her planned happy reunion turned into a horror of tending the wounded brought aboard her steamboat. That evening she received the news of her husband's death, his body left on the field. "God gave me strength," she later recalled, and she went on tending the wounded throughout the night.

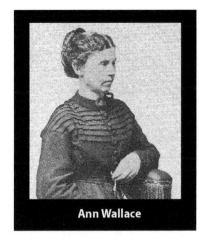

Ann Wallace

But the next day she was overjoyed when her beloved Will was brought in from the field, terribly wounded but conscious and able to recognize her voice and speak to her. Taken to Cherry Mansion in Savannah, Grant's pre-battle headquarters, the tenacious Wallace lingered for days, frequently conversing with his wife. Hope rose that he might actually recover. But on April 10th an infection set in and he sank rapidly. His last words were to his wife, "We meet in heaven."

"We meet in heaven."

Confederate Pvt. Jessie W. Wyatt, Co. B, 12th Tennessee, picked up a small pocket Bible on the battlefield that belonged to Federal Pvt. Samuel Lytle, Co. F, 11th Iowa. The Iowan greatly regretted the loss, as it was a keepsake from his father.

Two years later, on May 17, 1864, a private with the 73rd Illinois, C. W. Keeley, picked off a Confederate sharpshooter near Adairsville, Georgia. Pvt. Jessie Wyatt was his target. Rifling through the dead Confederate's haversack, Keeley found the bible with Lytle's address still in it. Some years after the war, Keeley sent it back to Lytle.

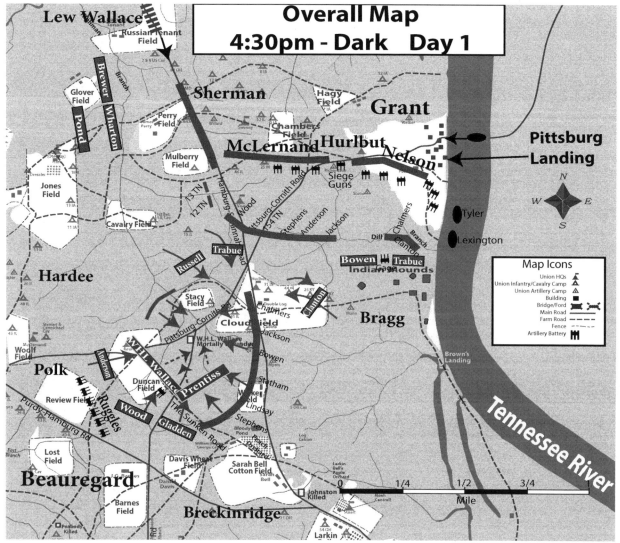

Overall Map
4:30pm - Dark   Day 1

Confederates close in on the southwestern side of Cloud Field, known as Hell's Hollow, capturing 2,200 Federals. Meanwhile, the remainder of the Federal army retreats to Grant's Last Line at Pittsburg Landing.

Google Map Links (scan with OC Reader to go to online maps)

Duncan Field

Cloud Field

Stacy Field

Cherry Mansion

Pittsburg Landing

Chapter 19   Grant's Last Line

5 PM – 6:30 PM

By 4:30pm, what remained of all three wings of Grant's army – left, right and center – had been pushed back to the muddy road leading from Pittsburg Landing.

In the west, Grant's right wing under Sherman and McClernand had made a fighting retreat from Shiloh Branch, then back to the Crossroads, then back to Jones Field, then back to Tilghman Branch. There they made another stand against Pond's Confederate brigade before finally falling back to the Savannah-Hamburg Road where they cobbled together a shaky line only a half mile west of Pittsburg Landing.

And that was the good news. Grant's left wing was completely shattered, as was his center, where 2,200 of his men had been trapped and forced to surrender, with the survivors fleeing back to Pittsburg Landing in various degrees of disorder. The Landing itself was in chaos, crammed with 10,000 to 15,000 soldiers – a quarter or a third of Grant's army – including many officers, who had simply thrown away their weapons and quit the battle. No one, including Grant, could rally them. They simply sat or wandered aimlessly, looking for opportunities to run even further. The transports, now crammed with wounded, cut their cables and dropped anchor in the middle of the river so as to avoid being swamped with fugitives. But periodically some of the panicked soldiers would drown trying to swim out to the boats. Many tried to float across the river on logs.

But on the front line, the remainder of the army continued to fight stubbornly hour after hour, resisting Confederate onslaughts, and buying Grant what he needed most – time.

Musician 4th Class John Cockerill, who seemed to wander all over the battlefield that day, stood on the bluff above the Landing and observed the pandemonium.

"Below lay thirty transports, at least," he recalled, *"all being loaded with the wounded, and all around me were baggage wagons, mule teams, disabled artillery teams and thousands of panic-stricken men. Some of the stragglers were being forced to carry sandbags up to fortify batteries of heavy siege guns."*

Modern view of Grant's Last Line, looking east toward the Tennessee River, about 500 yards away. The guns are pointing south toward Dill Creek, the direction of the last Confederate attack of the day.

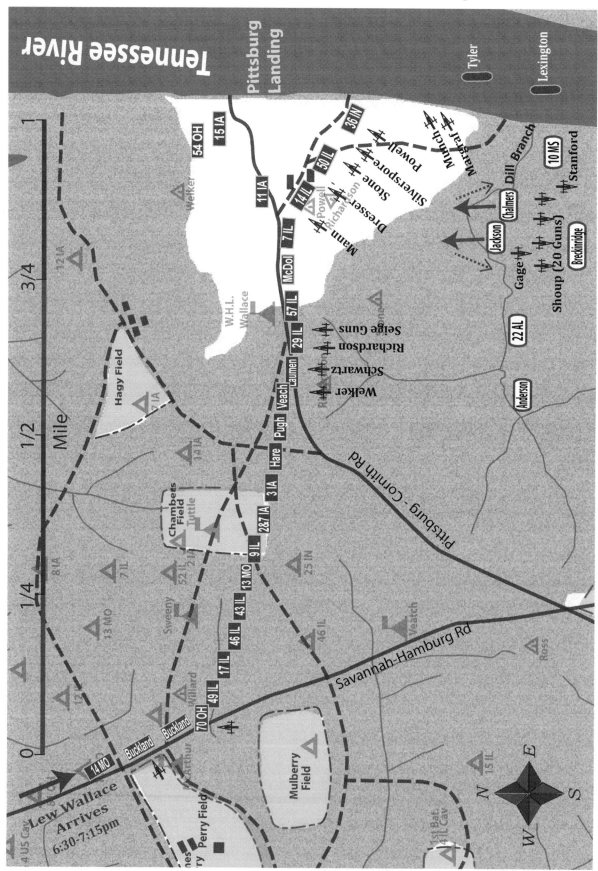

Cockerill also noted that the cabin on the bluff was *"turned into a temporary field hospital where hundreds of wounded men, brought down in wagons and ambulances, were being unloaded, and where their arms and legs were cut off and thrown out to form gory, ghastly heaps."* (Surgery on the boats was more convenient, as buckets of amputated limbs were simply dumped in the river).

Amazingly, given the situation, Grant seemed as confident as a Presbyterian holding four aces. At one point, chewing on a cigar, he stared at the battleline and said to one in particular, *"Not beaten yet. Not by a damn sight."*

And in fact he did have a couple of aces up his sleeve. One was Lew Wallace's division of 7,500 fresh troops out there, somewhere; he had expected Wallace by noon. The other ace was Buell's reinforcements, expected within the hour. Also nightfall was coming – Civil War armies rarely fought at night for many good reasons. So time was on Grant's side. All he had to do was hold out another 90 minutes, after which reinforcements would surely arrive from east or west or, if nothing else, at least he could count on darkness.

But Grant wasn't just waiting on reinforcements. He had spent much of the afternoon building a final defense line here at Pittsburg Landing, and a formidable line it was – the most formidable defense the Confederates would encounter that day.

Early that afternoon, Grant ordered his Chief of Staff, Col. Joseph D. Webster, to collect every artillery piece he could lay hands on, and stack them hub to hub facing the oncoming enemy. Webster went to work with a vengeance, collecting the guns of two uncommitted batteries, plus the surviving guns from batteries that had fallen back to the Landing. He even dragged the army's big siege guns, intended for later use at Cornith, up to this line. By 6pm, Grant's Last Line bristled with 41 cannon, 10 of them in two batteries deployed on a ridge jutting out from the river, allowing them to fire straight up the hollow of Dill Branch Ravine – the most likely point of assault – a high bluff, almost a fortress, from which the Federals could fire down on attacking Confederates.

Two gunboats – the USS Tyler and USS Lexington – bolstered Grant's firepower with their 8 inch

cannon. Far larger than even the army's big siege guns, they could throw shells "bigger than a hog." (In fact, the gunboats weren't of much help in the close-in fighting around Dill Branch because they couldn't lower the elevation of their guns enough, but at least they *sounded* dangerous.)

Manning the line were about 18,000 Federal infantry, made up of retreating units of Grants five divisions who still had some fight in them.

Grant appeared at the landing about 4:30pm. He pleaded with the mass of stragglers to return to ranks. They ignored him. Grant then ordered a squadron of cavalry to drive the mob away from the river's edge. The cavalrymen drew their sabers, divided up at each end of landing, and drove toward each other, temporarily pushing the mob from the water's edge and back up the embankment. But by 5pm the mob had returned.

"I heard a thud and some dark object whizzed over my shoulder. It was Captain Carson's head."

At some point Grant and his staff were riding along the bluff when Captain Irving Carson (no relation to Kit Carson), one of Grant's cavalry scouts, rode up to make a report. He dismounted and was holding his horse by the bridle *"when a six pound shot carried away all of Carson's head, bespattering Grant's clothing with blood."* A Lt. Fisher, who was present, wrote later, *"I heard a thud and some dark object whizzed over my shoulder. It was Captain Carson's head."*

Earlier that day, Grant had at least one other close call when Rebel artillery caught him and his staff out in the open. A shell fragment broke Grant's sword scabbard. (Grant later showed the damaged scabbard to Buell, who was supremely unimpressed).

Strange Riders Appear

About this time some of skulkers at the Landing spotted two riders observing them from a cornfield on the opposite bank, one of them carrying a white flag with a red square in it. The jumpy spectators concluded it was Texas cavalry. But about 15 minutes later Col. Jacob Ammen's brigade, of Brig.

Battery of five 24-pounder siege guns set up along "Grant's Last Line" by Grant's Chief of Staff, Col. Joseph D. Webster. Photo taken a couple of days after the battle.

Gen. William "Bull" Nelson's Division, emerged from the woods. It was the van of Buell's army.

Ammen and his men stared in amazement at the spectacle on the opposite side of the river. Several transports packed with wounded were parked in mid-river. Two or three transports hugged the shoreline on the north end of the landing. But most amazing was the panorama of 10,000 to 15,000 Federals milling around the opposite river bank, pleading for Ammen and his 550 men to save them. The sight outraged Ammen's troops, who had made a brutally rapid march from Savannah to join the fight. *"I blush to describe it,"* wrote one 6th Ohio soldier. *"The entire bank of the river, for a mile up and down, was crowded with cowardly poltroons who were crowding down to be out of harm's way."*

Col. Jacob Ammen
1807 - 1894

Arriving with Buell's army was one Lt. Ambrose Bierce, a noted author of his time, who wrote that *"the air was full of thunder and the earth was trembling beneath [our] feet. Below us ran the river, vexed with plunging shells and obscured in spots by blue sheets of low-lying smoke."* In the distance, *"the battle was burning brightly enough; a thousand lights kindled and expired every second. There were deep shaking explosions and smart shocks, and faint, desultory cheers"* could be heard from the battlefield.

Finally the 36th Indiana of Ammen's brigade ferried across the river and splashed ashore on the west bank. Once on the Landing,

"Damn your souls! If you won't fight, get out of the way and let men come here who will!"

a mass of stragglers blocked their path. This was a crowd of cowards as far as Ammen's men were concerned. "Bull" Nelson – a giant of a man with a mean temper and a large, black ostrich feather stuck in his hat – was in a particularly nasty mood. Ordering up some cavalry, Nelson roared: *"Gentlemen, draw your sabers and trample these sons a bitches into the mud! Charge!"* As the troopers slashed at the skulkers, Nelson bellowed: *"Damn your souls, if you won't fight, get out of the way, and let men come here who will."* He then ordered his men to shout *"Buell!, Buell!, Buell!,"* and beat time with his saber as they chanted.

Somewhere in the midst of the insanity, a small drummer boy among the stragglers pounded furiously on his drum, possibly to welcome the reinforcements, or possibly because he didn't know what else to do. Drummer boys averaged pretty tough in Grant's army. A Lt. Crocker of the 55th Illinois remembered that *"the belligerent little drummers nearly all preferred to fight and were found along the line, gun in hand, as fierce as fighting cocks, with no notion of shirking."*

Also blocking the way was a chaplain who ran about shouting: *'Rally, men, rally, and we may yet be saved. Oh rally! For God and your country's sake, rally! Rally! Oh! Rally round the flag of your country!'* It was all too much for Ammen, who shouted, *"Shut up, you God damned old fool, or I'll break you head! Get out of the way!"*

Once he was up on the Landing, Lt. Horace C. Fisher, one of Nelson's aides, described the scene: "As we sat on our horses we saw the flotsam and jetsam of Gen. Grant's army drift by in flight toward The Landing. We saw double-decked ambulances galloping wildly with well men on the front seats prodding the horses with bayonets and swords, the ghastly load of wounded men inside shrieking in agony as the ambulances collided with each other or with trees in their flight. Shells were shrieking through the air and trees were breaking and casting their branches upon the ground. Nor were the bullets less vicious as they ripped around us. In a word, it was pandemonium broken loose."

Admittedly it wasn't pretty, but Grant had his defensive line - his "Last Line" - of about 18,000 men of his own and 550 from Buell, along with 41 cannon and two gunboats just off shore. The line stretched about a mile with Sherman and McClernand on the far right, Buell's fresh troops on the

Brig. Gen. William Nelson
1824 - 1862

Five months after the battle, Nelson got into an argument with one of his subordinates, Brig. Gen. Jefferson C. Davis, a Union regular army officer. Davis confronted Nelson in a hotel lobby. The massive Nelson slapped Davis (a brigadier general!) in the face. Davis departed, but soon returned with a gun and shot Nelson dead. The case against Davis was never prosecuted, with many considering it a justifiable homicide.

left, and a hodgepodge of battered but determined units in between.

Dill Creek

Fronting Grant's troops near the river - the most obvious point of attack - was a formidable barrier called Dill Creek. "Creek" is a misnomer; at least near the river it wasn't so much a creek as a deep, dense, jungle-like ravine, 60-90 feet high on both sides, where water flowed in and eroded the ravine as the river rose and fell. The ravine's sides were steep – probably 60 degrees or more. The bottom of the ravine, about 50 feet wide near the river, was a soggy marsh for a half mile inland, and with all the recent rain it currently held about three feet of water near the river. Grant's troops formed along the north side of this ravine, as well as on a spur that jutted out 200 feet towards the river on the far left of the Union line, where two Federal batteries of 10 cannon aimed down the length of the ravine. And anchored right behind them were the two gunboats with their massive 8 inch guns.

Federal skirmishers carefully worked their way over to the south side of the ravine, so as to give early warning of an attack.

The Day's Last Attack

Several hundred yards to the south, Braxton Bragg gathered about 4,000 Confederate troops, mainly from Jackson's and Chalmer's brigades, and ordered them to attack this last line, promising, *"One more charge my men, and we shall capture them all!"* But the attack fizzled miserably – the exhausted Confederate troops wilted under the blistering artillery fire and fell back just as the sun set.

Bragg and his division com-

"My God, when is victory ever sufficiently complete?!

Modern photo looking west into Dill Branch Ravine. The Tennessee River is about 50 yards behind the camera.

mander, Jones Withers, looked about for more troops to add to their force in preparation for a larger assault. Just then a courier arrived from Beauregard, who was well to the rear near Shiloh Church. Beauregard's message ordered the attack halted and to pull the troops back, stating that "*Victory was sufficiently complete.*" Bragg muttered, "*My God, when is victory ever sufficiently complete?!*" He later claimed he was tempted to disregard the order, but other units were already withdrawing, and there wasn't time to reverse their movements and make another assault before nightfall.

At last blessed darkness arrived, shielding Grant's line from more attacks until daybreak. Later that night, resting against a tree near the Landing, Grant tried to catch some sleep but it soon began to rain and he decided to move to one of the nearby shacks. But the building was filled with the stench of blood and the moans of the wounded, and eventually Grant hobbled back to his tree – he was still on crutches due to a badly sprained leg. (Grant had a cabin on the nearby steamer, moored a few yards away. Why didn't he spend the night there? Probably because he didn't want it reported that he was sleeping comfortably in the boat's cabin while his men were in the rain.)

"Lick'em tomorrow, though."

Around midnight Sherman, his arm in a sling, went looking for Grant, assuming the next step was "*to put the river between us and the enemy and recuperate.*" But when he found Grant alone in the pouring rain, propped against his tree, his collar up and his hat covering his head from the downpour, Sherman later said he was "*moved by some wise and sudden instinct*" not to talk about retreat. Instead, he said, "*Well, Grant, we've had the devil's own day, haven't we?*" Grant replied, "*Yep. Lick'em tomorrow though.*"

Could the Confederates Have Won on that First Day?

During the afternoon, after Johnston was killed, Beauregard received faulty intelligence that Buell's army would not join Grant for several more days after all. So Beauregard believed that he had Grant's army at his mercy and could destroy it at leisure in the morning. The Confederate general therefore canceled the attack with probably about an hour of at least partial daylight remaining.

Beauregard's decision to halt the attack is yet another of the great what-ifs of the battle. What if he had continued attacking? Could he have broken Grant's line and destroyed his army before Union reinforcements arrived? Probably not. Grant's line, with 41 cannon, naval support, 18,000 Federal infantry well situated behind the steep Dill Creek Ravine, and their flanks protected by the river and the swamp, was far stronger than the Federal position on the Sunken Road, and it had taken the better part of the day for the Confederates to break that line.

Especially with Buell's fresh troops beginning to trickle in, boosting morale, it's extremely unlikely that the Confederates, exhausted and badly disorganized after a day's fighting, could break the Union line in the 30 minutes or less of remaining full-daylight.

But you'll never convince die-hard Confederate supporters of that!

Beauregard was so confident of victory on the evening of the first day that he sent a telegram to Jefferson Davis, informing him of Johnston's death and also announcing a "complete victory" of Confederate arms. His telegram went on to say that the enemy was thoroughly beaten and "the remnant of his army driving in utter disorder to the immediate vicinity of Pittsburgh and we remained undisputed master of his ... [camps]."

Checking the Confederate Advance on the Evening of the First Day.
Battles & Leaders, Vol 1, pg 475

Union gunboats, the Tyler and Lexington, bombard Confederate positions. Mariners Museum; Newport News; VA

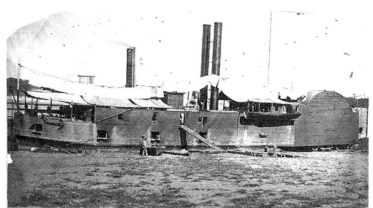

USS Tyler moored at a river bank on laundry day.

Modern photo of a naval gun used by the Tyler and Lexington. They were larger than even Grant's siege artillery.

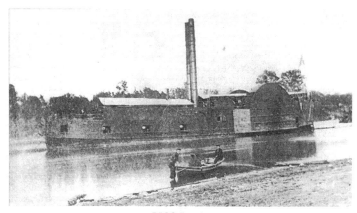

USS Lexington

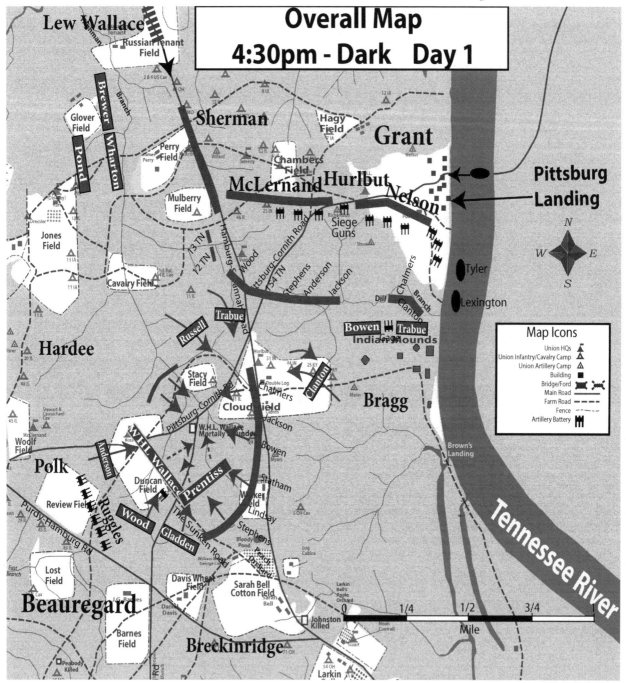

Overall Map 4:30pm - Dark Day 1

Google Map Links (scan with OC Reader to go to online maps)

Pittsburg Landing   Shiloh Church   The Crossroads   Jones Field

Chapter 20   Lew Wallace Finally Arrives

12 NOON – 7:15 PM

By noon that first day, as the fighting raged at Shiloh, with the Federal line teetering on the verge of collapse and being pushed back ever closer to the Landing, Grant kept looking north, anxiously awaiting Lew Wallace's arrival with his 3rd Division of 7,500 men (about 5,000 trigger-pullers). Wallace was deployed near Crump's Landing, just five or six miles north of Pittsburg Landing by the shortest route, which was the River Road. But, unknown to Grant, Wallace hadn't taken the shortest route, and he would spend the next 40 years of his life explaining why it took him almost eight hours to cover the six miles to Pittsburg Landing, at a time when Grant so desperately needed him.

**Maj. Gen. Lew Wallace
1827 - 1905**

The heart of the problem was that most of Wallace's division wasn't actually located at Crump's Landing. His division was initially posted there, but Grant suspected that Crump's Landing would be the most likely target for a Southern attack, and in the event of such an attack, Wallace expected that nearest assistance would come from Sherman's division to the south, up a fine road called the Shunpike. Sherman's division was the farthest inland (west) from Pittsburg Landing. So, to put himself within easy reach of Sherman, Wallace left only one of his brigades at Crump's Landing, and moved the other two a couple of miles inland – westward – near the small villages of Adamsville and Stoney Lonesome. This was done with Grant's knowledge and approval.

But on the morning of April 6th, the Confederates struck Grant's main army at Pittsburg Landing instead of Wallace's isolated division at Crump's Landing. Hearing the firing, Wallace alerted his troops and concentrated them near his center brigade at Stony Lonesome, 2 ½ miles inland from Crump's Landing. Wallace himself was still at Crump's Landing about 8:30am when Grant's boat steamed up from Savannah, heading to Pittsburg Landing. On the way, Grant briefly halted his vessel to confer with Wallace. The commander wasn't yet sure what was happening at Pittsburg Landing, but in a shouted conversation between boats, he ordered Wallace to have his division to be ready to march, and await orders.

Upon reaching Pittsburg Landing, Grant soon realized his army was fighting for its life, and he directed his adjutant general, Capt. John A. Rawlins, to order Wallace's 3rd Division to come quickly. Rawlins, a personal friend of Grant's, was sort of the general's PR man whose unofficial duty was to make sure Grant stayed sober. (Sherman, for one, was unimpressed with Rawlins as a staff officer.)

Rawlins in turn repeated the Grant's command to another staff officer, Capt. A. S. Baxter, who was assigned to relay the message to Wallace. Capt. Baxter requested the message in writing. Rawlins hastily scrawled a message and handed it to the captain. Baxter then boarded a steamboat back north to Crump's Landing, reaching Wallace at around 11:30am or slightly earlier. The written message was later lost. Exactly what the message said has always been a matter of heated dispute, creating a controversy that ultimately ended Lew Wallace's military career. Rawlins claimed the order he wrote directed Wallace to march on the road "nearest the river" – the River Road (aka the Savannah-Hamburg Road). Wallace swore that the message didn't specify a route. (Assuming it was so

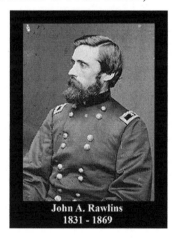

**John A. Rawlins
1831 - 1869**

As Grant and Rawlins were riding around during the day to visit the divisions on the firing line, they were accompanied by Capt. Douglas A. Putnam, a paymaster, who was serving as one of Grant's aides for the day. Riding with Rawlins behind the general as they approached the fighting, Putnam heard a steady patter on the surrounding leaves and asked how could it be raining under a clear sky.

"Those are bullets, Douglas," Rawlins informed him.

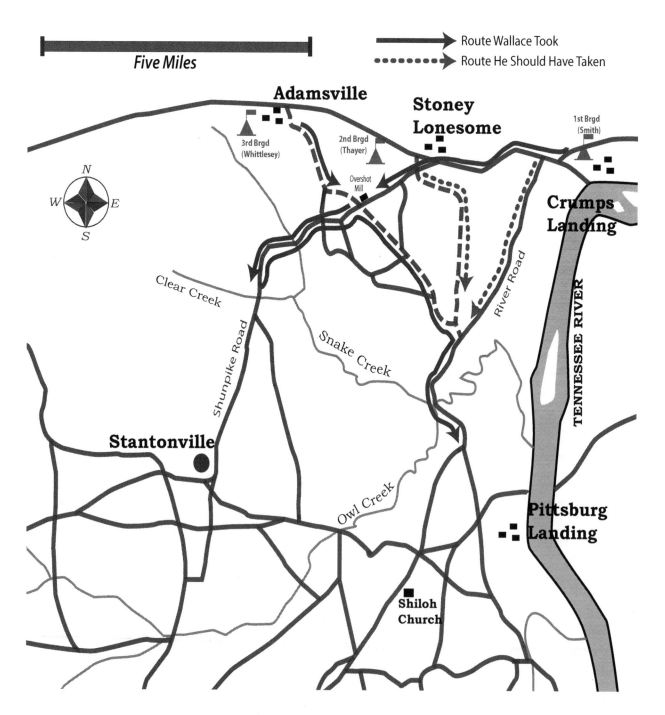

obvious to Grant and Rawlins that Wallace would use the River Road, it does seem odd that Rawlins would bother to specify the road in his hasty message).

Grant, back at Pittsburg Landing, had no idea Wallace would do anything other than haul his troops down to Pittsburg Landing as fast as possible using the shortest route – the River Road.

For whatever reason – whether deliberately disobeying orders as to which road to use or because he thought he was free to make his own choice – Wallace chose to march his division via the Shunpike, the better road and the one roughly in the center of his three brigades at Stoney Lonesome. His intent was to arrive at the northwest side of Sherman's camps, north of Shiloh Church, and hopefully strike the left flank of the Confederate army, winning the battle and perhaps the war.

Using the wrong road was one problem. But the other problem was that Wallace just never seemed to appreciate the urgency of the situation. When the courier, Capt. Baxter, arrived at 11:30am, Wallace inquired about the progress of the battle. Baxter responded that the Rebels were being repulsed. (It should be remembered that Grant, when he encountered Buell at Pittsburg Landing around mid-day, he informed Buell that "*all looks well.*") So, based on the courier's optimistic view, Wallace was under the impression that the battle was being won, and his main purpose was to march down the Shunpike and strike the enemy a devastating blow on his left flank.

Grant expected Wallace to be on the battlefield by noon, but it was noon before Wallace even got his troops on the march.

Around 2pm, another of Grant's messengers reached Wallace: Capt. William R. Rowley, who found Wallace's division resting leisurely on the Shunpike, as if they were on a Sunday stroll. Reaching Wallace and his staff at the head of the column, the captain demanded to know why the general didn't have his division on the River Road. Wallace responded that the Shunpike was the only way to reach Sherman's and McClernand's camps. Rowley quietly stepped aside with Wallace and whispered: "*My God! Don't you know Sherman has been driven back? Why, the whole army is within a half-mile of the river, and it's a question if we are not all going to be driven into it!*"

Wallace then asked if Grant's order was peremptory. "*Yes!*" declared Rowley, "*He wants you at Pittsburg Landing – and he wants you there like hell!*"

So now Wallace would have to counter-march. But rather than simply about-facing his division, he insisted on turning the brigades in order from the lead brigade, so as to keep his best brigade, Col. Morgan Smith's, at the head of the column. But doing so wasted even more precious time while Smith's unit marched back along the entire length of the column so as to remain in the lead of the division.

"Grant wants you at Pittsburg Landing, and he wants you there like hell!"

Now more of Grant's staff officers arrived, increasingly frantic. All failed to impress upon Wallace the urgency of the situation. Once turned around, Wallace's troops made a respectable 2.5 miles per hour, but he nearly drove Grant's staff officers to distraction with the frequency and length of the division's rest halts, and also at his reluctance to leave his artillery behind or otherwise sacrifice marching order for speed.

Capt. Rowley even considered placing the general under arrest. But he didn't, and in the end Wallace's division was useless in the first day's fighting.

Finally, after the Confederate assaults had ended for the day, at around 6:30pm and possibly as late as 7:15pm, Lew Wallace's division joined Grant's army to the right of Sherman, seven hours after Grant had expected him.

Grant never forgave Wallace and, with Halleck's approval, he cashiered the division commander soon after the battle. Wallace spent years appealing to every authority he could in hopes of reviving his stalled military career, arguing that he had acted properly at Shiloh. And after the war he would continue arguing for decades. But Grant remained unmoved, and maintained for the rest of his life, including in his memoirs written just before his death in the 1880s, that Wallace had failed him in Grant's hour of need.

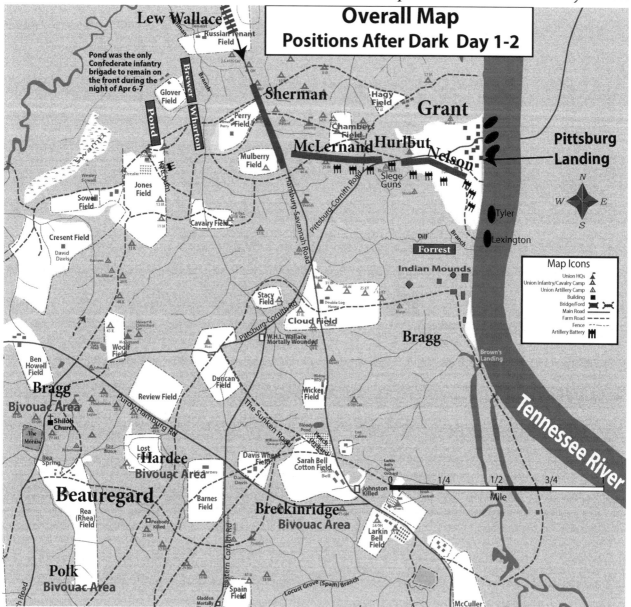

The Confederates fall back for the night, bivouacking in the abandoned Federal camps. Meanwhile, fresh Union troops disembark at Pittsburg Landing.

Google Map Links (scan with OC Reader to go to online maps)

Pittsburg Landing

Adamsville

Crump's Landing

Chapter 21 Day 2 - Buell Advances

DAY TWO OF THE BATTLE

5am - 10am   April 7

Throughout the night of April 6th - 7th, troops of Buell's Army of Ohio trickled in after being ferried from the east side of the Tennessee River, or steaming south ten miles from Savannah. In either case, when the reinforcements tramped down the steamers' gangplanks they entered the surreal world of Pittsburg Landing.

Milling around the Landing were thousands of beaten and frightened "stragglers," filled with horrifying tales about the Rebels. Wounded were everywhere, as was the stench of blood and cordite. In the darkness, nervous officers barked orders to form up the new arrivals and march them to the front-line, conveniently located just a 100 or so yards south of the Landing.

Along with the rest of the Union army, the new arrivals were in for a rough night. From about 10pm to 3am the sky unloaded sheets of rain, accompanied by massive peals of lighting and thunder. The rain was so heavy and the water so high that the troops couldn't lie down. They could only stand and stare out into the blackness toward their unseen foe; when the rain occasionally paused, they could hear pite-

Maj. Gen. Don Carlos Buell
1818 - 1898

ous cries of the wounded out there, somewhere. If anyone did manage to drift off to sleep he would be jolted awake about every 10 minutes by the blast from one of gunboat's massive 8 inch cannons. The USS Tyler and the Lexington dropped rounds intermittently throughout the night into suspected Rebel positions, just to hassle the enemy and hopefully kill a few.

Beauregard ordered his troops to fall back for the night into the abandoned Federal campsites. Though under the unpleasant harassing fire from the Union gunboats, most of the Confederates enjoyed their driest, best-fed night of the campaign, sleeping in tents and eating rations courtesy of the U.S. Government; though the Rebels did grumble that their accommodations leaked due to numerous bullet holes.

Buell had arrived a day ahead of his troops, spending a good part of the first day of the battle hunting for Grant. He had been on his way to meet Grant at his headquarters in Savannah but missed him when Grant heard the firing and immediately sailed down to Pittsburg Landing. The two finally connected around 1pm that day at the Landing.

The two generals – the scruffy Grant, with his reputation as a drunk, and the stern, cold Buell – were not on good terms. And it was not lost on either of them that Buell's army was in considerably better shape than Grant's. Buell was frankly appalled by what he saw – Grant hobbling around on crutches, with half his army a mob of deserters sitting in plain view, *right there in front of him,* on the Landing! At one point Sherman worried that Buell might even refuse to land his army.

Though Grant was technically senior by several weeks, under the circumstances he apparently couldn't summon the nerve to give Buell orders, and their attack the next day was only loosely discussed and coordinated, resulting in nothing more than a general understanding that Buell's army would attack on the left and Grant would attack on the right.

In his memoirs Buell would write about Grant and his army's situation:
"An army comprising 70 regiments of infantry, 20 batteries of artillery, and a sufficiency of cavalry, lay for two weeks and more in isolated camps, with a river at its rear and a hostile army claimed to be superior in numbers 20 miles distant in its front, while the commander made his headquarters and passed his nights 9 miles away on the opposite side of the river. It had no line or order of battle, no defensive works of any sort, no outposts, properly speaking, to give warning, or check the advance of an enemy, and no recognized head during the absence of the regular commander."

Buell's Troops Debarking at Pittsburg Landing Sunday Night. Battles and Leaders Vol1; pg518

Restarting the War

Around 5am, an hour before daylight, Bull Nelson's division – Col. Jacob Ammen's, Col. Sanders Bruce's and Col. William Hazen's brigades – restarted the war when they quietly advanced southwest toward the Dill Branch Ravine. They tripped over many a corpse in the spooky blackness. "*The ground was strewn with dead bodies, some wounded, some with their legs shot off, some almost tore to pieces, groaning in the greatest agony*," according to a Union private. The nervous Federals advanced toward the unseen foe who had done all this terrible damage, lurking out there somewhere in the darkness, waiting to give the new arrivals the same reception. Col. Ammen ("Old Jakey"), riding in front of his brigade, chanted: "*Now, boys, keep cool. Give'em the best you got.*"

> **Now, boys, keep cool. Give'em the best you got."**

With constant halts to redress ranks in the dense timber, it took Nelson's wary men until 8am just to reach Cloud Field. By that time, Brig. Gen. Thomas Crittenden's division of Buell's army had joined up on Nelson's right. And to the right of Crittenden was Brig. Gen. Alexander McCook's division, also from Buell's army.

> **"No painter ever did justice to a battlefield such as this, I am sure."**

As the lines advanced, Lt. Ambrose Bierce notice that every single tree still standing was covered in bullet holes "*from the root to a height of ten to twenty feet and one could not have laid a hand [on the trunk] without covering several punctures.*"

Musician John Cockrell noted that one the most piteous sights, scattered all over the field, "*were the poor wounded horses, their heads drooping, their eyes glassy and gummy, waiting for the slow coming of death. No painter ever did justice to a battlefield such as this, I am sure.*"

Hazen's brigade first struck opposition about halfway across Cloud Field, near Hurlbut's old camp headquarters. Confederate skirmishers fired off some quick shots and raced back toward their lines. Hazen's men kept advancing for another thirty minutes, almost to Wicker Field, when they hit solid resistance. Confederate infantry and artillery opened on them. This being their first time under artillery fire, the men on Nelson's right flank wavered.

Friendly cannon are great confidence-boosters for nervous infantry, but Nelson's artillery was still back in Savannah, so Buell loaned him Capt. John Mendenhall's Battery from Crittenden's division. Soon Mendenhall's teams rolled up and unlimbered on the west side of the Savannah-Hamburg Road. Then Capt. William R. Terrill's battery of smooth-bore Napoleons raced up and deployed across from Mendenhall on the east side of the road. Both batteries came under accurate fire from a Confederate battery hidden somewhere near W. Manse George's cabin to the southwest. The Federals couldn't see the battery, only the smoke puffs rising above the trees after each discharge. Then another Confederate battery to the west began lobbing shells into them, forcing both Mendenhall and Terrell to re-face their guns so as to return fire. Finally, after a spirited half-hour fight, which included Federal infantry advancing and sniping at the Rebel guns, the Confederate batteries withdrew.

Nelson's division now swept past Bloody Pond. Emerging from the timber, Bruce's brigade fronted the Peach Orchard, while Ammen's brigade deployed east of the Savannah-Hamburg Road, along the deep ravine that had proven such a handy barricade for McArthur's brigade the day before. Hazen's brigade, on Bruce's right, reached the Sunken Road. All of these areas – scenes of bitter fighting the day before – would have been blanketed with dead and wounded. And now the Federals saw the main Confederate line, arrayed from the Larkin Bell Field in the east to the Eastern Corinth Road in the west.

Nelson ordered a halt to assess the situation.

Aftermath

Even from their rocking chairs in the 1880s, Grant and Buell were still arguing about the effect of Buell's arrival on the Shiloh battle. Buell swore that the arrival of his army late that afternoon of the first day saved Grant's army from disaster. Grant disagreed, pointing out that only a couple of Buell's regiments were deployed on the battleline by nightfall, though he did concede that the arrival of even a few of Buell's troops was "probably" a morale-booster for his men.

Google Map Links (scan with OC Reader to go to online maps)

Bloody Pond

Cloud Field

Savannah

Larkin Bell Field

Pittsburg Landing

W. George Manse cabin

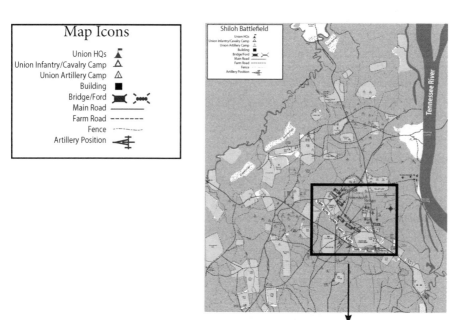

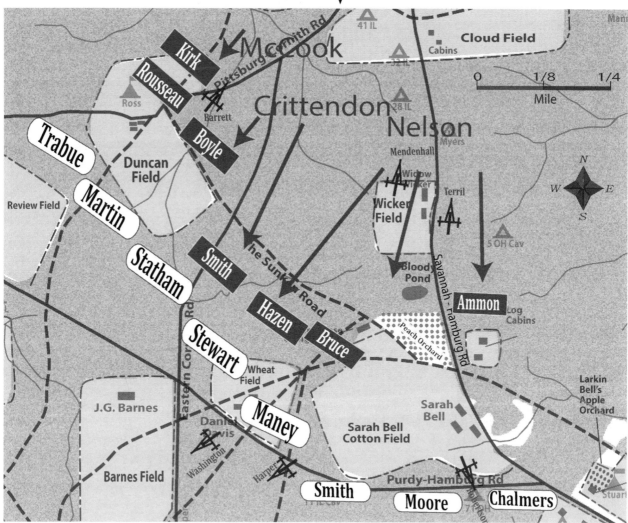

Buell's army counterattacks on the morning of the second day.

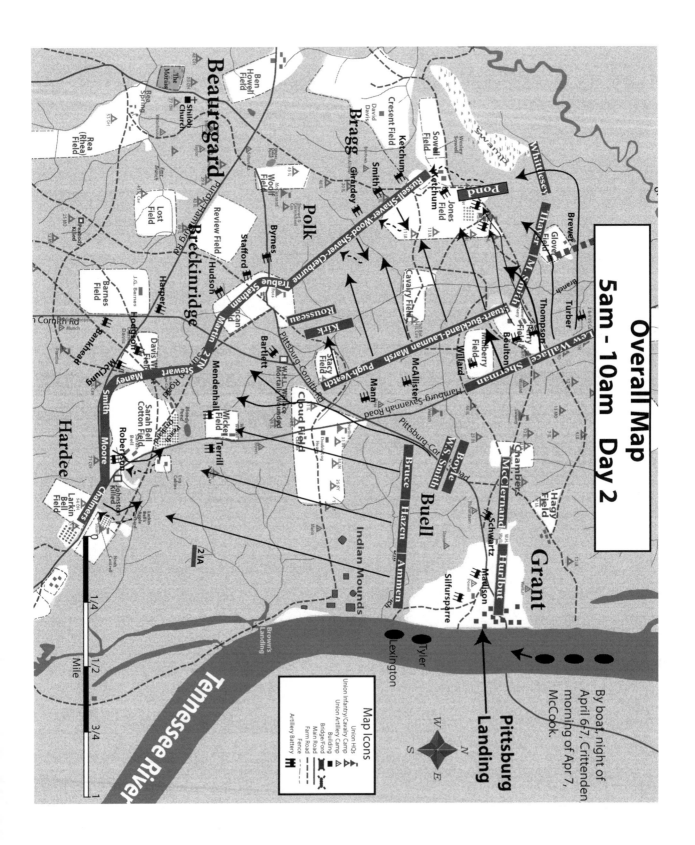

Chapter 22   Confederate Counterattack

Bloody Fighting Across Davis Wheatfield

10am to 11am, April 7

With the surrender of thousands of Federals late in the afternoon of the first day's fighting – Sunday, the 6th – most Southerners assumed the battle was all but over. Also, a message reached Beauregard the previous evening reporting that Buell's Army had diverted to some other destination, and so Grant's Army was ripe for plucking the next morning, even after including the arrival of Grant's long-lost 3rd Division commanded by Lew Wallace. (Beauregard's scouts kept him well appraised of Wallace's progress, or lack of same, to the battlefield).

So the Confederates got a nasty surprise around mid-morning of the second day when they realized Grant had been heavily reinforced.

But during the night, in the pouring rain, the fierce Col. Nathan Bedford Forrest ordered some of his men to slip on dead Yankees' overcoats, and sent them sliding into the cold, black waters of the Dill Ravine swamp, slithering in the rain through the Union lines to spy on Pittsburg Landing. In what must have been a memorable trip, the spies made it, there and back, and reported seeing Yankee soldiers by the thousands unloading from transports.

Forrest decided the only way to win the battle was with an immediate night attack. He tramped around the muddy battlefield in the rainy blackness, trying to find Beauregard. But the Confederate army was so disorganized that no one knew where Beauregard was. It turned out that Beauregard and Bragg were sharing Sherman's old tent near Shiloh Church, not that there was the slightest possibility that Beauregard could have ordered an attack at that hour.

Beauregard and his generals spent the early hours of April 7 organizing a coherent battle-line. On the eastern side of the battlefield, five badly mauled infantry brigades and four artillery batteries manned a line commanded by Hardee and Breckinridge. The two divided their command, with Hardee controlling Confederate forces from the southwest end of Sarah Bell's Old Cotton Field to the river, and Breckinridge taking responsibility from the western edge of the cotton field to the Eastern Cornith Road.

Around 9am, Beauregard gave Hardee the order *"to charge the enemy in conjunction with General Breckinridge."* In fact the two generals' assaults were uncoordinated since they had no time to consult prior to the attacks.

Hardee's men launched their assault from the Davis Wheatfield, angling toward the Bloody Pond, striking Hazen's and Bruce's brigades, and threatening to overrun Mendenhall's battery in the process. The sweating Federal gunners blasted the onrushing Rebels with case shot (air-bursts) and canister. Desperate to hold his line, Hazen personally led the 6th Kentucky in a bayonet charge. Finally, the combination of canister and infantry broke the Confederate attack. *"They run!"* cried some of Bruce's men, and the cheer echoed up and down the Union line.

The Confederates fell back and formed a new battle line along the Purdy-Hamburg

Col. William B. Hazen
1830 - 1887

Road, centered approximately at the Davis Wheatfield. Some of the fiercest fighting of the second day occurred around this field and the area to the immediate east. By 10:30am, having fought off Hardee's spoiler attack, Nelson's division advanced across Sarah Bell's Cotton Field, scene of so much carnage the day before. At the south end of the field, the Federals came under a storm of fire from Confederate infantry deployed just south of Purdy-Hamburg Road, as well as enfilading fire from Davis Wheatfield to the west where the Washington

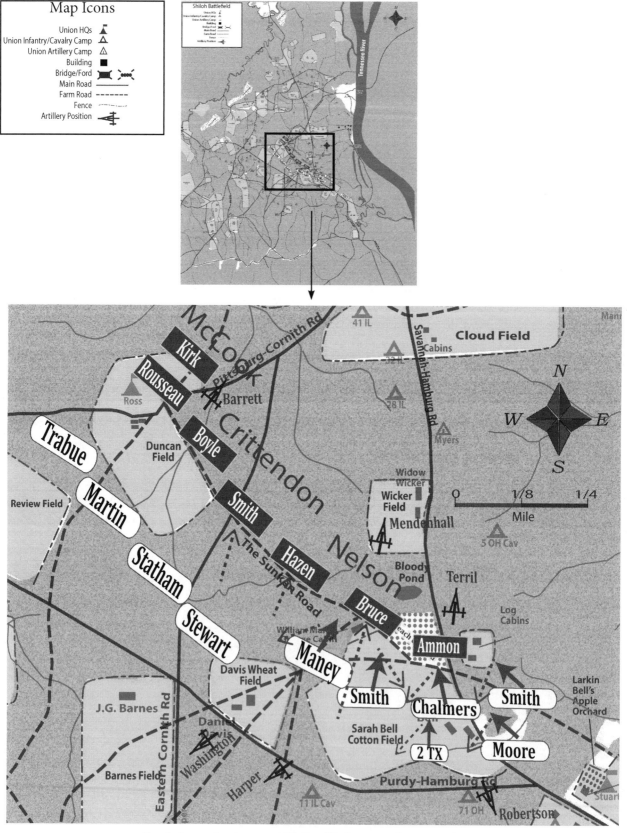

Confederates counter-attack Buell's force on the second day.

(New Orleans) Artillery and McClung's Tennessee battery were posted. Ammen's and Bruce's brigades were badly shot up.

Furious Attacks and Counterattacks, Seemingly Without End

Seeing the Yankees wavering, Hardee, nicked in his arm and his uniform shredded by several bullets, decided to counterattack using Col. John Moore's brigade. But the attack got only as far as the W. Manse George cabin before Hazen's brigade drove the Southerners back once again. Now Hazen, along with Col. William Sooy Smith's 11th Brigade of Crittenden's neighboring division, counterattacked the counterattackers, leading yet another charge across Sarah Bell's field. This time the Federals drove the Confederate infantry back from the Purdy-Hamburg Road and surged toward the Washington Artillery battery.

The New Orleans gunners pumped some 60 rounds of canister into the onrushing Yankees, slowing but not checking them. The gunners decided it was time to leave. According to Louisiana cannoneer, John Pugh, the decision was a bit late: "*The balls [bullets] were falling around us like hail,*

Col. John C. Moore
1824 - 1910

and before we could get ready three horses at my piece and the same at two others were killed, our sergeant was killed, and Lieut. Slocomb wounded, and we had to run, leaving these three pieces on the field."

An artillery officer galloped up to the 19th Louisiana and the Crescent Regiment, both on reserve south of the road. "*For God's sake, boys, hurry up or our battery is gone!*" he cried. The two regiments charged the Yankees at the abandoned battery. In fierce hand-to-hand fighting, 6th Kentucky (Union) Col. W. C. Whita-

ker used his sword to cleave the skull of at least one young Rebel who tried to yank him off his horse. In the confusion and smoke, Union Sooy Smith's men unleashed a volley into Hazen's Union brigade, creating even more chaos. The Federals finally gave up and fell back, but not before spiking the three guns – jamming their fuse ports with mud and rendering them temporarily useless.

But the issue was far from settled. The Federals regrouped, counterattacked and pushed the Louisianans back well past the Purdy-Hamburg Road. Then the Confederate 1st Missouri, hidden beneath the brow of a hill, rose up and blasted the Federals, sending *them* reeling. With the Yankees now on the run, the Crescent Regiment charged again, driving the blue soldiers back through the Davis Wheat Field and into the underbrush; once there, the Federals about-faced

Brig. Gen. William Sooy Smith
1830 - 1916

and ambushed the Confederates, now forcing *them* to withdraw. But Hazen's brigade was shattered in the crazy, see-saw battle, having suffered more than half the loss of Nelson's entire division during the battle.

The Sarah Bell Cotton Field

While the fighting raged in the Davis Wheat Field, just to the east, Union Col. Bruce's Kentucky brigade fought to regain control of the Sarah Bell Field. Again it was a bloody, see-saw battle. The Union 13th Kentucky lost a third of its men on this same field where so much blood had been spilled the day before. The Union 2nd Kentucky regained the woods between the Sarah Bell Field and the Davis Wheatfield, overrunning one gun in the process - probably from Capt. Hugh McClung's Tennessee Battery. Bruce eventually retired his brigade when Hazen's and Smith's brigades to the west fell back.

For the moment, the increasingly frazzled Confederates had barely managed to check Bull Nelson's tough, fresh division.

"We Don't Give a Damn!"

Just prior to Hardee's counterattack around 11:30am, Confederate Moore's troops were warned that Col. John Martin's brigade (Breckinridge's Corps) was somewhere to their front and under no circumstances should they fire on it. The 2nd Texas, the left wing of Moore's brigade, had the hard part – advancing out of the underbrush and into the open of Sarah Bell field, west of the Savannah-Hamburg Road. According to one of the Texans, "*The silence was oppressive. I do not remember that on our way across the open space, a command was given or a word spoken.*"

> "*The silence was oppressive. I do not remember that on our way across the open space, a command was given or a word spoken.*"

Some 200 yards ahead, on the northern edge of the field, a large unit of troops appeared. The Texans were cautioned not to fire – that must be Martin's brigade. The Texans kept advancing. Suddenly, the mysterious unit unleashed a terrific volley, decimating the Texan ranks. "*Our line seemed actually to wither and curl up,*" according to one Texan. When one Confederate raised his rifle to fire back, an officer threatened to blow his head off, still insisting those were friendlies in front.

The Texans had enough of *this*! They fled the field, and no amount of threats or pleas could coax them back in ranks. Hardee sent word that he would call them "*a pack of cowards*"; the Texans sent his courier back with their reply: "*We don't give a damn if you do!*"

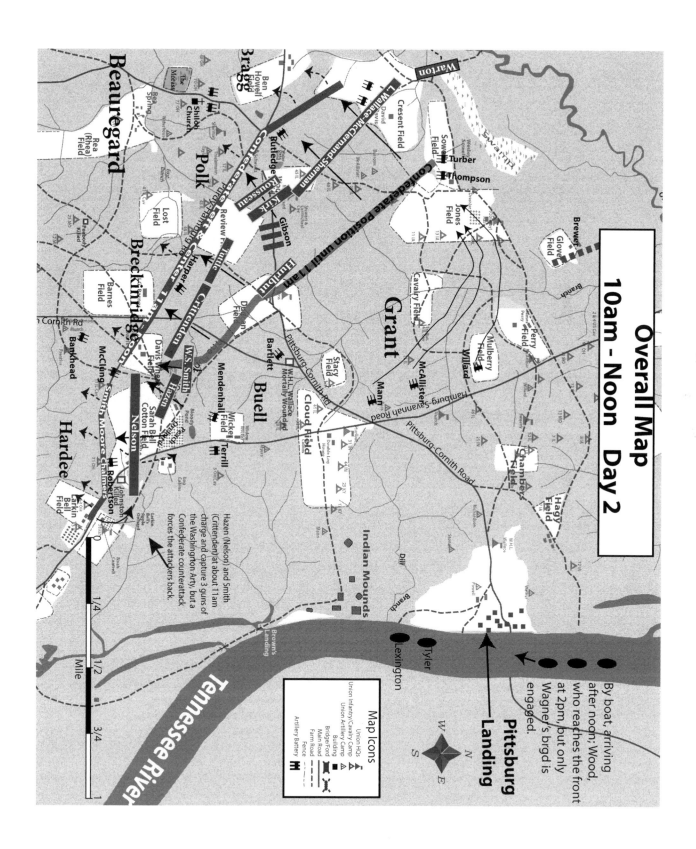

Overall Map
10am - Noon Day 2

By boat, arriving after noon; Wood, who reaches the front at 2pm, but only Wagner's brgd is engaged.

Hazen (Nelson) and Smith (Crittenden) at about 11am charge and capture 3 guns of the Washington Arty, but a Confederate counterattack forces the attackers back.

Map Icons

Union HQs
Union Infantry/Cavalry Camp
Union Artillery Camp
Building
Bridge/Ford
Main Road
Farm Road
Fence
Artillery Battery

Google Map Links (scan with OC Reader to go to online maps)

Shiloh Church

Sarah Bell's Cotton Field

Bloody Pond

Davis WheatField

Pittsburg Landing

W. Manse George cabin

Chapter 23   Grant Attacks

DAY TWO OF THE BATTLE

Tilghman Branch
6:30am – 9am, April 7

Early on the morning of April 7th, Grant ordered Lew Wallace to advance to the west, crossing the valley of Tilghman Branch. Waiting on the high bluff on the opposite side of the branch was Confederate Capt. William Ketchum's Alabama Battery, supported by Col. Preston Pond's brigade, newly deployed into line along the top of the bluffs. Pond's unit, by accident, was the most advanced Confederate infantry that morning; somehow he hadn't gotten the word to pull back to the Yankee tents the previous evening.

Wallace, probably wisely, elected not to immediately send his infantry across Tilghman Branch and up its 50-60 feet ravine. First, he wanted to soften up the Rebel position, particularly its artillery. He called up Lt. Charles Thurber's and Capt. N. S. Thompson's batteries for the job. The two Federal gun crews engaged in a 30 minute duel with Ketchum's gunners before one of the Federals' shots dismounted one of Ketchum's guns, causing Pond to withdraw both the battery and his infantry back to the south end of Jones Field.

So now Wallace's troops crossed the ravine of Tilghman Branch with no losses and scaled the bluffs on the far side. Wallace had managed his advance over the ravine well, except for one thing – it was slow; a consistent problem with him.

Jones Field
9am – 12 noon

Having seized the bluffs on the west side of Tilghman Branch, Wallace faced virtually no opposition, with his men on the left flank of the Confederate army, exactly where he had hoped to be on the previous day. Using the swamps along the Owl Creek bottoms to shield his own right flank, he initially decided to wheel his division left, from the west to the southwest, and attack the exposed Confederate flank. The general had overwhelming numbers in this sector, and a perfect opportunity to destroy the Confederate army. Had he attacked immediately, Lew Wallace would today probably be famous as the Union hero of Shiloh.

But again he halted his advance; this time because Sherman's division hadn't yet caught up to support Wallace's left flank. And he continued to remain stationary in the face of even more temptation – Confederate Gen. Ruggles unwisely ordered Pond's brigade to another part of the field, leaving only scattered Confederate units to resist any Federal advance.

Detecting Pond's departure, Thurber's Federal artillery shelled the marching column. This in turn drew counter fire from a Confederate battery at the south end of the field, creating *"a fine artillery duel,"* according to Wallace. Taking advantage of the uneven terrain, Wallace ordered his men into the woods and the lower ground, sheltering his troops from the barrage. Capt. Emmons, for one,

Modern photo of Tilghman Branch, looking north.

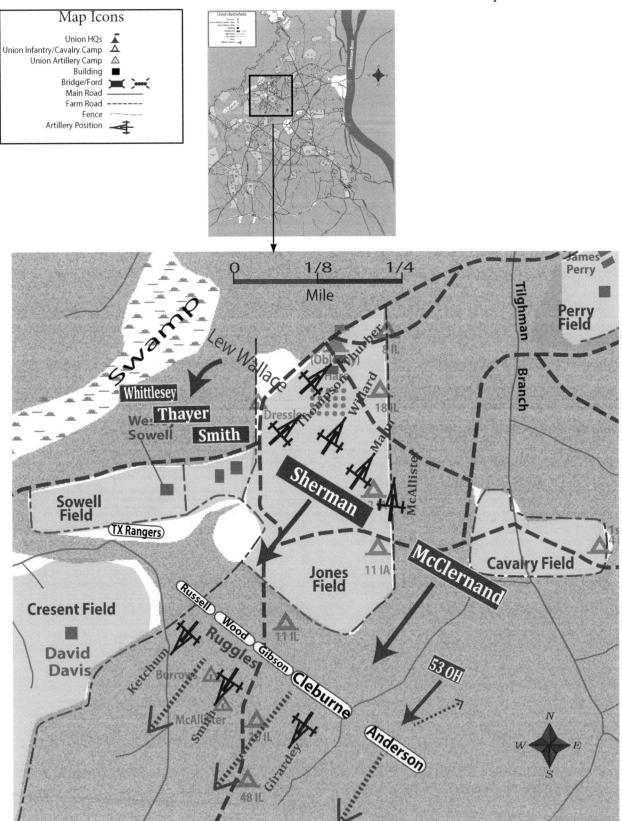

Map Icons

Union HQs	
Union Infantry/Cavalry Camp	△
Union Artillery Camp	△
Building	■
Bridge/Ford	
Main Road	
Farm Road	- - -
Fence	
Artillery Position	

Swamp

Lew Wallace

Whittlesey

Thayer

Smith

West Sowell

Dressler

Sherman

Sowell Field

TX Rangers

Jones Field

11 IA

McClernand

Cresent Field

David Davis

Russell

Wood

Ruggles

Gibson

Cleburne

Ketchum

Burrow

McAllister

Smith

Girardey

48 IL

11 IL

Anderson

53 OH

Cavalry Field

McAllister

Mahn

Willard

Thompson

(Objective)

Hare

8 IL

18 IL

James Perry

Perry Field

Tilghman Branch

N
W E
S

0   1/8   1/4
Mile

Grant's men retake the ground lost the previous day, constantly pushing the Confederates back step by step.

appreciated it, writing of "*the skill of our commander in taking advantage of the hills and causing us to lie down, shells and cannonballs flying close overheads.*"

Then Louisiana and Arkansas infantry from Gibson's brigade, and even Confederate cavalry, got the order to attack Thurber's battery. As Gibson's men prepared to charge, a soldier in the 4th Louisiana discovered a fife on the ground. Having been a fifer in the Regular Army during the Mexican War, the soldier picked up the instrument and began playing "Dixie." Both sides listened as the shrill notes drifted over the still battlefield. Then Beauregard rode down the line shouting, "*The day is ours! One more charge and we have the victory!*" With a storm of cheers, the weary Southern farm boys surged forward, as they had countless times in the last two days.

They succeeded in getting in among the guns in hand to hand fighting, and for some moments the blue cannoners defended their guns by swinging hammers, axes, and ram rods, while the gray infantry surged in with gun butts and bayonets. Finally Union infantry from Morgan Smith's brigade arrived and drove off the attackers, rescuing the cannon.

Sherman's division now lined up on Wallace's left. Sherman's men may have been recruits yesterday, but they were veterans today – at least those who survived Sunday and remained in ranks, and today they formed a splendid, though short and ragged, line of battle.

Finally convinced that his left flank was safe, Wallace renewed his advance, continuing to wheel his three brigades left in echelon with Smith leading on the left, Thayer in the middle, and Whittlesey bringing up the rear on the right. Smith's and Thayer's brigades, both out in the open field at the same time, apparently made quite an impressive sight with their neat formation and fluttering flags; at least they impressed the Confederates on the other side of Jones Field, who quickly withdrew.

Meanwhile, just to the east, Sherman's and McClernand's decimated divisions also advanced across Jones Field, where they were soon checked in the timber south of the field by three equally decimated Confederate brigades under Brig. Gen. Ruggles. The Federals halted and reformed their line before continuing their advance around 10:30am. The troops were freshly inspired after just learning of the arrival of Buell's army.

Col. Morgan L. Smith
1822 - 1874

Col. John M. Thayer
1820 - 1906

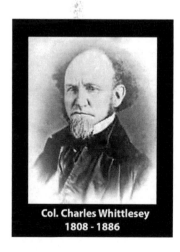

Col. Charles Whittlesey
1808 - 1886

Wallace's brigade commanders - Smith, Thayer and Whittlesey

Making a fighting withdrawal, Ruggles' exhausted men soon fell back toward Woolf Field.

Increasingly desperate to stop the Union tide, Bragg ordered what remained of Cleburne's brigade, less than 800 men, to counterattack. Cleburne protested that his left flank would be completely in the air. The courier returned with Bragg's command to proceed with the charge. Clerburne did, but his attack was soon broken.

Now Anderson's brigade surged forward to try to blunt the Federal drive. The first Yankee regiment they encountered was the 53rd Ohio, formerly commanded by Col. Jesse Appler, who had fled the field on the morning of the first day. Though the 53rd was one of Sherman's regiments, today it was attached to McClernand. When Anderson's men opened fire, the Buckeyes immediately raced for the rear – running had now become a habit. McClernand, disgusted at their "*disgraceful and cowardly*" action, ordered the regiment from the field, which was fine with the 53rd Ohio.

With his remaining two brigades McClernand quickly broke Anderson's attack and pressed the Federal advance toward the Crossroads.

In Hindsight

Wallace commanded a fresh and well rested division, his men had full ammo pouches and they outnumbered Confederate Pond's brigade five to one. Grant expected Wallace to strike like a tiger. But Wallace advanced timidly both at Tilghman Branch and at later at Jones Field. This didn't endear him to Grant, who already was extremely annoyed with Wallace's tardy arrival on the field the evening before.

Wallace's concern about his men's welfare did pay off with a low casualty rate. Of the 7,337 men in his division, there were only 491 casualties (6.7% - very low by Civil War standards). But a more aggressive advance earlier in the day might have won the battle.

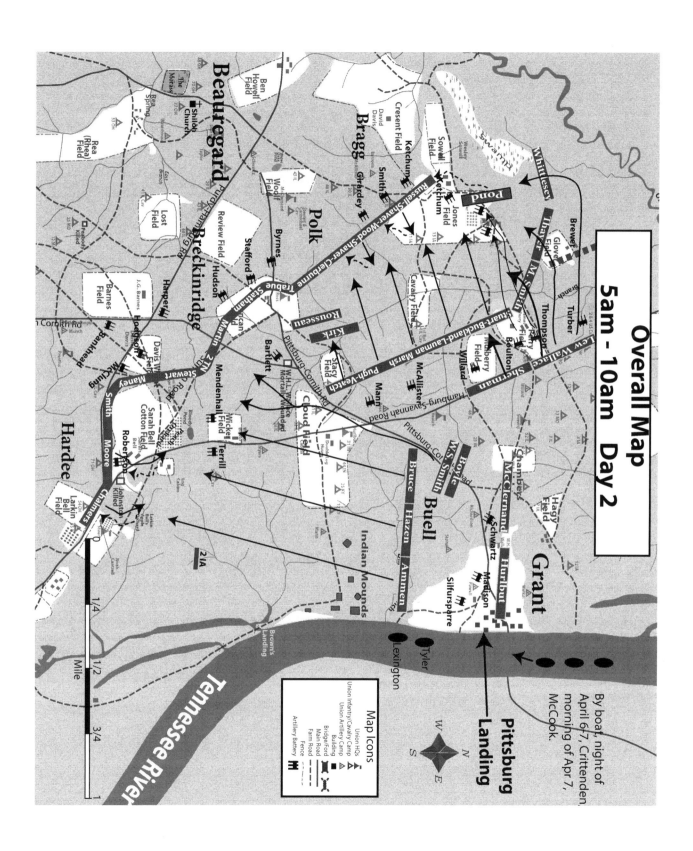

Overall Map
5am - 10am Day 2

Beauregard

Bragg

Polk

Breckinridge

Hardee

Shiloh Church

Rea (Rhea) Field

Lost Field

Barnes Field

Ben Howell Field

Cresent Field

David Davis

Ketchum

Sowell Field

Smith

Gibson

Woolf Field

Stafford

Byrnes

Review Field

Harper

Hodgson

McClung

Maney

Stewart

Martin

Robertson

Sarah Bell Cotton Field

Larkin Bell Field

Chalmers

Smith & Moore

Bankhead

Davis Wheat Field

Trabue Statham

Cleburne

Russell-Shaver-Wood-Shaver-

Stuart-Buckland-Lauman Marsh

Kirk

Rousseau

Cavalry Field

Jones Field

Ketchum

Glover Field

Brewer

Turner

Thompson

Whittlesey

W.H.L. Wallace Mortally Wounded

Stacy Field

Bartlett

Mendenhall

Wicker Field

Terrill

Cloud Field

Mann

Pugh-Veatch

McAllister

Boulton

Mulberry Field

Willard

McClernand

Chambers

Hagy Field

Lew Wallace

Sherman

W.S. Smith

Boyd

Bruce

Hazen

Ammen

Indian Mounds

Buell

Grant

Schwartz

Hurlbut

Madison

Silfursparre

Johnston Killed

Pittsburg Landing

Lexington

Tyler

By boat, night of April 6-7, Crittenden, morning of Apr 7, McCook.

Tennessee River

Brown's Landing

0   1/4   1/2   3/4   1
Mile

Map Icons
- Union HQs
- Union Infantry/Cavalry Camp
- Union Artillery Camp
- Building
- Main Road
- Farm Road
- Bridge/Ford
- Fence
- Artillery Battery

Google Map Links (scan with OC Reader to go to online maps)

Jones Field   Woolf Field   The Crossroads

Chapter 24   Sowell Field

DAY TWO OF THE BATTLE

9am - 10am, April 7

By 9am, Pond's Confederate infantry had been pushed back toward the Purdy-Hamburg Road, leaving Ketchum's battery and the Texas Ranger cavalry to conduct a rear-guard action.

By now the Confederate army was flailing wildly like an exhausted boxer, determined to remain on its feet and still swinging, but hopelessly overmatched,

Wallace's fresh Union division finished clearing out the southern edge of Jones Field, and then continued its left wheel into another field to the west, Sowell Field, until the battleline faced south. Thayer's brigade had ended up on the far right flank of the Union line since Whittlesey's men had not been able to keep up in the wheel due to the rough terrain on the outside end of the line.

Still engaging retreating Confederate infantry to his front, Thayer noticed a band of Rebel cavalry attempting to pass his right flank. This was Col. John A. Wharton's Texas Ranger Regiment, ordered by Beauregard to ride around the Yankee flank and strike the Union line in the rear in one of the few cavalry actions of the battle. To avoid being flanked, Thayer ordered his right flank regiment, the 23rd Indiana, to shift its battle line 100 yards farther to the right, directly blocking the path of the Texas horseman. The Texans, riding in single file due to the rugged terrain, were now themselves flanked because the Federals could fire straight down their line.

Wharton and his troopers in the lead opened fire with their fast-shooting carbines, hoping the rest of the troopers behind them would have time to catch up and spread out in a battle line before they were shot to pieces. But it was no use. Wharton went down when his horse was shot from under him, and many of his troops were toppled from their saddles. Desperate, Wharton pulled his men back and ordered them to dismount, hoping to form a proper skirmish line on foot. But in a cavalry vs. infantry slugging match, the Texans were getting the worst of the exchange. Mercifully, orders came from Beauregard to fall back and cover the retirement of other Confederate forces on the left.

As Wharton later described it, *"I was sacrificing the lives of my men, fighting 30 men against at least a regiment, [which had] the advantage of position, and with no prospect but that the men would all be killed as they came into view, as they could only advance in single file."*

After a brief pause to again regroup and allow Whittlesey's brigade to catch up, Wallace's division pressed onward. At around this same time, Confederate Brig. Gen. Ruggles directed Gibson's brigade to attack toward Jones Field, as discussed in the previous chapter.

Col. John A. Wharton (w)
1828 - 1865

Wharton, a former Texas attorney, would survive the war only to be shot dead during a quarrel in a Houston hotel in April 1865. The shooter was Col. George W. Baylor, an aide to Albert Sidney Johnston.

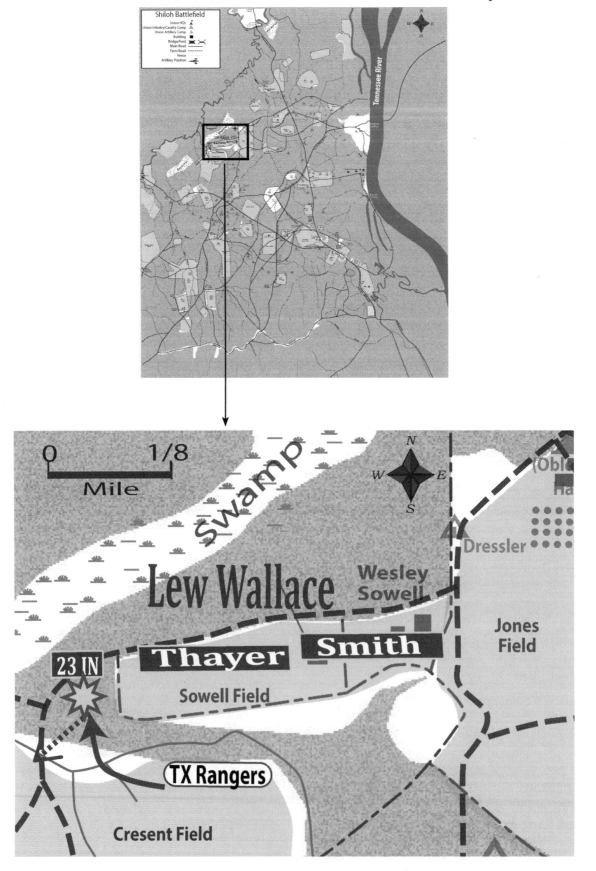

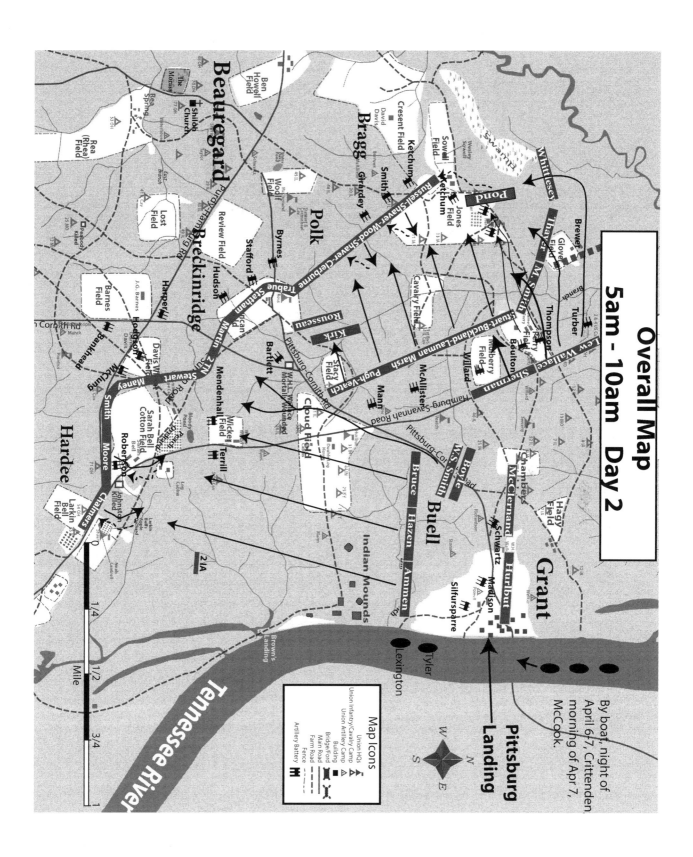

**Overall Map
5am - 10am Day 2**

By boat, night of
April 6-7, Crittenden,
morning of Apr 7,
McCook.

Pittsburg
Landing

Tennessee River

Map Icons

Union HQs
Union Infantry/Cavalry Camp
Union Artillery Camp
Building
Bridge/Ford
Main Road
Farm Road
Fence
Artillery Battery

0   1/4   1/2   3/4   1
Mile

Beauregard

Bragg

Polk

Breckinridge

Hardee

Smith

Moore

Cloud Field

Buell

M.L. Smith

M.S. Smith

McClernand

Grant

Hurlbut

Sherman

Lew Wallace

Whittlesey

Pittsburg Landing

Google Map Links (scan with OC Reader to go to online maps)

Jones Field

Sowell Field

Chapter 25 Final Attacks & Withdrawal

DAY TWO OF THE BATTLE

12pm - 2pm, April 7

While Grant's Army of Tennessee in Jones and Sowell fields battled its way closer to the Crossroads, with McClernand and Sherman approaching from the north and Lew Wallace from the northwest, elements of Buell's Army of the Ohio slugged its way southwestward from Pittsburg Landing, linking up with Grant's line.

The Confederate left was being overwhelmed, with Bragg desperately trying to stitch together a defense line he hoped would halt the Federal advance at least temporarily. Ironically, help came from Lew Wallace. Having repulsed the minor cavalry attack by the Texas Rangers, and finally advancing after Sherman's arrival on his left flank, Wallace now grew concerned that if he pursued the enemy farther in the current direction (southeast) his men would become entangled with Sherman's neighboring division. So he again halted his division and began the time-consuming process of wheeling his line back to the right in order to scoot some distance west before turning south and continuing the attack.

Bragg was the main beneficiary of this maneuver since it gave him time to reform his lines. That done, he put up a stiff fight not only against Grant's columns, but also against Buell's troops advancing from the northeast.

But the exhausted Confederates were coming to believe that damn Yankees just sprouted out of the ground like mushrooms.

Responding to an urgent order from Bragg, Maj. Gen. Cheatham rushed five regiments past Shiloh Church, formed a line of battle, and advanced to the Crossroads, where they were joined by Wood's brigade, now down to less than 650 men. At Bragg's order, the Confederates stepped off their counterattack. Woods, at the head of his men, plunged straight across the waste-deep water of Water Oaks Pond – the same pond Confederates fought their way across the day before. Cheatham

meanwhile rode back and forth in front of his line, waving a battle flag and encouraging his men. In some of the heaviest fighting of the second day, the attack then continued on across Woolf field, pushing Sherman's and McClernand's division back 300 yards.

Though Bragg's counterattack had driven Sherman's and McClernand's divisions back, it also exposed the Confederate's left flank to Wallace, who was now once again in a position to destroy the Confederate army. Instead, he went over to the defensive and even momentarily considered retreating. The Confederates attacked him but couldn't drive him back – particularly due to his right flank regiment, the 11th Indiana, which fought fiercely to hold its position.

Now more fresh Federal troops joined the battle; McCook's division of Buell's Army of Ohio, with Brig. Gen. Lovell Rousseau's brigade in the lead, marched up Cornith Road and struck the right flank of Bragg's line

"[It was] the severest musketry I have ever heard."

in Woolf Field. Once again fierce fighting erupted, with the two sides surging back and forth across the ground with charge and counter-charge. Sherman declared that the firing was *"the severest musketry fire I've ever heard."*

To support the Confederate line, Capt. Arthur Rutledge's Tennessee Battery raced up and dropped trails just east of the Crossroads, firing into the Yankee positions for a half hour.

At one point a desperate Beauregard galloped up to the 18th Louisiana and Orleans Guards Battalion (now acting as one unit) and seized the colors of the latter. The flagstaff holding the banner was a hollowed relic of Fort Sumter, and had been sent by Beauregard to New Orleans earlier in the war. He now personally led the Louisianans to the left of Bragg's line, shouting *"Charge them, charge them my braves!"* A private pleaded with the general not to expose himself to the enemy's fire. Beauregard's blood was up and he snapped: *"Never mind my*

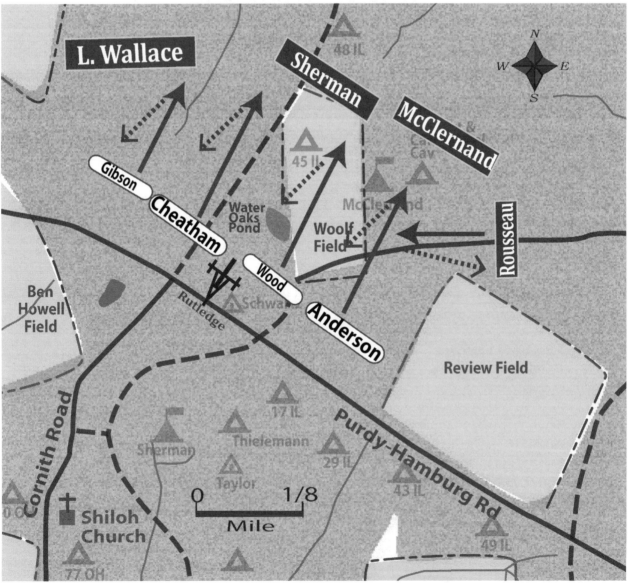

In the Wake of Battle.   Battle & Leaders, Vol II, pg 686

good fellow, you do your duty and I'll do mine." The private replied that it was his duty to die and not to general's. The Army commander smiled and moved to the rear. Then the general, who doctors thought should be in bed, returned to the church and led two Tennessee regiments into position, although he was too frail to carry their large and heavy battle flags.

But gradually the Confederates were pushed back to the Purdy-Hamburg Road. The fighting now rippled east into the southern edge of Review Field. Reduced to plugging holes, the Confederates rushed troops into Review Field, including the 20th Tennessee and remnants of Col. August Reichard's and Col. Charles Wickliffe's brigades. They were met on the opposite side of the road by the fresh Union regiments of Colonels William Gibson, James Veatch and George Wagner. Confederate Wickliffe, a West Pointer and Mexican War veteran, was mortally wounded with a shot to the head. Slowly, very slowly, the Southerners gave ground, until by 2:00pm the Federals held the Purdy-Hamburg Road.

Retreat
2pm - 5pm

By early afternoon the Confederates were clearly being overwhelmed. Though they refused to quit, fighting for every foot of ground, the disorganized and exhausted men teetered on the verge of collapse. Col. Thomas Jordan, the officer who had drawn up the initial battle plan, now asked Beauregard, *"General, do you not think our troops are in the condition of a lump of sugar, thoroughly soaked with water, but yet preserving its original shape, though ready to dissolve?"* Beauregard sadly agreed, stating that he intended with withdraw in a few minutes.

At 3pm, the retreat commenced. *"It was sad beyond measure ..."* Bragg later wrote to his wife. The retreat was orderly, covered by a rear-guard of about 2,000 infantry of Wood's and Trabue's brigades, along with 12 to 15 guns. At one point,

"It was sad beyond measure."

to keep the Yankees at bay, the Southerners even launched a quick counterattack, allowing Beauregard and the rest of his army to depart through Rea Field - the same field where they began their attack the day before – a thousand years ago, before they'd seen the elephant.

By 5pm, the Confederates were gone.

Grant Doesn't Follow

The Federal army did little to hinder the Confederates' departure. Grant later claimed he didn't feel he had the authority to order Buell's fresher troops to pursue the retreating enemy, while Buell stated that Grant was the senior commander and he gave no order to pursue. The truth probably is that everyone in the Union army, probably most of all Grant, had more than enough of the Confederate army for the moment – much like McClellan after Antietam, and Meade after Gettysburg.

In fact, Sherman said as much when asked years later why there was no pursuit of the Rebels: "I assure you, my dear fellow, we had had quite enough of their society for two whole days, and were only too glad to be rid of them on any terms."

And so the Battle of Shiloh was over. The battle was the Confederacy's best chance to break the string of Union victories that had begun with Forts Henry and Donelson the preceding February. The Confederates had fought valiantly and nearly pulled it off. But not quite.

Postscript: The Battle of Fallen Timbers
April 8th

Col. Nathan Bedford Forrest (w)
1821 - 1877

Actually, there *was* a minor, but mean, scrap the day after the battle, on April 8th, notably mainly for the ferocity of one man who would remain a thorn in the side of the Union army, and especially in Sherman's side, for the rest of the war. That man was Nathan Bedford Forrest – a former Memphis slave trader.

Tuesday morning Forrest and 350 cavalry – consisting of about 150 of his own men, plus some Texas Rangers and a few other cavalry – were patrolling the Ridge Road, guarding the Confederate rear from any pursuing Yankees. Meanwhile, to make sure the Confederates were indeed retreating, and not merely reforming for another attack, Grant ordered Sherman to scout the roads south of the Landing.

So down the road came Sherman with two infantry brigades and the 4th Illinois Cavalry regiment. Presently, the Federals spotted some Southern horsemen in a muddy cotton field bordered by a clearing of fallen timber – trees cut down by farmers – several hundred yards wide.

"Suddenly a fierce yell filled the air."

Sherman sent forward two companies of the 77th Ohio as skirmishers, followed by the remainder of the regiment - about 240 men in all - to scout the roads south of the Landing. Sherman's skirmishers proceeded to push back the small group of the Confederate troopers, who fought dismounted and slowly retreated. But it was a trap. Forrest, who could see that the Yankees had trouble maneuvering through the fallen timber and a small creek, ordered the bulk of his force to charge.

Suddenly *"A fierce yell filled the air,"* according to a 77th Ohio lieutenant, and hundreds of Rebel horsemen, armed with shotguns, pistols and sabers, thundered over a ridge straight at the Yankee skirmish line. The Federals took off on a dead run back to their main line. But the surprised Federal infantrymen on the main line fired their weapons prematurely; they then tried to make a stand in a double line of fixed bayonets. But the Confederates, with Forrest in the lead, smashed through their ranks, shooting, slashing and cutting down Federals. Even Sherman admitted that he and his staff were put on the run, *"through the mud, with pistols already emptied, closely followed by Forrest and his men."*

With a loss of no more than 20 of his men, Forrest had killed 15, wounded 25 and captured 53 Yankees. (Forrest grumbled that he wished the Yankee prisoner hadn't surrendered, so he could have killed them all).

Sherman began reforming his line and called up his second brigade. Forrest, either out of excitement or because his horse bolted, depending on who tells the story, charged on his own, crashing into the waiting line of blue infantry. Federals, shouting *"Kill him!", Knock him off that horse!"* tripped over themselves to get at the rider, who slashed at them right and left with his saber. Finally one Federal shot Forrest at point-blank range, the ball lodging against his left hip next to the spinal column, numbing one of his legs and leaving it dangling. Forrest spurred his horse and escaped in the woods to the south. According a biography written in 1906, Forrest yanked a Yankee soldier up on the saddle behind him to cover his escape. But that seems a stretch, given Forrest's wound, and Forrest never mentioned anything about it.

Sherman, who probably witnessed the action, would in the coming years have plenty of reasons to wish his men had killed Forrest that day. The two implacable foes shared many traits, including genius and possibly a touch of madness.

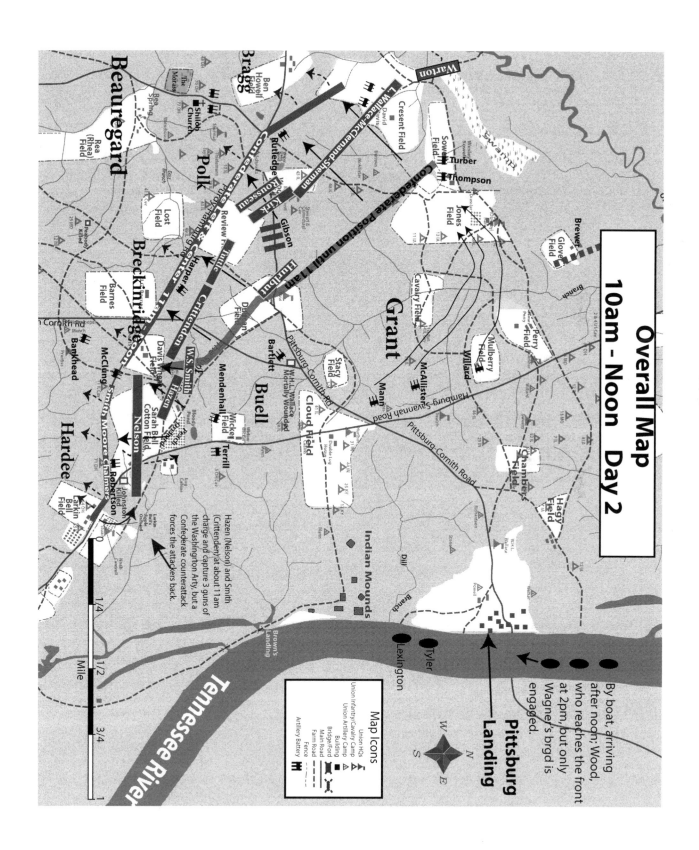

Overall Map
10am - Noon Day 2

By boat, arriving after noon: Wood, who reaches the front at 2pm, but only Wagner's brgd is engaged.

Pittsburg Landing

Hazen (Nelson) and Smith (Crittenden) at about 11am charge and capture 3 guns of the Washington Arty, but a Confederate counterattack forces the attackers back.

Map Icons

Union HQs	⚑
Union Infantry/Cavalry Camp	△
Union Artillery Camp	△
Building	◩
Bridge/Ford	■
Main Road	— — —
Farm Road	· · · ·
Fence	⚏⚏⚏
Artillery Battery	⚑

Tennessee River

Lexington

Tyler

Brown's Landing

Indian Mounds

Confederate Position until 11am

Grant

Buell

Beauregard

Bragg

Polk

Breckinridge

Hardee

Nelson

Crittenden

W.S. Smith

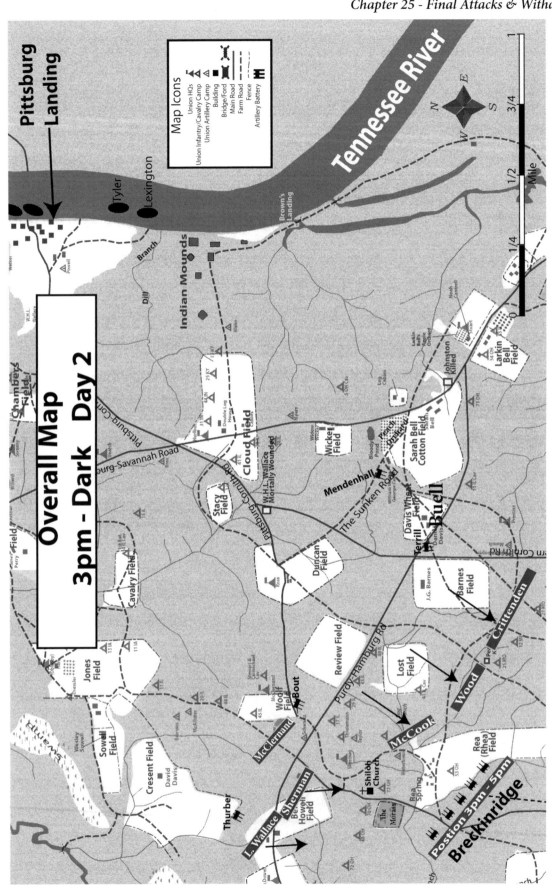

Overall Map
3pm - Dark   Day 2

Pittsburg Landing

Tennessee River

Map Icons
Union HQs
Union Infantry/Cavalry Camp
Union Artillery Camp
Building
Bridge/Ford
Main Road
Farm Road
Fence
Artillery Battery

Tyler
Lexington

Brown's Landing

Indian Mounds

Larkin Bell Field

Johnston Killed

Sarah Bell Cotton Field

Peach Orchard

Buell

Cloud Field

W.H.L. Wallace Mortally Wounded

Mendenhall

The Sunken Road

Davis Wheat Field

Wicker Field

Stacy Field

Duncan Field

Barnes Field

J.G. Barnes

Crittenden

Chambers Field

Cavalry Field

Jones Field

Bout

Wolf Field

Review Field

Lost Field

Wood

McClernand

McCook

Sowell Field

Cresent Field

David Davis

Shiloh Church

Rea (Rhea) Field

Rea Spring

The Morass

L. Wallace

Sherman

Howell Field

Thurber

Position 3pm - 5pm

Breckinridge

Pittsburg-Savannah Road

Purdy-Hamburg Rd

1/4   1/2   3/4   1   Mile

But anyway it was clear that the Confederate cavalry was just a rear guard, protecting the
withdrawal of the army, and so Sherman withdrew.
Even though he had just received something of
a bloody nose in this scrap, when he returned to
the main battlefield he was cheered wildly. Despite
their stormy beginning, Sherman and the volunteer troops had now bonded. He would soon be
calling them "*his boys*," and they would be calling
him "*Uncle Billy*." It was the start of one of the Civil
War's great love stories.

Amazingly, though painfully wounded, Forrest
would be back in the saddle within two months.
He was probably the last casualty of the battle of
Shiloh.

Google Map Links (scan with OC Reader to go to online maps)

Sowell Field	Jones Field	The Crossroads	Shiloh Church

Woolf Field	Pittsburg Landing	Water Oaks Pond

Rea Field	Review Field	Fallen Timbers

Chapter 26   Aftermath

The Battlefield

The departed Confederates left in their wake a man-made disaster the likes of which had never been seen on the American continent, and rarely seen since. The exhausted Union army, almost in shock, had to immediately contend with thousands of mangled corpses of men and horses, and even more thousands of wounded, all of whom threatened to spread disease. And of course the field was littered with the debris of battle – wrecked wagons and tents, artillery pieces, and discarded weapons. Food was scarce to nonexistent. Grant's men had no food or personal effects because their tents had been raided. Buell's men had no food or personal effects because they had left everything back at Savannah in their haste to reach Pittsburg Landing.

McClernand found his tent perforated with 27 bullet holes. *"Within a radius of 200 yards of my headquarters tent the ground was literally covered with dead."* He found that a wounded Rebel had staggered inside his tent, dying with his head resting on the general's desk.

The dead horses were gathered into huge mounds, doused with kerosene, and burned. The sickening

> *"Within a radius of 200 yards of my headquarters tent the ground was literally covered with dead."*

smell of burning flesh wafted over the battlefield for days. By Thursday most of the dead soldiers on both sides were buried, though for decades thereafter bones would be discovered throughout the timber and brush.

The Union dead were buried in trenches. It was only after the war that their bodies were re-interred into what is now the National Cemetery overlooking the Tennessee River.

The Park Service today identifies five Confederate mass-grave locations, but there were almost certainly more. It's also very likely that many exhausted and hungry Union privates, who after all hadn't joined the army to be grave diggers for their enemies, simply pitched many Rebel body parts into the fires along with the horses, or dumped them into the many tree-covered ravines.

It took until Friday and possibly Saturday, four or five days after the battle, before the last of the wounded would be located on the field and removed to a field hospital. For the wounded laying out in the woods, wild hogs were a serious threat. Droves of hogs could be heard wandering about, devouring dead and wounded men alike,

Dead horses burned on the battlefield near the Peach Orchard.   Library of Congress

Shiloh Field Hospital

their sounds *"unmistakable, quarreling over their carnival feast."*

And the field hospitals - houses, barns and tents woefully inadequate in the best of circumstances - were overwhelmed with thousands of Union and Confederate wounded. The surgeons worked 20 hour days, much of that time spent sawing off limbs (Doctors back then were called "surgeons" or "sawbones" for good reason.

According to one 9-year-old, possible witness and probable Confederate sympathizer, Elsie Duncan, "The Yankees didn't bury the Confederate dead. They threw them into the gullies and ravines and covered them with leaves and left them for the hogs to root up and eat up. This I know to be the truth. I could not understand anyone to be so heartless to leave a human being unburied even if they were a rebel - they were dead."

Their primary tool was a small saw that looked like a modern hacksaw, and was used in exactly the same manner). And once a young soldier lost a limb, his future was grim – there not being much demand for one-legged farmers.

It would be a week after the battle before the army could deliver provisions by steamer to Pittsburg Landing. When the steamers did arrive, as many as 40 boats lined up two or three deep at the Landing. Scores of sacks of corn were scattered over the muddy bank to create better footing.

Grant's Problems

Grant's head was definitely on the chopping block; even his troops knew he had grossly underestimated the threat of a Confederate attack. And the Northern public was stunned at the butcher's bill. The casualties in the two-day battle exceeded the combined casualties of all of America's previous wars. Grant was criticized for being caught by surprise without fortifications, which was true, and for being drunk during the battle, which was not true. Many of the "stragglers" who fled the battle were the first on the transports back north and once safely in taverns at the various river towns, for the price of a beer, they were more than happy to tell any reporter how fouled up the whole operation was.

Halleck, arriving at the Landing four days after the battle, was also more than happy to take up one of his favorite projects – shelving Grant and removing a potential rival.

Taking personal command of Grant and Buell's armies, Halleck also summoned the army of Maj. Gen. John Pope, which had just seized Island Number 10 and New Madrid on the Mississippi River the day after the Shiloh battle ended. With his consolidated army now numbering almost 125,000 men, Halleck planned to assault Cornith. Rather than leaving Grant in command of the largest component in this new force, the Army of Tennessee, Halleck turned the command over to Maj. Gen. George H. Thomas, and instead named Grant to the meaningless post of second-in-command.

Grant considered resigning, but Sherman talked him out of it. Grant and Sherman had not really known each other prior to Shiloh but they

> *"I can't spare this man; he fights."*

were quickly becoming good friends.

Actually, Grant *did* have one other friend – Abraham Lincoln. When it was clear that Grant had made major mistakes at Shiloh, and when the appalling casualty list was known, and when everyone in the country was yelling for Grant's head, Lincoln famously responded, "*I can't spare this man; he fights.*"

Grant would keep his job.

Retreat to Cornith

No matter how miserable the Federals were back at Shiloh, their problems paled in comparison to those of the Confederates, for their return march to Cornith was a true horror. First of all, the Southerners had no choice but to use the same two muddy roads used in their march to Shiloh – Monterey Road and Ridge Road. Bragg notified Beauregard on April 8th, "*Troops utterly disorganized and demoralized. Road almost impassable ... Our artillery is being left all along the road by its officers; indeed, I find but few officers with their men.*" According to a sergeant of the 17th Louisiana, "*The trip back to Cornith used me up worse than the battle as we were gone five days and slept about ten hours during that time. We ate nothing almost, traveled very hard, and it rained on us every night,*"

The wounded suffered the most. "*Some of them as they jostled along over the rough road in springless wagons gave most pitiful groans, which made me forget I was hurt,*" recalled one passenger. About 300 wounded died in the retreat and were dumped along the road. Some of the more seriously wounded were left to die in homes along the way. Only those who couldn't walk were allowed to ride in the wagons. The walking wounded with only mangled arms and gouged eyes had to trudge through the mud.

It rained not only every night of the march but every night for 10 days after the battle. It also turned cold, and the rain became hail. The roads, already badly churned during the Confederate advance, were now quagmires. Monterey Road was by far the worst. "*I am not exaggerating when I inform you that all the way the mud was knee deep,*

and we were obliged to wade several streams which were waist deep,*" Pvt. Thomas Robertson wrote his mother.

According to a 47th Tennessee private, "*We have been without anything to eat but two crackers per day since Sunday morning & traveled in water & mud waist deep all day.*" An artilleryman of Ketchum's battery said, "*The men looked as if they did not have life enough left in them to move ... Completely saturated with rain, and .. standing in mud ankle deep all night.*"

> *"Every train brings some anxious parent looking after their sons."*

When the men finally stumbled into Cornith, their ordeal wasn't over. The surgeons now got busy with their saws. "*The Railroad platform is almost covered with coffins and wounded soldiers – every train brings some anxious parents looking after their sons,*" wrote one soldier. Another soldier from Louisiana, walking past a church filled with wounded, noticed a ghastly sight, casually sitting out back – a large box "*filled with feet and arms & hands. It was so full that horrible & bloody feet protruded out of the top.*"

Cornith was now a gigantic hospital, with wounded jammed for days in churches, schools, and homes. Running out of space, hundreds were simply laid out on porches, sidewalks and railroad platforms. The sweet smell of gangrene was everywhere. Not surprisingly, many of the men died of pneumonia – a killer at that time – especially given the soldiers' weakened condition.

Morale was a rock bottom. "*The camp, once so gay, so joyous, now lay under the pall of death. Everywhere prevailed a mournful silence,*" according to one of the Orleans Guardsmen. "*Everyone was hushed in sadness.*"

> *"The camp, once so gay, so joyous, now lay under the pall of death. Everywhere prevailed a mournful silence. Everyone was hushed in sadness."*

There were 2 main methods used to amputate large limbs during the War: Flap and Circular Amputations. In the field the flap method was more widely used where time was a factor. With this method the bone was dissected and flaps of deep muscle and skin were used to close the operation. When implementing the flap method it was imperative to cut the bone away a few inches above the place where the flaps were brought together.

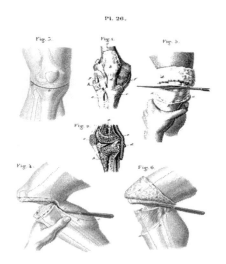
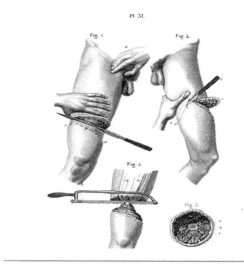

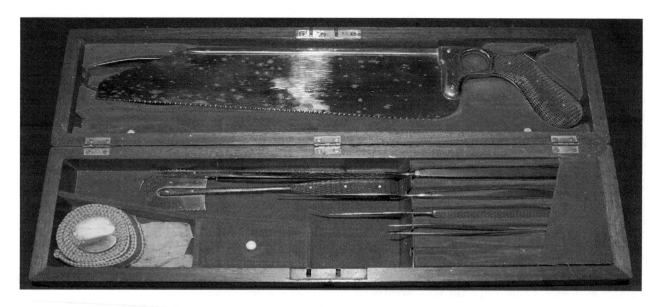

Civil War Surgeon's Kit

The Cornith Campaign
April 8 - May 30, 1862

Halleck's 22 mile advance on Cornith after the battle of Shiloh has been almost universally described as "*glacial*." It took Halleck three weeks to begin rolling his massive army southward, after which it averaged two thirds of a mile per day for the next month. Determined not to be caught by a surprise like Grant, each night Halleck ordered his 125,000 troops to entrench, much like the Roman army.

His snail's pace practically begged the Confederates to take back the initiative. But doing so required a daring commander, which Beauregard was not. In any case, he was in poor health, and burdened with some real problems – including being badly outnumbered and facing serious supply and transportation problems.

On May 29 with the town about to be surrounded, Beauregard realized he could no longer hold Cornith. Overnight he carried out a crafty evacuation, complete with ordering his troops to cheer when the trains chugged into Cornith, giving the Yankees the impression that reinforcements were arriving – when in fact they were departing. Beauregard and his army would take up a new position in Tupelo, Mississippi, two day's march south of Cornith.

The next morning Halleck's troops crept into Cornith, only to find it deserted. But they'd finally seized the vital railroad junction.

Halleck's slow pace and his failure to snare any part of the Confederate Army disappointed Lincoln, but at least Halleck had captured Cornith. This was more than the Army of the Potomac was doing at that time back in Virginia. Halleck's solid though unspectacular success earned him a promotion to General in Chief of all Union armies. The promotion had two benefits: first, it put Halleck and his hemorrhoids permanently behind a desk, for which he was far better suited than a field command, and being sent to Washington was, for a bureaucrat, like being summoned to Mecca. From his new post Halleck could fuss with files and papers to his heart's content, parsing words, and slipping in sly innuendos; eventually he would succeed in making himself despised by nearly every general in the United States Army.

The second benefit was that he was out of Grant's hair.

Halleck's Confederate opponent had more serious political problems. Beauregard spun his withdrawal from Cornith in glorious terms, suggesting it amounted to a great victory. But President Davis wasn't impressed. He was sour because he convinced himself that Beauregard halted the Shiloh attack prematurely, after Davis' old West Point friend, Johnston, was killed with victory in his grasp. A couple of weeks after arriving in Tupelo, Beauregard took an unauthorized sick leave. Davis quickly replaced him with the recently-promoted Bragg.

The Civil War in the West would drag on for years. Many soldiers who faced each other for the first time at Shiloh would meet again and again at Stones River, Perryville, Champions Hill, Vicksburg, Chickamauga, and more. But the growing Union war machine would slowly, inexorably, grind down Southern resistance. And the South would never again have as great a chance of complete victory in the West, and come as close to achieving it, as it had in the woods and fields around Shiloh Church in April of 1862.

Cornith, MS

Modern Photo of Shiloh National Cemetery

Appendix A - Order of Battle
Army of Tennessee - Order of Battle
Maj. Gen. U. S. Grant, Commanding

k = Killed   w = Wounded   mw = Mortally Wounded   d = Disabled   c = Captured

1st Division
Maj. Gen. John A. McClernand

1st Brigade
Col. Abraham M. Hare (w)
Col. Marcellus M. Crocker

8 IL
Capt. James M. Ashmore (w)
Capt. William H. Harvey (k)
Capt. Robert H. Sturgess

18 IL
Maj. Samuel Eaton (w)
Capt. Daniel H. Brush (w)
Capt. William J. Dillion (k)
Capt. Jabez J. Anderson

11 IA
Lt. Col. William Hall (w)

13 IA
Col. Marcellus M Crocker

2nd Brigade
Col. C. Carroll Marsh

11 IL
Lt. Col. T. E. G. Ransom (w)
Maj. Garrett Nevins (w)
Capt. Lloyd D. Waddell
Maj. Garrett Nevins

20 IL
Lt. Col. Evan Richards (w)

45 IA Col. John E. Smith

48 IA
Col. Isham N. Hayniea
Maj. Manning Mayfield

3rd Brigade
Col. Julius Raith (mw)
Lt. Col. Enos P. Wood

17 IL
Lt. Col. Enos P. Wood
Maj. Francis M. Smith

29 IL
Lt. Col. Charles M. Ferrell

43 IL
Lt. Col. Adolph Endelmann

49 IL
Lt. Col. Phineas Pease (w)

Artillery
Dresser's Btry D, 2 IL Arty
Capt. James P. Timothy

McAllister's Btry D, 1 IL Arty
Capt. Edward McAllister (w)

Schwartz's Btry E, 2 IL Arty
Lt. George L. Nispel

Burrows' Btry, 14 OH Arty
Capt. Jerome B. Burrows (w)

Cavalry
1st Bn, 4 IL Cavalry
Lt. Col. William McCullough

Carmichael's Co. IL Cavalry
Capt. Eagleton Carmichael

Stewart's Co. IL Cavalry
Lt. Ezra King

2nd Division
Brig. Gen.W. H. L. Wallace (mw)
Col. James M. Tuggle

1st Brigade
Col. James M. Tuggle

2 IA
Lt. Col. James Baker

7 IA
Lt. Col. James C Parrott

12 IA
Col. Joseph J. Woods (w & c)

14 IA
Col. Wm. T. Shaw (c)

2nd Brigade
Brig. Gen. John McArthur (w)

9 IL
Col. August Mersy

12 IL
Lt. Col. Augustus L. Chetlain

13 MO
Col. Crafts J. Wright

14 MO
Col. B. S. Compton

81 OH
Col. Thomas Morton

3rd Brigade
Col. Thomas W. Sweeny (w)
Col. Silas D. Baldwin

8 IA
Col. James L. Geddes (w & C)

7 IL Maj. Richard Rowett

50 IL
Col. Moses M. Bane (w)

52 IL
Maj. Henry Stark
Capt. Edwin A. Bowen

57 IL
Col. Silas D. Baldwin
Capt. Gustav A. Busse

58 IL
Col. Wm. F. Lynch (c)

Artillery

Willard's Btry A 1 IL Arty
Lt. Peter P. Wood

Richardson's Btry D, 1 MO Arty
Capt. Henry Richardson

Welker's Btry H, 1 Mo Arty
Capt. Frederick Welker

Stone's Btry K, 1 Mo Arty
Capt. George H. Stone

Cavalry
Co. A, 2 IL Cavalry
Capt. John R. Hotaling

Co. B, 2 IL Cavalry
Capt. Thomas J. Larison

Co. C, 2 US Cavalry
Lt. James Powell

Co. I, 4 US Cavalry
Lt. James Powell

Army of Tennessee - Order of Battle (page 2)

k = Killed   w = Wounded   mw = Mortally Wounded   d = Disabled   c = Captured

3rd Division
Maj. Gen. Lew Wallace

1st Brigade
Col. Morgan L. Smith

11 IN
Col. George F. McGinnis

24 IN
Col. Alvin P. Hovey

8 MO
Lt. Col. James Peckham

2nd Brigade
Col. John M. Thayer

23 IN
Col. William L. Sanderson

1 NE
Lt. Col. William D. McCord

58 OH
Col. Valentine Bausenwein

68 OH
Col. Samuel H. Steadman
(Not engaged at Shiloh - remained at Crump's Landing)

3rd Brigade
Col. Charles Whittlesey

20 OH
Lt. Col. Manning F. Force

56 OH
Col. Peter Kinney
(Not engaged at Shiloh - remained at Crump's Landing)

76 OH
Col. Charles R. Woods

78 OH
Col. Mortimer D. Leggett

Artillery
Thompson's Btry, 9 IN Arty
Lt. George R. Brown

Buel's Btry I, 1 MO Arty
Lt. Charles H. Thurber

Cavalry
3 Bn, 11 IL Cavalry
Maj. James F. Johnson
(not engaged at Shiloh - remained at Crump's Landing)

3 Bn, 5 OH Cavalry
Maj. Charles S. Hayes
(not engaged at Shiloh - remained at Crump's Landing)

4th Division
Brig. Stephen A. Hurlbut

1st Brigade
Col. Nelson G. Williams (w)
Col. Isaac C. Pugh

28 IL
Col. Amory K. Johnson

32 IL
Col. John Logan (w)

41 IL
Col. Isaac C. Pugh
Lt. Col. Ansel Tupper (k)
Maj. John Warner
Capt. John N. Nale

3 IA
Maj. William M. Stone (c)
Lt. George W. Crosley

2nd Brigade
Col. James C. Veatch

14 IL
Col. Cyrus Hall

15 IL
Lt. Col. Edward F. W. Ellis (k)
Capt. Louis D. Kelly
Lt. Col. William Cam

46 IL
Col. John A. Davis (w)
Lt. Col. John J. Jones

25 IN
Lt. Col. William H. Morgan (w)
Maj. John W. Foster

3rd Brigade
Brig. Gen. Jacob G. Laumen

31 IN
Col. Charles Cruft (w)
Lt. Col. John Osborn

44 IN
Col. Hugh B. Reed

17 KY
Col. John H. McHenry, Jr

25 KY
Lt. Col. Benjamin H. Bristow
Maj. William B. Wall (w)
Capt. B. T. Underwood
Col. John H. McHenry

Artillery

Ross's Btry, 2 MI Arty
Lt. Cuthbert W. Laing

Mann's Btry C, 1 Mo Arty
Lt. Edward Brotzmann

Myer's Btry, 13 OH Arty
Capt. John B. Myers

Cavalry

1st & 2nd Bn 5 OH Cav
Col. William H. H. Taylor

Army of Tennessee - Order of Battle (page 3)

k = Killed   w = Wounded   mw = Mortally Wounded   d = Disabled   c = Captured

5th Division	6th Division
Brig. Gen. William T. Sherman (w)	Brig. Gen. Benjamin M. Prentiss (c)

5th Division

1st Brigade
Col. John A. McDowell (d)

40 IL
Col. Stephan G. Hicks (w)

6 IA
Capt. John Williams (w)
Capt. Madison M. Walden

46 OH
Col. Thomas Worthington

2nd Brigade
Col. David Stuart (w)
Lt. Col. Oscar Malmborg
Col. T. Kilby Smith

55 IL
Lt. Col. Oscar Malmborg

54 OH
Col. T. Kilby Smith
Lt. Col. James A. Farden

71 OH
Col. Rodney Mason

3rd Brigade
Col. Jesse Hildebrand

53 OH
Col. Jesse J. Appler
Lt. Col. Robert A. Fulton

57 OH
Lt. Col. Americus V. Rice

77 OH
Lt. Col. Willis De Hass
Maj. Benjamin D. Fearing

4th Brigade
Col. Ralph P. Buckland

48 OH
Col. Peter J. Sullivan (w)
Lt. Col. Job R. Parker

70 OH
Col. Joseph R. Cockerill

72 OH
Lt. Col. Herman Canfield (k)
Col. Ralph P. Buckland

Artillery
Maj. Ezra Taylor, Chief of Arty

Taylor's Btry B, 1 IL Arty
Capt. Samuel E. Barrett

Waterhouse's Btry E, 1 IL Arty
Capt. Allen C. Waterhouse (w)
Lt. Abial R. Abbott (w)
Lt. John A. Fitch

Morton's Btry, 6 IN Arty
Capt. Frederick Behr (k)

Cavalry
2nd & 3rd Bns, 4 IL Cav
Col. T. Lyle Dickey

Thielemann's Two Cav Cos.
Capt. Christian Thielemann

6th Division

1st Brigade
Col. Everett Peabody (k)

12 MI
Col. Francis Quinn

21 MO
Col. David Moore (w)
Lt. Col. H. M. Woodyard

25 MO
Lt. Col. Robert T. Van Horn

16 WI
Col. Benjamin Allen (w)

2nd Brigade
Col. Madison Miller (c)

61 IL
Col. Jacob Fry

18 MO
Lt. Col. Isaac V. Pratt (c)

18 WI
Col. James S. Alban (k)

Not Brigaded

15 IA
Col. Hugh T. Reid (w)

16 IA
Col. Alexander Chambers (w)
Lt. Col. Addison H. Sanders

(the 15 and 16 IA were on the west side of the field in an independent command)

23 MO
Col. Jacob T. Tindall (k)
Lt. Col. Quin Morton (c)

(23 MO arrived on field about 9am on Apr 6th)

Artillery

Hickenlooper's Btry, 5 OH Arty
Capt. Andrew Hickenlooper

Munch's Btry, 1 MN Arty
Capt. Emil Munch (w)
Lt. William Pfaender

Cavalry

1st & 2nd Bns, 11 IL Cav
Col. Robert G. Ingersoll

Army of Ohio - Order of Battle
Maj. Gen. Don Carlos Buell, Commanding

k = Killed   w = Wounded   mw = Mortally Wounded   d = Disabled   c = Captured

2nd Division
Brig. Gen. Alexander McD. McCook

4th Brigade
Brig. Gen. Lovell H. Rousseau
6 IN
Col. Thomas T. Crittenden

5 KY
Col. Harvey M. Buckley

1 OH
Col. Benjamin F. Smith

1st Bn, 15 US
Capt. Peter T. Swain,
Maj. J. H. King

1st Bn, 16 US
Capt. Edwin Townsend,
Maj. J. H. King

1st Bn, 19 US
Maj. Stephen D. Carpenter,
Maj. J. H. King

5th Brigade
Col. Edward N. Kirk (w)

34 IL
Maj. Charles N. Levanway (k)
Capt. Hiram W. Bristol

29 IN
Lt. Col. David M. Dunn

30 IN
Col. Sion S. Bass (mw)
Lt. Col. Joseph B. Dodge

77 PA
Col. Frederick S. Stumbaugh

6th Brigade
Col. William H. Gibson

32 IN
Col. August Willich

39 IN
Col. Thomas J. Harrison

15 OH
Maj. William Wallace

49 OH
Lt. Col. Albert M. Blackman

Artillery
Terrill's Btry H, 5 US Arty
Capt. William R. Terrill

4th Division
Brig. Gen. William Nelson

10th Brigade
Col. Jacob Ammen

36 IN
Col. William Grose

6 OH
Lt. Col. Nicholas L. Anderson

24 OH
Lt. Col. Frederick C. Jones

19th Brigade
Col. William B. Hazen

9 IN
Col. Gideon C. Moody

6 KY
Col. Walter C. Whitaker

41 OH
Lt. Col. George S. Mygatt

22nd Brigade
Col. Sanders D. Bruce

1 KY
Col. David A. Enyart

2 KY
Col. Thomas D. Sedgewick

20 KY
Lt. Col. Charles S. Hanson

5th Division
Brig. Gen. Thomas L. Crittenden

11th Brigade
Brig. Gen. Jeremiah T. Boyle
9 KY
Col. Benjamin C. Grider

13 KY
Col. Edward H. Hobson

19 OH
Col. Samuel Beatty

59 OH
Col. James P. Fyffe

14th Brigade
Col. William Sooy Smith

11 KY
Col. Pierce B. Hawkins

26 KY
Lt. Col. Cicero Maxwell

13 OH
Lt. Col. Joseph G. Hawkins

Artillery
Bartlett's Btry G, 1 OH Arty
Capt. Joseph Bartlett

Mendenhall's batteries H & M, 4 US Arty
Capt. John Mendenhall

6th Division
Brig. Gen. Thomas J. Wood (Division arrived on field 2pm April 7th)

15th Brigade
Col. Milo S. Hascall

17 IN
Col. John T. Wilder

58 IN
Col. Henry M. Carr

3 KY
Col. Thomas Bramlette

26 OH
Col. Edward P. Fyffe

20th Brigade
Brig. Gen. James A. Garfield

13 MI
Col. Michael Shoemaker

64 OH
Col. John Ferguson

65 OH
Col. Charles G. Harker

21st Brigade
Col. George D. Wagner

15 IN
Lt. Col. Gustavus A. Wood

40 IN
Col. John W. Blake

57 IN
Col. Cyrus C. Hines

24 KY
Col. Lewis B. Grigsby

Army of Mississippi - Order of Battle
Gen. Albert Sidney Johnston (k), Gen. P. G. T. Beauregard, Commanding

k = Killed   w = Wounded   mw = Mortally Wounded   d = Disabled   c = Captured

I Corps
Maj. Gen. Leonidas Polk

1st Division
Brig. Gen. Alexander P. Stewart
Brig. Gen. Charles Clark (w)

1st Brigade
Col. Robert M. Russell

11 LA
Col. Samuel F. Marks (w)
Lt. Col. Robert H. Barrow

12 TN
Lt. Col. Tyree H. Bell
Maj. Robert P. Caldwell

13 TN
Col. Alfred J. Vaughan Jr.

22 TN
Col. Thomas J. Freeman (w)

Bankhead's TN Btry
Capt. Smith P. Bankhead

2nd Brigade
Brig. Gen. A. P. Stewart

13 AR
Lt. Col. A.D. Grayson (k)
Maj. James A. McNeely (w)
Col. James C. Tappan

4 TN
Col. Lt. Col. A.D. Grayson (k)
Maj. James A. McNeely (w)

5 TN
Lt. Col. Calvin D. Venable

33 TN
Col. Alexander W. Campbell (w)

Stanford's MS Btry
Capt. Thomas J. Stanford

2nd Division
Maj. Gen. Benjamin F. Cheatham (w)

1st Brigade
Brig. Gen. Bushrod R. Johnson (w)
Col. Preston Smith (w)

Blythe's MS Bn
Col. A. K. Blythe (k)
Lt. Col. David L. Herron (k)
Maj. James Moore

2 TN
Col. J. Knox Walker15 TN

154 TN (Senior)
Col. Preston Smith (w)
Lt. Col. Marcus C. Wright (w)

Polk's TN Btry
Capt. Marshall T. Polk (w)

2nd Brigade
Col. William H. Stephens
Col. George Maney

7 KY
Col. Charles Wickliffe (mw)
Lt. Col. William D. Lannom

1 TN Bn
Col. George Maney
Maj. Hume R. Field

6 TN
Lt. Col. Timothy P. Jones

9 TN
Col. Henry L. Douglass

Smith's MS Btry
Capt. Melancthon Smith

II Corps
Maj. Gen. Braxton Bragg

1st Division
Brig. Gen. Daniel Ruggles

1st Brigade
Col. Randall L. Gibson

1 AR Col. James F. Fagan

4 LA Col. Henry W. Allen (w)
        Lt. Col. Samuel E. Hunter

13 LA
Maj. Anatole P. Avengno (mw)
Capt. Stephen O'Leary (w)
Capt. Edgar M. Dubroca

19 LA
Col. Benjamin L. Hodge
Lt. Col. James M. Hollingsworth

Bains's MS Battery
Capt. S. C. Bain

2nd Brigade
Brig. Gen. Patton Anderson

1 FL Bn
Maj. Thaddeus A. McDonell (w)
Capt. W. G. Poole
Capt. W. Capers Bird

17 LA
Lt. Col. Charles Jones (w)

20 LA Col. August Reichard

1 MS Cavalry
Col. Andrew J. Lindsay

Conf Guards Bn
Maj. Franklin H. Clack

9 TX   Col. Wright A. Stanley

Washington (LA) Artillery
Capt. W. Irving Hodgson

3rd Brigade
Col. Preston Pond
16 LA Maj. Daniel Gober

18 LA
Col. Alfred Mouton (w)
Lt. Col. Alfred Roman

(LA) Crescent Reg
Col. Marshall J. Smith

(LA) Orleans Guard Bn
Maj. Leon Querouze (w)

38 TN   Col. Robert F. Looney

Ketchum's AL Arty
Capt. Wm Ketchum

2nd Division
Brig. Gen. Jones M. Withers

1st Brigade
Brig. Gen. Adley H. Gladden (mw)
Col. Daniel Adams (w)
Col. Zach C. Deas

21 AL Lt. Col. Stewart W. Cayce
        Maj. Frederick Stewart

22 AL   Col. Zach C. Deas
        Lt. Col. John C. Marrast

25 AL   Col. John Q. Loomis (w)
        Maj. George D. Johnston

26 AL Lt. Col. John G. Coltart (w)
        Lt. Col. William D. Chadick

1 LA   Col. Daniel W. Adams
        Maj. Fred H. Farrar, Jr

Robertson's AL Battery
Capt. Felix H. Robertson

2nd Brigade
Brig. Gen. James R. Chalmers

5 MS Col. Albert E. Fant

7 MS Lt. Col. Hamilton Mayson

9 MS Lt. Col. Wm A. Rankin (mw)

10 MS Col. Robert A. Smith

52 TN Col. Benjamin J. Lea

Gage's AL Battery
Capt. Charles P. Gage

3rd Brigade
Brig. Gen. John K. Jackson

17 AL Lt. Col. Robert C. Fariss

18 AL Col. Eli S. Shorter

19 AL Col. Joseph Wheeler

2 TX Col. John C. Moore
        Lt. Col. William P. Rogers
        Maj. Hal G. Runnels

Girardey's GA Battery
Capt. Isadore P. Girardey

Clanton's AL Cav
Col. J. H. Clanton (w)

Army of Mississippi - Order of Battle (page 2)

k = Killed   w = Wounded   mw = Mortally Wounded   d = Disabled   c = Captured

III Corps
Maj. Gen. William J. Hardee

1st Brigade
Brig. Gen. Thomas C. Hindman (d)
Col. R. G. Shaver (d)

2 AR
Col. Daniel C. Govan
Maj. Reuben F. Harvey

6 AR Col. Alexander T. Hawthorn

7 AR
Lt. Col. John M. Dean (k)
Maj. James T. Martin

3rd Confederate
Col. John S. Marmaduek

Miller's TN Battery
Capt. William Miller

Swett's MS Battery
Capt. Charles Swett

2nd Brigade
Brig. Gen. Patrick R. Cleburne

15 AR
Lt. Col. Archibald K. Patton (k)

6 MS
Col. John J. Thornton (w)
Lt. Col. W. A. Harper

2 TN
Col. William B. Bate (w)
Lt. Col. David L. Goodall

5 (35th) TN
Col. Benjamin J. Hill

23 TN
Lt. Col. James F. Neill (w)
Maj. Robert Cantrell

24 TN
Lt. Col. Thomas H. Peebles

Soup's AR Battalion
Trigg's (Austin) AR Btry
Capt. John T. Trigg

Calvert (Helena) AR Btry
Capt. J. H. Calvert

Hubbard's AR Btry
Capt. George. T. Hubbard

3rd Brigade
Brig. Gen. Sterling A.M. Wood(d)
Col. William K. Patterson

16 AL
Lt. Col. John W. Harris

8 AR
Col. William K. Patterson

9 (14th) AR Bn
Maj. John H. Kelly

3 MS Bn
Maj. Aaron B. Hardcastle

27 TN
Col. Christopher H. Williams (k)
Maj. Samuel T. Love (k)

44 TN
Col. Coleman A. McDaniel

55 TN
Col. James L. McKoin

Harper's MS Battery
Capt. William L. Harper (w)
Lt. Putnam Darden

Georgia Dragoons
Capt. Isaac W. Avery

Reserve Corps
Brig. Gen. John C. Breckinridge

1st Brigade
Col. Robert P. Trabue

4 AL Bn Maj. James M. Clifton

31 AL
Lt. Col. Montgomery Gilbreath

3 KY
Lt. Col. Benjamin Anderson (w)

4 KY Lt. Col. Andrew R. Hynes (w)

5 KY Lt. Col. Thomas H. Hunt

6 KY   Col. Joseph H. Lewis

TN BN
Lt. Col. James M. Crews

Byrne's (Cobb's) KY Btry
Capt. Robert Cobb

Byrne's MS Btry
Capt. Edward P. Byrne

Morgan's Squadron KY Cav
Col. John H. Morgan

2nd Brigade
Brig. Gen. John S. Bowen (w)

9 AR
Col. Isaac L. Dunlop

10 AR
Col. Thomas H. Merrick

1 MO
Col. Lucius L. Rich

2nd Confederate
Col. John D. Martin
Maj. Thomas H. Mangum

Hudson's MS Btry
Capt. Alfred Hudson

Watson's LA Btry
Capt. Allen A. Burlsey

Thompson's Co. KY Cavalry
Capt. Phil B. Thompson

3rd Brigade
Col. Winfield S. Statham

15 MS
Maj. William F. Brantley (w)
Capt. Lamkin S. Terry

22 MS
Col. Frank Schaller (w)
Lt. Col. Charles S. Nelms (mw)
Maj. James S. Prestidge

19 TN
Col. David H. Cummings (w)
Lt. Col. Francis M. Walker

20 TN
Col. Joel A. Battle (w & c)
Maj. Patrick Duffy

28 TN   Col. John P Murrary

45 TN Lt. Col. Ephraim F. Lytle

Rutledge's TN Btry
Capt. Arthur M. Rutledge

Forrest's Reg TN Cavalry
Col. Nathan B. Forrest (w)

Unattached
Wharton's TX Reg Cavalry
Col. John A. Wharton (w)

Wirt Adams MS Reg Cav
Col. Wirt Adams

McClung's TN Battery
Capt. Hugh L. W. McClung

Roberts AR Battery
Capt. Franklin Roberts

Appendix B - Casualty Lists

Total Casualties

	Killed	Wounded	Missing	Total
Army of Tennessee	1,512	6,597	2,828	10,937
Army of Ohio	241	1,805	55	2,101
Total Union Losses	**1,753**	**8,402**	**2,883**	**13,038**
Confederate Losses	**1,728**	**8,012**	**959**	**10,699**
Total Shiloh Losses	**3,481**	**16,414**	**3,842**	**23,737**

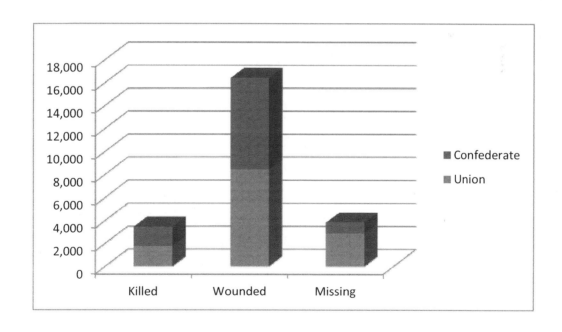

Union Casualties by Division

Army of Tennessee (Grant)
Casualties

First Division (McClernand)	Killed	Wounded	Missing	Total
First Brigade (Hare)	100	458	9	567
Second Brigade (Marsh)	80	475	30	585
Third Brigade (Raith)	96	392	46	534
Artillery	9	42	0	51
Cavalry	0	3	0	3
First Division Totals	**285**	**1,370**	**85**	**1,740**

Second Division (W. H.L. Wallace)	Killed	Wounded	Missing	Total
First Brigade (Tuttle)	39	143	676	858
Second Brigade (McArthur)	99	470	11	580
Third Brigade (Sweeny)	127	501	619	1,247
Artillery	4	53	0	57
Cavalry	1	5	0	6
Second Division Totals	**270**	**1,172**	**1,306**	**2,748**

Third Division (Lew Wallace)	Killed	Wounded	Missing	Total
First Brigade (Smith)	18	114	0	132
Second Brigade (Thayer)	20	99	3	122
Third Brigade (Whittlesey)	2	32	1	35
Artillery	1	6	0	7
Cavalry	0	0	0	0
Third Division Totals	**41**	**251**	**4**	**296**

Fourth Division (Hurlbut)	Killed	Wounded	Missing	Total
First Brigade (Williams)	112	532	43	687
Second Brigade (Veatch)	130	492	8	630
Third Brigade (Lauman)	70	384	4	458
Artillery	4	27	56	87
Cavalry	1	6	0	7
Fourth Division Totals	**317**	**1,441**	**111**	**1,869**

Fifth Division (Sherman)	Killed	Wounded	Missing	Total
First Brigade (McDowell)	136	439	70	645
Second Brigade (Stuart)	80	380	90	550
Third Brigade (Hildebrand)	70	221	65	356
Fourth Brigade (Buckland)	36	203	74	313
Artillery	3	27	0	30
Cavalry	0	6	0	6
Fifth Division Totals	**325**	**1,276**	**299**	**1,900**

Six Division (Prentiss)	Killed	Wounded	Missing	Total
First Brigade (Peabody)	113	372	236	721
Second Brigade (Miller)	67	311	352	730
Not Brigaded	48	215	418	681
Artillery	4	27	0	31
Cavalry	3	3	0	6
Six Division Totals	**235**	**928**	**1,006**	**2,169**

| **Unassigned Troops** | **39** | **159** | **17** | **215** |

Total Army of TN Casualties	1,512	6,597	2,828	10,937
	Killed	Wounded	Missing	Total

Army of Ohio (Buell)
Casualties

Second Division (McCook)	Killed	Wounded	Missing	Total
Fourth Brigade (Rousseau)	28	280	3	311
Fifth Brigade (Kirk)	34	310	2	346
Sixth Brigade (Gibson)	25	220	2	247
Artillery	1	13	0	14
First Division Totals	**88**	**823**	**7**	**918**

Fourth Division (Nelson)	Killed	Wounded	Missing	Total
Tenth Brigade (Ammen)	16	106	8	130
Nineteenth Brigade (Hazen)	48	357	1	406
Twenty-second Brigade (Bruce)	29	138	11	178
Second Division Totals	**93**	**601**	**20**	**714**

Fifth Division (Crittenden)	Killed	Wounded	Missing	Total
Eleventh Brigade (Boyle)	33	212	18	263
Fourteeth Brigade (Smith)	25	157	10	192
Artillery	2	8	0	10
Third Division Totals	**60**	**377**	**28**	**465**

Six Division (Wood)	Killed	Wounded	Missing	Total
Fifteenth Brigade (Hascall)	0	4	0	4
Twentieth Brigade (Garfield)	0	0	0	0
Twenty-First Brigade (Wagner)	0	0	0	0
Fourth Division Totals	**0**	**4**	**0**	**4**

Total Army of Ohio Casualties	241	1,805	55	2,101
	Killed	Wounded	Missing	Total

Army of Mississippi (Johnston)
Casualties by Corps

First Army Corps (Polk)

First Division (Clark)	Killed	Wounded	Missing	Total
First Brigade (Russell)	97	512	0	609
Second Brigade (Stewart)	93	421	3	517
First Division Totals	**190**	**933**	**3**	**1,126**
Second Division (Cheatham)				
First Brigade (Johnson)	120	607	13	740
Second Brigade (Stephens)	75	413	3	491
Second Division Totals	**195**	**1,020**	**16**	**1,231**
First Corps Totals	**385**	**1,953**	**19**	**2,357**

Second Army Corps (Bragg)

First Division (Ruggles)	Killed	Wounded	Missing	Total
First Brigade (Gibson)	97	488	97	682
Second Brigade (Anderson)	69	313	52	434
Third Brigade (Pond)	89	336	169	594
First Division Totals	**255**	**1,137**	**318**	**1,710**
Second Division (Withers)				
First Brigade (Gladden)	129	597	103	829
Second Brigade (Chalmers)	83	343	19	445
Third Brigade (Jackson)	86	364	194	644
Second Division Totals	**298**	**1,304**	**316**	**1,918**
Second Corps Totals	**553**	**2,441**	**634**	**3,628**

Third Army Corps (Hardee)

	Killed	Wounded	Missing	Total
First Brigade (Hindman)	109	546	38	693
Second Brigade (Cleburne)	188	790	65	1,043
Third Brigade (Wood)	107	600	38	745
Third Corps Totals	**404**	**1,936**	**141**	**2,481**

Reserve Army Corps (Breckinridge)

	Killed	Wounded	Missing	Total
First Brigade (Trabue)	151	557	92	800
Second Brigade (Bowen)	98	498	28	624
Third Brigade (Statham)	137	627	45	809
Reserve Corps Totals	**386**	**1,682**	**165**	**2,233**

Total Confederate Losses	**1,728**	**8,012**	**959**	**10,699**
	Killed	Wounded	Missing	Total

Army of Tennessee, Grant

Casualties by Brigade

Division Cmdr	Brgd #	Brigade Cmdr	Killed	Wounded	Missing	Total	% of Total
McClernand	1st Brgd	Hare	100	458	9	567	5%
	2nd Brgd	Marsh	80	475	30	585	6%
	3rd Brgd	Raith	96	392	46	534	5%
W.H.L. Wallace	1st Brgd	Tuttle	39	143	676	858	8%
	2nd Brgd	McArthur	99	470	11	580	6%
	3rd Brgd	Sweeny	127	501	619	1,247	12%
Lew Wallace	1st Brgd	M. Smith	18	114	0	132	1%
	2nd Brgd	Thayer	20	99	3	122	1%
	3rd Brgd	Whittlesey	2	32	1	35	0%
Hurlbut	1st Brgd	Williams	112	532	43	687	7%
	2nd Brgd	Veatch	130	492	8	630	6%
	3rd Brgd	Laumen	70	384	4	458	4%
Sherman	1st Brgd	McDowell	136	439	70	645	6%
	2nd Brgd	Stuart	80	380	90	550	5%
	3rd Brgd	Hildebrand	70	221	65	356	3%
	4th Brgd	Buckland	36	203	74	313	3%
Prentiss	1st Brgd	Peabody	113	372	236	721	0
	2nd Brgd	Miller	67	311	352	730	0
		No Brigade	48	215	418	681	0
					Total	10,431	100%

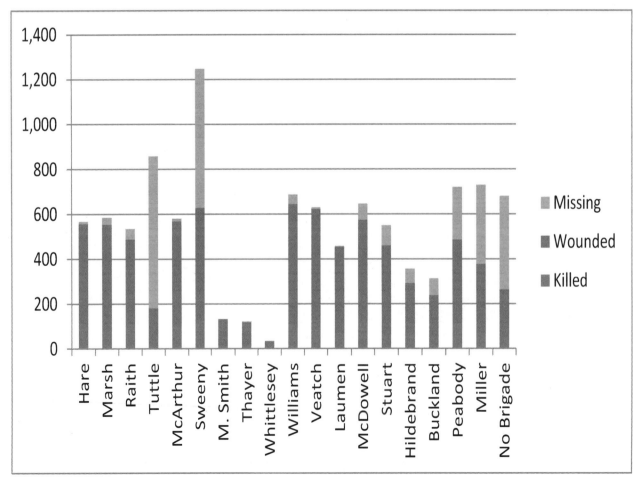

Army of Ohio, Buell

Casualties by Brigade

Division Cmdr	Brgd #	Brigade Cmdr	Killed	Wounded	Missing	Total	% of Total
McCook	4th Brgd	Rousseau	28	280	3	311	15%
	5th Brgd	Kirk	34	310	2	346	17%
	6th Brgd	Gibson	25	220	2	247	12%
Nelson	10th Brgd	Ammen	16	106	8	130	6%
	19th Brgd	Hazen	48	357	1	406	20%
	22nd Brgd	Bruce	29	138	11	178	9%
Crittenden	11th Brgd	Boyle	33	212	18	263	13%
	14th Brgd	W. Smith	25	157	10	192	9%
Wood	15th Brgd	Hascall	0	4	0	4	0%
	20th Brgd	Garfield	0	0	0	0	0%
	21st Brgd	Wagner	0	0	0	0	0%
					Total	2,077	100%

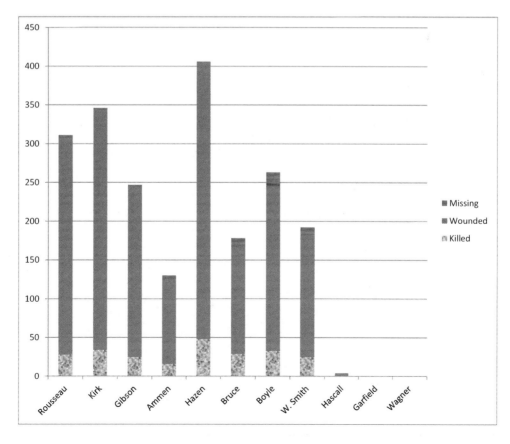

Army of Mississippi, Johnston

Casualties by Brigade

Corps	Division Cmdr	Brgd #	Brgd Cmdr	Killed	Wounded	Missing	Total	% of Total
Pope	Clark	1st Brgd	Russell	97	512	0	609	6%
		2nd Brgd	Stewart	93	421	3	517	5%
	Cheatham	1st Brgd	Johnson	120	607	13	740	7%
		2nd Brgd	Stevens	75	413	3	491	5%
Bragg	Ruggles	1st Brgd	Gibson	97	488	97	682	6%
		2nd Brgd	Anderson	69	313	52	434	4%
		3rd Brgd	Pond	89	336	169	594	6%
	Withers	1st Brgd	Gladden	129	597	103	829	8%
		2nd Brgd	Chalmers	83	343	19	445	4%
		3rd Brgd	Jackson	86	364	194	644	6%
Hardee	None	1st Brgd	Hindman	109	546	38	693	6%
		2nd Brgd	Cleburn	188	790	65	1,043	10%
		3rd Brgd	Wood	107	600	38	745	7%
Breckinridge	None	1st Brgd	Trabue	151	557	92	800	7%
		2nd Brgd	Bowen	98	498	28	624	6%
		3rd Brgd	Statham	137	627	45	809	8%
						Total	10,699	100%

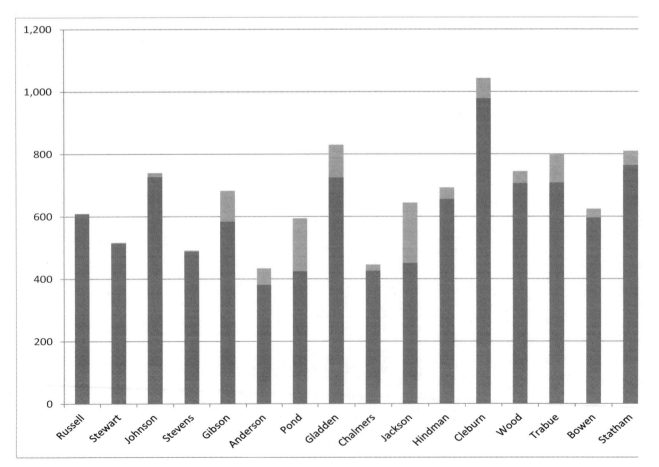

Appendix C - Army Organization

Theoretical Organization of Civil War Armies

This is the "ideal" army organization. But often there were major variances, especially early in the war. For example, in the Battle of Shiloh, the Union Army had no Corps, and half the Confederate Corps had no Divisions.

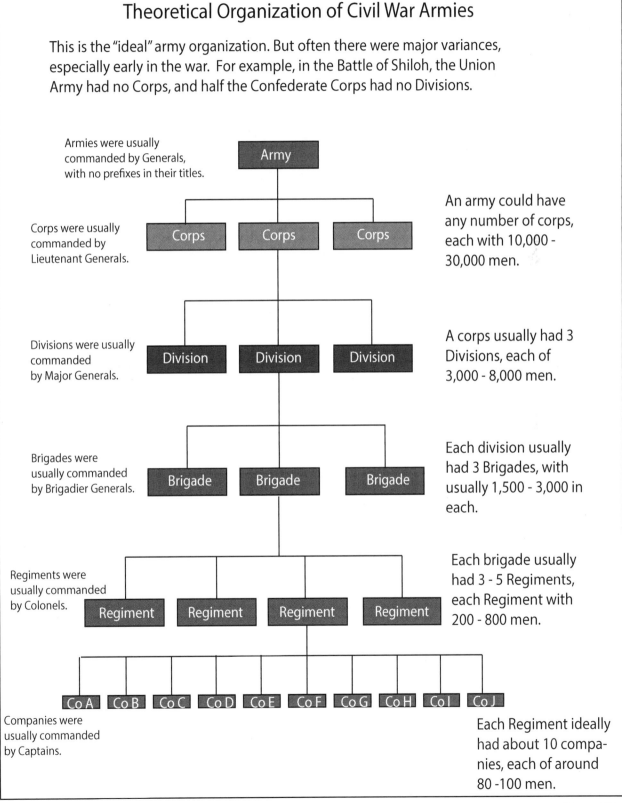

Armies were usually commanded by Generals, with no prefixes in their titles.

Army

An army could have any number of corps, each with 10,000 - 30,000 men.

Corps were usually commanded by Lieutenant Generals.

Corps **Corps** **Corps**

A corps usually had 3 Divisions, each of 3,000 - 8,000 men.

Divisions were usually commanded by Major Generals.

Division **Division** **Division**

Each division usually had 3 Brigades, with usually 1,500 - 3,000 in each.

Brigades were usually commanded by Brigadier Generals.

Brigade **Brigade** **Brigade**

Each brigade usually had 3 - 5 Regiments, each Regiment with 200 - 800 men.

Regiments were usually commanded by Colonels.

Regiment **Regiment** **Regiment** **Regiment**

Companies were usually commanded by Captains.

Co A   Co B   Co C   Co D   Co E   Co F   Co G   Co H   Co I   Co J

Each Regiment ideally had about 10 companies, each of around 80 -100 men.

Appendix D - Side Tours

MAPS & DIRECTIONS

If you're planning a trip to Shiloh you will of course be given a Park map when you arrive. However, for those of you who are *real* Civil War buffs, you might be interested in taking some out-of-Park side tours relating to the battle. I have included maps and directions here for three such tours. All of these come from the Blue & Gray magazine referenced at the end of this book. The maps were created by Park historian, Stacy Allen. So if you get lost on any of these side trips, blame Stacy Allen!

Odom-eter	Battle of Fallen Timbers Route
0	Exit Shiloh Battlefield by turning left onto Rt. 22-S toward Cornith.
2.8	In 2.8 mi. turn right onto Pratt Lane and immediately bear left to proceed along Pratt Lane
5.4	In about 2.6 mil. you will enter the area of Fallen Timbers. The fighting took place on the rise to your right.
5.6	In .2 mi. the historical road through the Fallen Timbers action intersected the road you are on, but is not accessible to backtrack along the ridge. However, all around you at this point, Forrest's cavalry and other Confederate units struggled with Union forces under William T. Sherman.
5.8	In another .2 mil turn right onto Harrison Road.
6.8	About a mile along Harrison Road, Sherman's cavalry struck Breckinridge's rear guard and the Federal advance came to a halt. The Federal cavalry did not venture onto the high ground ahead, which might have held an ambush. Sherman's reconnaissance ended at this point and his men retired to their camps on the Shiloh battlefield.
7.3	In about a half-mile, turn left onto Chambers Store Road.
9.2	In 1.9mi. you will come to the intersection with Rt. 22. Turn left to return to Shiloh Battlefield, or right to go to Cornith.

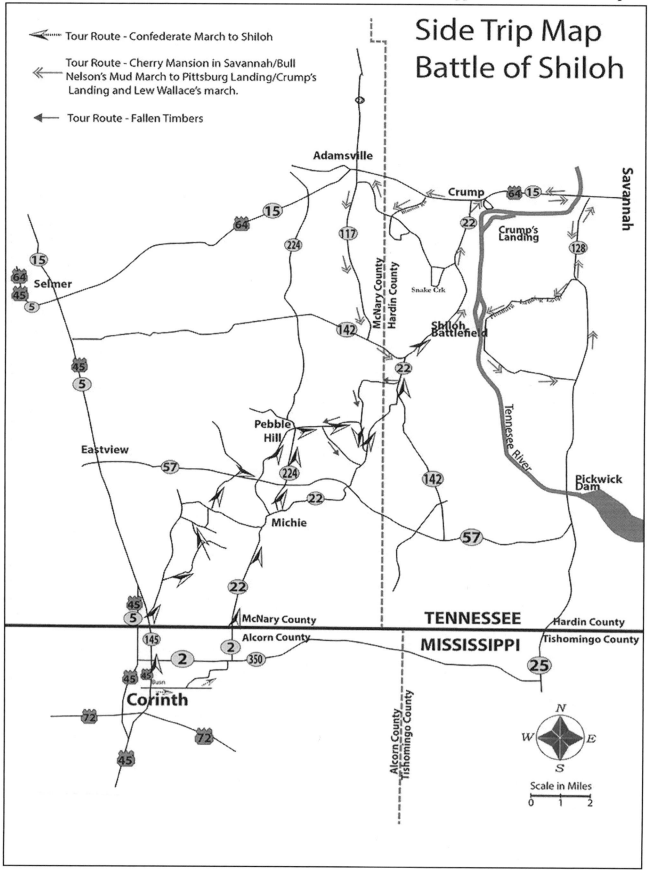

Side Trip Map
Battle of Shiloh

Tour Route - Confederate March to Shiloh

Tour Route - Cherry Mansion in Savannah/Bull Nelson's Mud March to Pittsburg Landing/Crump's Landing and Lew Wallace's march.

Tour Route - Fallen Timbers

Adamsville

Crump

Savannah

Crump's Landing

Selmer

Snake Crk

Shiloh Battlefield

Tennessee River

Eastview

Pebble Hill

Pickwick Dam

Michie

TENNESSEE

McNary County

Hardin County

MISSISSIPPI

Tishomingo County

Alcorn County

Corinth

Busn

N
W   E
S

Scale in Miles
0   1   2

	Crump's Landing and Lew Wallace's March
Odometer	After crossing the Tenn River Causeway, you will be in the town of Crump. Its principal connection to the Shiloh Campaign is Crump's Landing. Once in town, be on the lookout for the Flea Market stalls on your left.
0	In Crump, pass the first traffic light; turn left at the first intersection onto Crump Landing Road between the Flea Market and gas station (River Heights Grocery).
.5	In a half-mile is a boat landing on the Tenn River. This is Crump's Landing, where Lew Wallace's division was set ashore on March 13; still posted here on Apr 6 was M. L. Smith's brigade. Bear right onto Lew Wallace Road.
1.1	In about a half-mile bear left onto Crump Landing Road. Proceed the short distance to US 64-W, and turn left.
1.6	In a half-mile, pass through the intersection with Rt. 22-S and stay straight onto US 64/Rt. 22-N.
3.3	In 1.7 mi turn left onto Blanton Rd., and instantly bear right to stay on Blanton. This intersection was Stoney Lonesome in 1862, where Thayer's brigade of Wallace's division was posted. If Wallace had turned left, departing Blanton Rd, he would have passed to the River Road and come onto the battlefield where Grant wanted him. However, he bore to the right, as you have, staying on Blanton Rd and following the route he understood conformed to the plans to reinforce him.
4.5	In 1.2 mi turn right onto Caney Branch Rd, the old Shiloh road. Here too the road departs from the historical route taken by Wallace, which is impossible to track anymore. (Where you turned right onto Caney Branch Rd, Wallace proceeded straight. You will pick up his march again soon.)
5.2	In a little over a half-mile, bear right at the bend, now Old Shiloh Road.
6.3	In 1.1 mi, bear left to stay on the tour route.
6.8	In .5 mi, turn left onto Rt. 117-S in Adamsville, where Whittlesey's brigade of Wallace's division was posted.
8.1	In 1.3 mi you will cross Snake Creek. Three-quarters of a mile to your left is the site of Overshot Mill, where Wallace crossed Snake Creek then proceeded to climb the ridge to your left front.
8.9	In .8 mi, go straight through the intersection with Sharon Rd, here rejoining Wallace's march southward.
10.4	In 1.5 mi pull over if you can on the high ground at Smith's, overlooking Clear Creek. Here Wallace, his men in column and stopped in the road, was located by one of Grant's staff officers who redirected his march. Wallace turned around and eventually reached the battlefield later on the 6th. However, you will continue straight ahead.
10.9	Descend the slope and in a half-mile cross Clear Creek.
12.9	In 2 mi, turn left onto Rt 142-E.
13.7	In .8 mi, you will cross Owl Creek.

| 14.4 | In .7 mi, you will come to the intersection with Rt. 22. Turn left to proceed back to Shiloh Battlefield (1.8mi away), or right to leave the Shiloh area. |

	Bull Nelson's Mud March to Pittsburg Landing
Odometer	Most of the route has changed little since 1862. Many dirt roads are unmarked and can be extremely muddy. Narrow roads and tight turns may be difficult for large vehicles, such as campers.
	Since you have chosen to take Bull Nelson's mud March and are backtracking on Main St in Savannah after leaving the Cherry Mansion, you will soon arrive at the intersection with US 64)a busy multi-lane road called Bridge St, but here it becomes Main St). At the intersection is a flagpole and cannons to denote the locale of Grant's Savannah HQ.
0	Jog left onto this busy thoroughfare and almost immediately on the right is the Tenn River Museum.
.3	About a quart-mile past the Museum, turn right onto Pickwick Rd, which is Rt 128.
3	In 2.7 mi, turn right onto Pittsburg Landing Loop, also called Diamond Island Loop at Rt 128. Diamond Island Loop turns into 1st Pittsburg Landing Road, in about a mile from Rt 128.
3.8	A little over three-quarters of a mile away, bear left to stay on Pittsburg Landing Loop.
4.2	In .4 mi, bear left at an unmarked fork. As you drive along, note the mud, stagnant swampland, and an occasional cotton field, typical of the terrain that Nelson's men slogged across during their trek to Pittsburg Landing.
5.2	After a mile, bear right at an unmarked fork.
5.6	In .4 mi, continue straight at the T-intersection.
6.8	In 1.2 mi, bear left at the fork.
8.2	In 1.4 mi, pass the intersection with Couch Rd, to stay on Pittsburg Landing Loop. Be especially careful to NOTE THE MILAGE because you will pull over at the next stop.
8.7	In .5 mi, carefully pull over to the side of the road. A trail leads the short distance to the Tenn River. Directly across the river you can see Pittsburg Landing. From here Bull Nelson looked across at the scnene of mass confusion on the early evening of Apr 6, as many of Grant's demoralized and exhausted troops sought refuge below the bluffs. Here too, Nelson's division boarded transports to join Grant on the west side. After you have toured the area, return to your vehicle and continue along Pittsburg Landing Road.
11	In 2.3 mi, stay straight at the T-intersection, then cross a small bridge.
12.3	In about a mile and a quarter, pass through the intersection with Sunset Dr to stay on Pittsburg Landing Loop.
12.8	After a half-mile, turn left onto Rt 128 and proceed back toward Savannah.
16.8	Only as a point of reference, in 4.0 mi, you will pass the intersection with Pittsburg Landing Loop, where you turned off of this road during the first leg of Nelson's Mud March. Do not turn here.
19.6	In 2.8 mi, turn left onto US 64-W in Savannah.

20.3	In .7 mil you will cross the Tenn River bridge on your way to Crump's Landing and Lew Wallace's adventure on April 6, trying to reach the battlefield.

	The Bragg - Breckinridge Route to Shiloh
Odometer	From Cornith. Note that Breckinridge marched north from Farmington, joining Bragg on route to Pittsburg Landing.
0	Turn right onto Shiloh Rd, the old Cornith-Pittsburg Landing Road.
1.4	In 1.4 mi, turn left to stay on Shiloh Road
3.5	In 2.1 mi turn right onto Minor Road (Alcorn County Rt 152). After some departures from the historical route, this stretch follows the wartime road.
3.8	In .3 mi on the right is the Driver House, a private residence which stood during the war. The wartime road trace here departs from the modern-day route by cutting across the field to your left, following the ridgeline.
4	In .2 mi, turn left onto Alcorn Country Rt 143. In this vicinity, Breckinridge's column came into the road to join Bragg's. The Bragg-Breckinridge column is now intact.
5.2	In 1.2 mile turn onto Mississippi Rt 2-E, then make a quick left to stay on Rt. 2 A sign for Shiloh Battlefield points the way.
6.3	In 1.1 mi, you will cross the Mississippi-Tennessee state line into McNairy County. Rt 2 now becomes Tenn Rt 22. A small marker just past the Action city limits sign tells of Bragg's march.
8.3	In 2.0 mi, you will enter the town of Michie (pronounced Mickey) which is wartime Monterey.
10	In 1.7 mi is a marker for the Fallen Timers action. Shiloh park historian Stacy Allen says to ignore this sign as it is improperly placed by four miles, "as the crow flies." (more on this later).
10.6	In .6 mi, you will see Michie Rd, coming in on the left. DO NOT TAKE this road, but simply note its historical significance: Bragg was to send Ruggles's division (his left wing) onto this road to strike the Ridge road at Squire Moore's, but because of muddy roads and already being behind schedule, Bragg pressed on without releasing Ruggles. Polk was at Squire Moore's awaiting Ruggles, which caused further delays in the Confederate time-table.
10.7	In .1 mi is the Michie Post Office, and by a clump of trees on the right just past the building is a small marker to describe the Confederate approach.
10.9	In .2 mi, turn left onto Rt 224-N. There is a historical marker at the intersection describing Bragg's march, but its location makes it difficult and dangerous to read.
11.4	In .5 mi, the road begins dropping into Lick Creek valley.
11.9	In .5 mi is the intersection with Rt 57. DO NOT TURN onto Rt 57. Stay on Rt 224, but as you approach the intersection look to your left. Polk and Hardee marched their columns along the ridge in the distance toward a junction with Bragg and Breckinridge.
12.4	You will cross Lick Creek (right) in .5 mi.

13.9	In 1.5 mi you will ascend Pebble Hill. On your left you will soon see the intersection with Dillon Rd, but DO NOT TURN onto Dillon. However, slow down so as to be ready to make a right turn at the top of the hill. By Dillon Road, Polk and Hardee joined Brag and Breckiridge. On Pebble Hill was the hamlet called Micke's during the war. As you reach the crest of the hill, immediately turn right onto Chamers Store Rd, which is the wartime Ridge or Bark Road. The Mickey house, a corrupted spelling of the Michie family name on old maps, sat at this intersection. THE TURN ONTO CHAMBERS STORE ROAD IS EASY TO MISS, SO SLOW DOWN AS YOU ASCEND PEBBLE HILL. On Apr 5 a major traffic jam occurred here as Polk's corps arrived via the Ridge road and proceeded behind Wither's division of Bragg's corps. This cut off Ruggle's division which was still marching north from Monterey. The mishap was a result of Bragg not sending Ruggles to Squire Moore's where his column was scheduled to move ahead of Polk's corps. In the late afternoon, an angry General Johnston rode back from the front to locate Ruggle's missing division. Finding the route blocked by Polk, Johnston ordered his men and trains off the road so that Ruggles could pass forward to his assigned place in the attack order. Thus the Confederates missed an opportunity to attack on Apr 5.
15.1	In .9 mi after your turn onto Chambers Store Road, bear left onto Harrison Rd, a dirt and gravel road which is the wartime Bark Road.
16.5	In 1.4 mi, turn right onto Joe Dillon Rd. At this point the historical road disappears, so you must travel on modern roads to reach the next stretch of historical road.
17.6	In 1.1 mi turn left onto unmarked Rt. 22.
18.9	In 1.3 mi, at a bend in the road, the route picks up the historical Bark road. On teh night of Apr 5, Breckinridge's camps were located here.
19.1	In .2 mi you will enter Hardin County. As you cross the county line, General Johnston's HQ tent on the night of Apr 6-7 was about 150 yards to the left; there is a Tenn Civil War Trails waysid exhibit. Polk's corps, deployed in column of brigades, bivouacked along this section of road the night of Apr 5-6.
19.5	After traveling .4 mi beyond the county line you will come to the intersection with Bark Dr. DO NOT TURN HERE, but use it as a reference point as to where Bragg's corps was located, 300 yards in front of you. Some markers at the intersection describe the armies engaged at Shiloh. Also, Gen. Beauregard pitched his tent at this intersection on the night of Apr 5-6. It was here that Confederate generals held a council of war to discuss proceeding with the offensive.
20.2	In .7 mi, prepare to turn left to stay on Rt 22-N. As you approach the intersection, note that straight ahead is a slight break in the trees. This is where the old road continued past Fraley Field, which is just beyond the trees and is where opening shots of the Battle of Shiloh were fired. On this front, Hardee's corps bivouacked in line of battle the night of Apr 5-6, just one mile south of Sherman's camp at Shiloh Church. Make your left turn onto Rt 22 and begin looking for signs for Shiloh Battlefield.

23.6	In 3.4 mi, after the let turn onto Rt 22, turn right into the main park entrance and proceed the 1.1 mi to the Shiloh Visitor Center.

	The Polk - Hardee Route to Shiloh
Odometer	These instructions are for those who, in Cornith, chose to take the Polk-Hardee route to the battlefield.
0	Whereas the followers of the Bragg-Breckinridge column here turned right onto Shiloh Rd (the old Cornith-Pittsburg Landing road), to follow the Polk-Hardee route simply go straight at this intersection, staying on Business Rt 45, the old Purdy-Cornith Road.
3.5	In 3.5 mi, you will cross the Mississippi-Tennessee line into McNairy County. A marker at the state line tells of the Polk-Hardee march. Bear right at the marker then instantly turn left onto Sticine Rd.
5.2	After traveling 1.7 mi beyond the state line, turn right onto Melvin Qualls Rd. In about a mile you will come to the area reached by the Confederates on their first day of the march; here they set up camp for the night.
7.4	About 2.2 mi form your turn onto Melvin Qualls Rd, turn left onto Will Coln Rd, the old Purdy-Farmington road (Stay on Will Coln Rd - DO NOT TURN onto the jog for Melvin Qualls Rd).
7.6	In .2 mi, the wartime road departs the modern road and cuts across the ground to the right.
8.4	In .8 mi, turn right onto New Hope Rd, old State Line Road.
8.8	In .4 mi, note the clump of trees on the right. The wartime hamlet of Locust Grove once occupied that location. TURN LEFT onto S. Prather Rd, just past the clump of trees.
9.5	In .6 mi, turn right from S. Prather onto Hubert Manul Rd; then make a quick left onto N. Prather Rd, an unpaved road.
11.1	In 1.6 mi, pass through the intersection with Rt. 57 and stay on the extension of N. Prather, now called Taylor Road.
11.6	A half-mile after passing over Rt 57 you will come to a 4-way intersection. Prepare to turn right. Squire Moore's place, no longer standing, occupied the ground directly ahead of you at this intersection. Turn right onto Pleasant Site Rd. At this point you are 11 miles southwest of Pittsburg Landing. On the afternoon of Apr 4, this is where Polk, who at this intersection was joined by Cheatham's division (which had marched south from Purdy on the road to your left), awaited the arrival of Ruggle's division. Ruggles was to have been detached to Squire Moore's y Bragg, but was not detached because of muddy roads and the column being behind schedule. These delays forced Polk to bivouac here, while Hardee's corps, the vanguard of Johnston's army, had already moved to within five miles of Pittsburg Landing, and during the late afternoon of Apr 4, fought a heay skirmish with Sherman's infantry pickets and cavalry.
11.9	In .3 mil, turn left onto Rt 57.
12.3	In .4 mi, turn left onto Dillon Road.

13.2	In .9 mi, Dillon Rd picks up the historical stretch of road that took Polk and Hardee to a junction with the Bragg-Breckinridge column.
15	In 1.8mi you will strike Rt 224, the road the Bragg-Breckinridge column used. Turn left onto Rt. 224, then immediately make a right turn onto Chambers Store Road. The high ground you are on is Pebble Hill, location of the hamlet called Mickey's during the war. THE TURN ONTO CHAMBERS ROAD IS EASY TO MISS, SO SLOW DOWN! On Apr 5 a major traffic jam occurred here as Polk's corps arrived via the Ridge road and proceeded behind Wither's division of Bragg's corps. This cut off Ruggle's division which was still marching north from Monterey. The mishap was a result of Bragg not sending Ruggles to Squire Moore's where his column was scheduled to move ahead of Polk's corps. In the late afternoon, an angry General Johnston rode back from the front to locate Ruggle's missing division. Finding the route blocked by Polk, Johnston ordered his men and trains off the road so that Ruggles could pass forward to his assigned place in the attack order. Thus the Confederates missed an opportunity to attack on Apr 5.
15.9	In .9 mi after your turn onto Chambers Store Road, bear left onto Harrison Rd, a dirt and gravel road which is the wartime Bark Road.
17.3	In 1.4 mi, turn right onto Joe Dillon Rd. At this point the historical road disappears, so you must travel on modern roads to reach the next stretch of historical road.
18.4	In 1.1 mi turn left onto unmarked Rt. 22.
19.7	In 1.3 mi, at a bend in the road, the route picks up the historical Bark road. On teh night of Apr 5, Breckinridge's camps were located here.
19.9	In .2 mi you will enter Hardin County. As you cross the county line, General Johnston's HQ tent on the night of Apr 6-7 was about 150 yards to the left; there is a Tenn Civil War Trails waysid exhibit. Polk's corps, deployed in column of brigades, bivouacked along this section of road the night of Apr 5-6.
20.3	After traveling .4 mi beyond the county line you will come to the intersection with Bark Dr. DO NOT TURN HERE, but use it as a reference point as to where Bragg's corps was located, 300 yards in front of you. Some markers at the intersection describe the armies engaged at Shiloh. Also, Gen. Beauregard pitched his tent at this intersection on the night of Apr 5-6. It was here that Confederate generals held a council of war to discuss proceeding with the offensive.
21	In .7 mi, prepare to turn left to stay on Rt 22-N. As you approach the intersection, note that straight ahead is a slight break in the trees. This is where the old road continued past Fraley Field, which is just beyond the trees and is where opening shots of the Battle of Shiloh were fired. On this front, Hardee's corps bivouacked in line of battle the night of Apr 5-6, just one mile south of Sherman's camp at Shiloh Church. Make your left turn onto Rt 22 and begin looking for signs for Shiloh Battlefield.
24.4	In 3.4 mi, after the let turn onto Rt 22, turn right into the main park entrance and proceed the 1.1 mi to the Shiloh Visitor Center.

	Savannah & The Cherry Mansion
Odom-eter	From Shiloh Battlefield
0	Exit Shiloh Battlefield by turning right onto Rt 22-N toward Adamsville.
2.1	In 2.1 mi you will cross Snake Creek.
5	In 2.9 mi turn right onto US 64-E.
8.8	In 3.8 mi you will cross the Tennessee River. Move to the left lane and prepare to turn left.
9.1	In .3 mi, immediately after crossing the bridge, turn left onto S. Riverside Dr, then make a quick left onto Main St.
9.3	In less than a quarter-mile, Main St. dead-ends at the Cherry Mansion on the left, which was Grant's HQ on the morning of Apr 6. This is a private dwelling, but there's a marker at the site. As you face the Cherry Mansion from the street, Grant's room was on the second story, right side. Here too, Maj. Gen. Charles F. Smith died of a tetanus infection on Apr 25. Also dying here, on Apr 10, of his Shiloh wounds was Brig. Gen. William H. L. Wallace.

References

As you might suppose, I've read a number of books on the subject of Shiloh, though certainly not all of them. But the ones I've found most enlightening for my purposes are listed here:

Battles and Leaders of the Civil War: The Struggle Intensifies/Vol 1 (1883)

This book series was written in 1883 and is still one of the best historical references of the Civil War for my money. It is long out of print but you can buy it used, and for very little cost.

Shiloh (1997) Larry J. Daniel

One of the definitive modern works on the battle. I used this book constantly in my own research.

Shiloh and the Western Campaign of 1862 (2007) O. Edward Cunningham

Contains a detailed discussion of the Shiloh battle, as well as the events and policies leading up to it. For the serious student, this book makes a good companion to Daniel's book, already mentioned.

Shiloh: A Battlefield Guide (2006) Mark Grimsley and Steven E. Woodworth

This book is intended only to be a tour guide it therefore heavily summarizes the events of the battle. But I found it to be a good starting point in figuring out exactly what happened, where it happened, and when it happened, on the battlefield.

Shiloh, 1862 (2012) Winston Groom

This book came out as I was finishing up my own. As the author intended, I found it fairly light on actual battlefield maneuvers, but helpful on background information on the participants.

Shiloh (2012) Blue & Gray Magazine - Sesquicentennial Edition

This is a single magazine edition, not a book, but all on the subject of Shiloh. Written or at least edited by the Shiloh Park's historian, Stacy Allen. Very good maps, and in color, although at a higher level than where I targeted my maps and discussion. Overall, a very helpful guide in my research.

Index

About the Author

Describing myself gets me kind of depressed. At my advanced age, it doesn't look like I'm going to make President or even become a nice dentist. (Sorry, Mom!)

But I console myself with my pipe, a shot or two of bourbon, and decent health. When not sitting at home on my duff behind a computer, I can often be found tooling around the country in a beat-up old van, along with my attack-cat, Pepper, my chief critic.

The stated purpose of these trips is to gather data and photos for books – all four of them at present - but I do love walking battlefields and writing about them.

The Civil War has always fascinated me. I can remember when I was a kid in Illinois, reading about the clash of the Blue & the Gray and being amazed that Americans could fight each other with such fury. Back then the Civil War seemed to have happened a zillion years ago. But as I've grown older and time passes faster, I've come to realize that the Civil War wasn't that long ago at all. The last Civil War veteran died in 1956, in my lifetime, and there were thousands of them still around when my parents were born.

Anyway, I decided to combine my interest in the Civil War with a couple of others - writing and computer technology

I consider myself more of a "splainer" rather than a true historian. For one thing I've never been to historian school, and for another I haven't spent years pouring through letters, newspapers and journals of the era. I greatly admire those who do and in my next life I might join them, but right now my goal is to take their consolidated research to the next step by explaining what happened in a way that readers can easily relate to, taking full advantage of computer technology that was only available to a limited extent, if at all, to previous writers - technology that includes the lavish use of photography, map illustrations, GPS, and whatever other visual and audio tools I can lay hands on. It's due to technology that we probably know a lot more detail today about what happened in Civil War battles than did the participants themselves.

All of this is not to say I don't research my books. I do, usually for months. But I try not to get lost in research or technology. My ultimate goal is to explain in plain terms what happened back then, and to do so in an entertaining fashion, and also to get across to the reader what it was really like to be a participant in these terrible battles.

The result is the book you see (or listen to) here.

And that's pretty much the story of my life - so far. Hope you enjoy this book and have a good day!

Jack Kunkel (and Pepper)

Books by This Author

Battle of Gettysburg: A Visual Tour

The Battle of Shiloh: A Step-by-Step Account of One of the Greatest Battles of the Civil War

A Gettysburg Photo Tour: Then & Now Photos with Map Locations and GPS Coordinates

Showdown at Antietam: A Battlefield Tour of America's Bloodiest Day

Made in the USA
Middletown, DE
21 October 2017